Library of
Davidson College

The Poetics of Epiphany

The Poetics of Epiphany

NINETEENTH-CENTURY ORIGINS OF THE MODERN LITERARY MOMENT

Ashton Nichols

THE UNIVERSITY OF ALABAMA PRESS
TUSCALOOSA AND LONDON

Copyright © 1987 by
The University of Alabama Press
Tuscaloosa, Alabama 35487
All rights reserved
Manufactured in the United States of America

Designed by Laury A. Egan

LIBRARY OF CONGRESS CATALOGING-IN-PUBLICATION DATA

Nichols, Ashton, 1953–
   The poetics of epiphany.

   Bibliography: p.   Includes index.
   1. English poetry—19th century—History and criticism. 2. Epiphanies in literature. I. Title.
PR585.E85N53   1987   821'.7'09   86-16042
ISBN 0-8173-0327-8

        British Library Cataloguing-in-Publication Data is available.

TO MY MOTHER,
Grace Ashton Nichols,
AND TO THE MEMORY OF MY FATHER,
Jesse Brooks Nichols, Jr.

For the other gods are too far removed from us, or they hear us not. Either they do not exist at all, or they do not concern themselves about us. But thee we can see with our own eyes.

> —song sung for the epiphany of Demetrius Poliorketes, king of Macedonia, 336–283 B.C. (transcribed by Athenaeus)

For in this Period the Poet's Work is Done: and all
    the Great
Events of Time start forth & are conceived in such a
    Period,
Within a Moment, a Pulsation of the Artery.
> —Blake, *Milton*

His thinking was a dusk of doubt and selfmistrust lit up at moments by the lightnings of intuition, by lightnings of so clear a splendour that in those moments the world perished about his feet as if it had been fireconsumed.

> —Joyce, *A Portrait of the Artist as a Young Man*

Contents

	Preface	xi
1.	*The New Epiphany*	1
	THE BACKGROUND OF THE MODERN EPIPHANY	1
	FROM INSPIRATION TO INTERPRETATION	13
	FROM INTERPRETATION TO EPIPHANY	20
2.	*Wordsworth and the Origins of Epiphany*	35
	WORDSWORTH'S ORIGINALITY	35
	"SPOTS OF TIME": FROM DREAD TO BENEDICTION	49
3.	*Flashes of Internal Inspiration*	70
	"RESOLUTION AND INDEPENDENCE": THE ORDINARY TRANSFORMED	70
	COLERIDGE: "PHANTASY" IN "FROST AT MIDNIGHT"	80
	SHELLEYAN "MOMENTS": A DEFENSE OF THE EPIPHANIC IMAGINATION	93
4.	*Browning's Modernism*	107
	THE INFINITE MOMENT AS EPIPHANY	107
	THE POET AS MAGUS: *The Ring and the Book*	122
5.	*Victorian Versions of Epiphany*	144
	TENNYSON'S SECULAR MYSTICISM: THE EPIPHANIC TRANCE POEM	144
	HOPKINS AND THE RETURN TO THEOPHANIC EPIPHANY	166
6.	*Epiphany in Twentieth-Century Poetry*	181
	YEATS: THE ARTIFICER OF THE "GREAT MOMENT"	181

Contents

Eliot: History as a "Pattern of Timeless Moments"   *190*
Stevens: "Moments of Awakening"   *198*
Heaney: "Description Is Revelation!"   *204*

Notes   *213*
Bibliography   *239*
Index   *250*

Preface

NUMEROUS COMMENTATORS have noted the extent to which nineteenth-century writers record a particular form of experience, characterized by its brief duration and notable for its intense personal significance over time. But critics have so far failed to suggest that these experiences represent a new source of literary inspiration and become a new way of attributing value to events. This type of momentary insight has been described in various ways and has been given various names but has received, as M. H. Abrams suggests, "what seems destined to become its standard name" from James Joyce's use of the term "epiphany."

The Poetics of Epiphany begins by suggesting that the epiphanies of Joyce originate in the nineteenth century, specifically in Wordsworth's "spots of time." The notion that a powerfully felt, momentary experience can be transformed by the mind into a significant image plays a central role in Romantic theories of poetic meaning. The new literary epiphany reverses traditional ideas about inspiration by providing a poetic technique in which meaning emerges only after the interpretation of the revelatory moment. *The Prelude* and a number of Wordsworth's lyrics suggest that the "manifestation" in the new epiphany is found not in experience itself but in its imaginative transformation into a work of art. Coleridge's "phantoms" and Shelley's "trances" develop Wordsworth's idea by emphasizing the role of the mind in such elevations of ordinary events into moments of extraordinary significance. Jung's term "synchronistic" provides a useful model for describing these "meaningful coincidences of external and internal events." Coincidences become meaningful, however, only under certain conditions.

The literary epiphany develops in important ways during the Victorian period. Browning's "infinite moment" reveals the mind's ability to focus emotion and perception in a fleeting, illuminated instant. The *chronos* of temporal duration gives way to the *kairos* of eternity in what Browning calls the "good minute." His conceptions of the complex sources of human love and the problematic nature of poetic truth, as expressed in *The Ring and the Book,* originate in such moments. Likewise, Tennyson's "trances" derive from an imaginative power that produces a "sudden spiritual manifestation" out of an otherwise ordinary object or event. Tennyson's often-discussed mysticism is, in fact, much more closely related to the Wordsworthian spot of time than it is to any traditional form of mystical vision. The general Victorian sense of evolutionary developments based on sudden, small changes that interrupt vast periods of historical time leads to a similar concern with powerful moments of seeming significance.

Toward the end of the nineteenth century, the literary epiphany moves in two directions. It returns, via the theophanies of Hopkins, to a theological framework, suggesting that the epiphany is defined not by its specific content but by its potential for infusing certain experiences with meaning. Hopkins's poems contain epiphanies whenever significance is attributed directly to experiences which may then lead to religious interpretations. At the same time, the literary epiphany emerges—by way of the symbolist aesthetic—as the dominant form of purely secular revelation. In the modern epiphany, the moment of revelation is absolute and determinate, but the meaning provided by the inspiration is relative and indeterminate. As Northrop Frye has noted, the accidental becomes oracular in such moments of transformed consciousness. But modern oracles, like their traditional counterparts, tend to speak in equivocal ways.

The nineteenth-century origins of epiphany reveal important changes in the kinds of experiences that were seen as suitable poetic subjects and also suggest a uniquely modern approach to questions of literary meaning. *The Poetics of Epiphany* concludes by commenting on the literary "moment" in the poetry of Yeats, Eliot, Stevens, and Heaney, thereby suggesting the continuing importance of epiphany in modern poetry. The concept of epiphany becomes a way of momentarily balancing the dynamic opposition between the closure called for by traditional theories of literary interpretation and the openness demanded by recent approaches to verbal discourse. As epiphany closes in on the determinate moment of verbal power, it opens out onto multiple manifestations of meaning.

I WOULD LIKE to thank all those who contributed to the completion of this project. My greatest debt is to Robert Langbaum; his

Preface

enthusiastic support and exacting encouragement helped at every stage in the writing of this book. Leo Damrosch provided advice and encouragement in the early stages. Paul Cantor made useful suggestions on each chapter. Cecil Lang read the manuscript with an insightful editorial eye. John Beer made it possible for me to spend a worthwhile summer at Cambridge. I would also like to thank those whose willingness to discuss these matters added coherence to portions of my argument, as well as those who provided other forms of assistance and encouragement: Elma H. Ashton, Effie Bousoulopoulos, Sidney Burris, Charles Lloyd Garrettson III, W. Bertram Hitchcock, Susan Tyler Hitchcock, Samuel Lloyd, Jay Losey, Richard B. Miller, Thomas Newbolt, Alan Richardson, Anthony Roche, and P. Kingsley Smith. I thank the Auburn Office of Research for a grant-in-aid. Judith Knight at the University of Alabama Press helped to move the project toward completion. Two anonymous readers for the press made a number of useful suggestions. Craig Noll copyedited the manuscript with care and concern. I am grateful to all of these individuals.

Parts of chapters 4 and 5 have appeared in a slightly different form in *Browning Institute Studies* 11 (1983) and *Victorian Poetry* 24:2 (1986). I am grateful to the editors of these journals for permission to reprint this material in a revised form. I would also like to thank the following publishers and holders of copyright for permission to reproduce copyrighted material: quotations from the fourth edition of *The Poems of Gerard Manley Hopkins*, ed. W. H. Gardner and N. H. Mackenzie (copyright © 1967 by The Society of Jesus) reprinted by permission of Oxford University Press on behalf of The Society of Jesus; selections from *The Workshop of Daedalus*, ed. Robert Scholes and Richard M. Kain (copyright © 1965 by Northwestern University Press and the Estate of James Joyce), reprinted by permission; extracts from *Stephen Hero* by James Joyce (copyright © 1963 by the Estate of James Joyce) reprinted by permission of The Society of Authors Ltd., and Jonathan Cape; material from *Moments of Being* by Virginia Woolf (copyright © 1976 by Quentin Bell and Angelica Garnett) and *The Waves* by Virginia Woolf (copyright © 1931 by Harcourt Brace Jovanovich Inc., renewed 1959 by Leonard Woolf), reprinted by permission of Harcourt Brace Jovanovich and Hogarth Press; quotations from *The Collected Poems of W. B. Yeats* (copyright © 1916 by Macmillan Publishing Company, renewed 1944 by Bertha Georgie Yeats), reprinted by permission of Macmillan Publishing Company; selections from *Four Quartets* by T. S. Eliot

Preface

(copyright © 1943 by T. S. Eliot, renewed 1971 by Esme Valerie Eliot), reprinted by permission of Harcourt Brace Jovanovich and Faber and Faber Ltd.; quotations from *The Collected Poems of Wallace Stevens* (copyright © 1954 by Wallace Stevens) and *Opus Posthumous* by Wallace Stevens (copyright © 1957 by Elsie Stevens and Holly Stevens), reprinted by permission of Alfred A. Knopf; and excerpts from *Poems 1965–1975* by Seamus Heaney (copyright © 1966, 1969, 1972, 1975, 1980 by Seamus Heaney), from *Field Work* by Seamus Heaney (copyright © 1976, 1979 by Seamus Heaney), and *Preoccupations* by Seamus Heaney (copyright © 1980 by Seamus Heaney), reprinted by permission of Farrar, Straus, and Giroux Inc., and Faber and Faber Ltd.

Finally, I give special thanks to my wife, Kimberley, and our daughters—Amy, Molly, Elizabeth, and Tessa—who all, in their own ways, understand that *claritas* is *quidditas*.

The Poetics of Epiphany

1
The New Epiphany

THE BACKGROUND OF THE MODERN EPIPHANY

THE TERM "epiphany" has become almost a literary commonplace. The British poetry journal *Agenda* recently included a poem by Anne Beresford entitled "Epiphany Minsmere 1983." Alexander Coleman, reviewing the Spanish poet Antonio Machado in the *New York Times Book Review,* compared Machado to Yeats and Rilke and described him as a poet of "quiet epiphanies." In a recent article in *Studies in Romanticism,* Martin Bidney attempted to "sketch a phenomenology of epiphanic imagery in the major lyrics of Coleridge."[1] Such references are not surprising if we consider the importance of the literary technique first called "epiphany" by James Joyce in his description of Stephen Daedalus's secular revelations. Indeed, momentary manifestations of significance in ordinary experience have become a defining characteristic of twentieth-century fiction. Roger Cardinal has suggested that "intermittent and ephemeral" poetic epiphanies are central to a wide range of modern poetry, and Jonathan Culler has boldly asserted that one solution to the problem posed by certain modern poems is to "read any brief descriptive lyric as a moment of epiphany."[2]

It is surprising that no one has yet offered a complete exploration of the nineteenth-century origins of this new way of establishing poetic meaning. Several critics have pointed out that Joyce actually coins a term for a literary technique that has already been in use for over a century when Stephen Daedalus begins collecting his "epiphanies." Robert Langbaum is perhaps the first to note that the experiences described in *Stephen Hero* do not originate with Joyce:

The Poetics of Epiphany

> Joyce has taught us, in connection with the latest form of the short story, to call this way of meaning an *epiphany*—a manifestation in and through the visible world of an invisible life. But the epiphany does not begin in literature with the short stories of Joyce or Chekov. It is the essential innovation of *Lyrical Ballads*.[3]

Langbaum adds that this new form of momentary insight characterizes the "poetry of experience," a poetry that relies on the structure of human experience for its values and creates a new mythos out of imaginative insights into the enduring nature of things. Langbaum sees epiphany in this sense as discontinuous from all earlier forms of inspiration and as a characteristic aspect of modern literature.

Northrop Frye likewise connects Wordsworth with the Joycean "epiphany" and relates the term to a particularly Romantic aspect of the imagination:

> Joyce uses the word as a critical term in *Stephen Hero*, and appears to have adopted it because of his full agreement with the Romantic tendency to associate all manifestations of divinity with the creative spirit of man. But Joyce seems to have thought of the basis of the epiphany, in its literary context, as an actual event, brought into contact with the creative imagination, but untouched by it, so that it preserves the sense of something contained by the imagination and yet actual in its own terms. As Stevens says, one is more apt to confide in what has no concealed creator. Wordsworth was the great pioneer, almost the discoverer, of epiphany in this sense, as something observed but not essentially altered by the imagination, which yet has a crucial significance for that imagination.[4]

Frye sees such epiphanies as important to modern literature because of their ability to produce an "association between the random and the oracular." Earlier, in *Anatomy of Criticism*, Frye connects epiphany with an "archetypal" form of criticism, that is, one that rests on a theory of myths. In this context he characterizes the "point of epiphany," which he parallels to the Wordsworthian spot of time, as the point at which the "undisplaced apocalyptic world and the cyclical world of nature come into alignment." He also describes "demonic epiphanies," where the central manifestation is of the reality of evil.[5]

The New Epiphany

In *Epiphany in the Modern Novel*, Morris Beja traces the origins of the distinctively modern epiphany to Wordsworth. Like Langbaum, he sharply distinguishes the Joycean sense of the term from earlier accounts of divine visitation and inspiration:

> We are gradually coming from the moment of divine revelation of Augustine to the secular "epiphany"—the great new interest in which, as a matter of fact, dates from the Romantic movement. . . . Indeed the epiphany, at least as it usually appears in literature from now on, seems essentially a "Romantic" phenomenon. The most influential Romantic statement on inspiration is probably Wordsworth's "Preface" to the *Lyrical Ballads*, an essay packed with phrases showing an awareness of the poetic value of moments of illumination.[6]

Beja proceeds to define epiphany in Joycean terms and trace its appearance and importance in the prose of the twentieth century, with emphasis on the work of Mann, Woolf, and Faulkner. He does not, however, attempt to trace in detail its development in the poetry of the nineteenth century, though he does note this evolution in his introductory chapter.

In recent years, the term "epiphany" has come into widespread use in a variety of critical contexts. M. H. Abrams calls such experiences "moments" and characterizes them as times during which "an instant of consciousness, or else an ordinary object or event, suddenly blazes into revelation." Abrams draws his term from Augustine's *momentum* and the German *der Moment* and suggests, unlike many other critics, that these Romantic moments possess affinities with instants of inspiration recorded "over the Christian centuries." In fact, Abrams does not fully distinguish traditional religious revelation from its modern, and, as I will argue, essentially dissimilar, counterpart. He does admit, however, that the term "epiphany" has given the Romantic moment "what seems destined to become its standard name."[7]

Geoffrey Hartman uses "epiphany" to refer to a central characteristic of poems by Gray, Blake, Wordsworth, and Keats. He claims that late eighteenth-century poets Gray, Percy, Macpherson, and Blake inflate "neoclassical 'godkins and goddesslings' as giant epiphanic forms." In Keats's "Hyperion," says Hartman, epiphany serves to "abort historical vision" by concentrating on moments of overwhelming significance instead of a gradual temporal progress.[8] This notion of a contrast between time conceived in mo-

3

mentary terms and time conceived as a gradual progression is central to any understanding of the new literary epiphany. Elsewhere Hartman uses the phrase "accidental epiphany" to describe Wordsworth's experience on the summit of Snowdon—a sudden, unexpected perceptual phenomenon that draws the poet from his train of thought and startlingly confirms a preexisting disposition in the mind.[9] This particular type of epiphany, Hartman adds, has become "almost a modern staple."

Critics have so far failed to provide a comprehensive discussion of the origins and defining characteristics of the new literary epiphany. Although many critics have employed the term "epiphany," no one has yet traced its development in the poetry of the nineteenth century. This omission is particularly surprising when we consider the important role that epiphany has come to play in modern poetry and prose. The following chapters will offer just such a discussion of the Romantic origins of the new literary epiphany, its development by the Victorians, and its role as a precursor of twentieth-century literary techniques. The modern literary epiphany, I argue, offers a new form of meaning in which the moment of inspiration is absolute and determinate, while the significance provided by the epiphany is relative and indeterminate.

The long shadow cast by Wordsworth over nineteenth-century poetic theory and practice is, in one sense, the result of his insight into a new way of deriving significance from certain sensations which are transformed by a complex mental process. The literary epiphany is also one of the most important formal techniques in nineteenth-century poetry. It plays a role in the lyrics of Wordsworth, Coleridge, Shelley, Keats, Browning, Arnold, Tennyson, and Hopkins. In addition, it becomes an important transitional device between the poems of the nineteenth century and the poems and prose of the twentieth century. Insofar as the roots of modernism are contained in Romantic and Victorian poetry, they are contained to an important extent in the structure of epiphany. The literary epiphany, originating in Wordsworth and developing over the next century, represents an important departure from forms of experience with which it has often been confused: divine inspiration, religious conversion, and mystical vision. The phenomenon Joyce calls "epiphany" is a literary technique that has its origins in a particular, historically locatable, interpretation of experience. Beginning with Wordsworth, a formal relationship is established between certain momentary perceptual events in the life of an individual and the emotional importance of these events as they are later recalled and expressed in poetry. A form of experience becomes a new way of meaning.

The structure of the epiphany—in which a commonplace event takes on a revelatory quality in the mind of the observer—becomes a standard means of organizing lyric poems during the nineteenth century. Wordsworth's spots of time bear comparison not only to Joyce's epiphanies but to Coleridge's "flashes," Shelley's "best and happiest moments," Keat's "fine isolated verisimilitude," Browning's "infinite moment," Arnold's "gleaming" moments, and Tennyson's "little things . . . that strike on a sharper sense." In the twentieth century, the same interpretive structure plays a role in Yeats's "masterful images," Ezra Pound's emphasis on imagistically focused instants, and Wallace Stevens's "moments of awakening." Coleridge and Shelley provide important developments of the Wordsworthian epiphany, while Browning becomes a central transitional figure, in whose increasingly narrative monologues the new epiphany begins the movement from lyric poem to novel. In Tennyson and Arnold the epiphany helps to create a new tone, while at the same time providing a source of solace amid Victorian uncertainties about language and meaning. The epiphany that begins in Wordsworth also gives rise to what I call the "epiphanic imagination." Epiphany is not to be identified with imagination. Rather, literary epiphany is used by authors to show one way that the verbal imagination operates, by heightening a perception through language to suggest psychic intensity and emotional importance. The epiphanic imagination, exemplified in various but related ways in all of these authors, is a continuing source of imagery and meaning in modern poetry and prose.

THE TERM "epiphany" derives from the Greek *phainein* "to show" and the prepositional prefix *epi,* which means variably "on," "over," "at," and "after." Phainein can also be translated "to bring to light" or "cause to appear." In this sense it is the root of "fantasy," "phantom," and "phenomenon." The term originally referred only to the notion of literal illumination. The Greek forms *epiphainein* and *epiphaneia* mean respectively "to manifest" and "appearance" or "manifestation." The adjectival form, *epiphanēs,* means "manifest" or "evident" (when it refers to objects) and "conspicuous" or "distinguished" (when it refers to persons).

Greek literature and religion commonly recorded appearances of gods and goddesses, which were described as "epiphanies." Stories of such visitations testified to the interpenetration of the divine and the mundane. They can be traced as far back as the earliest known examples of the Greek oral tradition. Dionysius's "manifestation" in the tree at Magnesia aided the development of the subsequent cult of Dionysiac mysteries. Often the cult motive was central to recorded epiphanies. Followers of a particular god or goddess reported an appearance of their chosen divinity in order to influence potential converts. In addition, actual appearances of human rulers were also recorded as epiphanies. The term "epiphaneia" was used to refer to supposedly miraculous occurrences, with or without the visible presence of a deity. In this sense the word referred only to a manifestation of the power of the divinity, not to a vision of the god itself. The Hindu notion of an avatar derives from this idea that gods could send their agents to earth to participate in human affairs. In these cases, only power was made manifest, leaving divinity itself inscrutable.

As the oral tradition gave way to a written literature, descriptions of direct interaction between gods and humans were common. The most typical of these appearances led to procreation, affected the outcome of a battle, or healed the sick. The *Iliad* recounts a series of epiphanic interventions that determine the outcome of the Trojan War. The plots of Euripides' *Alcestis* and *Electra* both depend on epiphanies at crucial points in the story. Herodotus's fictionalized history recounts numerous instances of divine intervention, particularly for the punishment of human arrogance. Around 200 B.C. the Greek author Istrus composed a treatise entitled *Epiphanies of Apollo*. At approximately the same time, Phylarchus collected various accounts of epiphanies in a work he called *On the Appearance of Zeus*. The notion was by no means unique to the Greeks. An anonymous Egyptian papyrus recounts a typical healing epiphany of the god Imouthes. In the document a young man recovering from a deathly illness recounts the story told him by his mother: "She saw the figure (whether it was the god or his attendant). . . . She found me rid of the fever and streaming with sweat, so she gave glory to the god for his epiphany. . . . The pains in my side ceased."[10] In all such cases the effect of the epiphany is immediate and powerful. The force of divinity has effected a fundamental change in a state of affairs on earth.

The cultural role of such epiphanies has been discussed by anthropologists and developmental sociologists. In psychological terms, the phenomenon has been seen as a clear example of psychic extension. Primitive cultures do not acknowledge an unbridgeable gap between human beings and gods. Gods tend to represent intensifications of powers that exist in a limited form in humans. Divine power can thus be directed, cajoled, or initiated by earthly men and women. Such gods tend to be the victims of the human emotions of jealousy, greed, and selfishness, which helps to explain why the notion of epiphany was widely accepted in classical antiquity. Gods were not so far removed from earth that their direct influence might not be felt on occasion. As Frazer noted, this view helps to explain the origins of sorcerers and magicians: "As the gods are commonly believed to exhibit themselves in the likeness of men to their worshippers, it is easy for the magician, with his supposed miraculous powers, to acquire the reputation of being an incarnate deity."[11] Short of incarnation, individuals in almost all cultures have testified to moments of temporary divine inspiration that most often produce religious conviction or creative impulses. An important corollary to this state is its effect on the individual: "Certain persons are supposed to be possessed from time to time by a spirit or deity, while the possession lasts their own personality lies in abeyance."[12]

The most widespread historical use of the term "epiphany" derives from its place in the Christian calendar. The early Christians adopted January 6 as the Feast of Epiphany to celebrate the manifestation of Christ's divinity to the magi.[13] For the Christian the Feast of Epiphany celebrates that moment in human history when God clearly and directly made himself manifest in the lives of men. The Gospels offer an account of a humble, strikingly ordinary birth that brings the power of divinity to earth. The circumstances could not be more lowly or mundane: a homeless wandering, a pregnancy which Joseph at first feels may be illegitimate, a birth amid barnyard animals. But the magi carry away a vision of a world transformed, of direct divine intervention into the affairs of humanity. The promise of salvation has been conveyed to them in an epiphany. As in earlier classical epiphanies, a visible manifestation of something invisible records the arrival of divinity on earth for the purpose of aiding mankind.

"Epiphany" is used almost solely in this theological sense until the twentieth century, when Joyce appropriates it into his aesthetic and literary theory. In the process of redefining the term, he focuses attention on a central psychological question: what is the relationship between an immediate perception and the value we ascribe to that perception? The answer to this question has important consequences, not only for psychology and literature, but for any epistemology based on the primacy of perception. Joyce defines the new literary epiphany in *Stephen Hero,* when Stephen Daedalus (later "Dedalus") is discussing his desire to collect trivial incidents which possess a unique intensity into a volume of epiphanies: "By an epiphany he meant a sudden spiritual manifestation, whether in the vulgarity of speech or of gesture or in a memorable phase of the mind itself."[14] Joyce's definition suggests a return to the original, literal meaning of the Greek term that referred to appearances, illuminations based on actual light, and physical objects suddenly revealed.

Joyce is not, however, the first to use "epiphany" in this sense. As Abrams has noted, Emerson expands the meaning of the term in the nineteenth century, when he refers to "facts, dull, strange despised things," which the aroused intellect finds to be "an Epiphany of God." Abrams quotes from Emerson's *Journals* but does not note that Emerson expanded on this use of the term in a lecture on December 19, 1838:

> Day creeps after day, each full of facts, dull, strange despised things that we cannot enough despise, call heavy, prosaic, and desart. The time we seek to kill. The attention it is elegant to divert from things around us. And presently the aroused intellect finds gold and gems in one of these scorned facts, then finds that the day of facts is a rock of diamonds, that a fact is an Epiphany of God, that on every fact of his life he should rear a temple of wonder and joy.[15]

In the draft version of this lecture, Emerson noted that "the facts . . . have no value until they take their order from conscious intelligence." The lecture takes this standard of value and applies it to the mind's ability to produce meaning and value out of seemingly insignificant events. Our life, says Emerson, is "nothing but an endless procession of facts or events like the pulsations of the heart or the beats of the pendulum." But the mind can act on these events, to manifest a new power: "The place of the fact is always the value of it. . . . Putrefaction is loathsome; but putrefaction seen as a step in the circle of nature, pleases. A mean or malicious act vexes me: but if I can raise myself to see how it stands related to past and future . . . it becomes comic, pleasant, fair, and prophetic." Emerson ends with a strikingly Wordsworthian description of this new form of epiphanic revelation: "The least fact to the [seeing soul] is full of meaning.... A flute heard out of a village window, a prevailing strain of a village maid will teach a susceptible man as much as others learn from the orchestra of the Academy."[16] We can only speculate whether Joyce knew of Emerson's use of "epiphany," but this little-known lecture reveals an important strand of nineteenth-century thought that connects the Wordsworthian spot of time with the Joycean epiphany.

The first epiphany recorded in *Stephen Hero* is the transcript of a brief, almost inaudible conversation between a young man and woman on a doorstep:

> The Young Lady—(drawling discreetly) ... O, yes ... I was ... at the ... cha ... pel ...
> The Young Man—(inaudibly) ... I ... (again inaudibly) ... I ...
> The Young Lady—(softly) ... O ... but you're ... ve ... ry ... wick ... ed ...

We note immediately that the silences and not the spoken words are most significant in this passage. Joyce suggests in the preceding paragraph what makes this seemingly trivial incident epiphanic. Stephen has been thinking of his own girlfriend when he eavesdrops on this exchange. As a result of overhearing this conversation, he sets about composing "some ardent verses," which he entitles "The Villanelle of the Temptress." He is predisposed by his own thoughts to respond to the undercurrents of this overheard conversation. The young girl's response to the young man's presumably indiscreet sexual suggestion creates in Stephen "an impression keen enough to afflict his sensitiveness very severely." A powerful imaginative response results from a trivial event.

Just how severely Stephen is affected by this epiphany does not become apparent until *A Portrait of the Artist as a Young Man*, where Joyce once again refers to the process of inspiration that is set in motion by an overheard conversation: "The instant flashed forth like a point of light and now from cloud on cloud of vague circumstance confused form was veiling softly its afterglow." In the sensitive mind of Stephen the trivial incident starts to take on a new shape—"O! In the virgin womb of the imagination the word was made flesh." A literal and figurative conception is set in motion by the seed of experience. As Emerson had pointed out in an essay written in the year of Wordsworth's death: "The finest poetry was first experience: but the thought has suffered a transformation since it was an experience. . . . In the poet's mind, the fact has gone quite over into the new element of thought, and has lost all that is exuvial."[17] This aspect of the modern epiphany has been largely ignored by critics. It records a moment when trivial circumstances are elevated to a new significance by the mind. The result is a new kind of poetry that values the ordinary and finds meaning in the seemingly insignificant.

Joyce describes epiphany as a psychological event. The majority of the epiphanies recorded by Joyce serve the same function as this first overheard conversation. A predisposition is triggered by a trivial event which takes on emotional and artistic significance by bringing an unrealized potential to light. Joyce applies the overheard conversation to Stephen's state of mind. In the process a truth about Stephen's predisposition is revealed. On the same page of *Portrait of the Artist*, Joyce defines the artist's role as that of a "priest of the eternal imagination, transmuting the daily bread of experience into the radiant body of everliving life." The daily bread—the commonplace—becomes revelatory and epiphanic at the point where it takes on the radiance of something beyond itself. The process occurs in the mind, where the raw data of consciousness are transformed into illuminated manifestations of meaning.

Recent commentators have noted two distinct, but related, uses of the term "epiphany" in Joyce. On the one hand, he uses "epiphany" to describe the moment of revelation, in which an object (often a person) or an experience reveals itself. On the other hand, Joyce uses the term to describe the verbal strategy by which numerous details in a poem or story are coalesced into a sudden disclosure of meaning. William T. Noon notes both of these senses of the term and says that epiphany in Joyce moves from Aquinas's epistemological *claritas* to become a completely verbal strategy. In *Stephen Hero*, according to Noon, epiphany is considered almost solely as a quality of experience, while in *Portrait of the Artist* experiential epiphany is not mentioned, having been subsumed by a general theory of aesthetics. Epiphany becomes central to a literary theory as early as Joyce's collection of manuscript "Epiphanies"—dream fragments, overheard conversations, naturalistic descriptions of vivid perceptions—and remains important, though modified, as late as *Finnegans Wake*, where the druid, as Noon points out, speaks of epiphany as a "sensible clue given by experience which leads the mind to interior philosophical insight, to the wisdom of 'the Ding hvad in idself id est.'"[18]

As early as 1946, Irene Hendry noted Joyce's tendency to shift back and forth "from the actuality of life experience to the experience of literature."[19] As Joyce evolved a more conscious literary theory, he moved away from autobiographical epiphanies to the suggestion that the artist could represent a symbolic imaginative essence as an epiphany in literature. Essential to my argument is Noon's claim that

> a literary application of the Joycean epiphany . . . would seem to differ little from the literary strategy which Wordsworth described as the aim of the *Lyrical Ballads:* "to choose incidents and situations from common life, and to relate or describe them, throughout, as far as possible, in a selection of language really used by men, and, at the same time, to throw over them a certain colouring of imagination, whereby ordinary things should be presented to the mind in an unusual aspect."[20]

Noon does not point out that Wordsworth's desire to trace the "primary laws of our nature: chiefly, as far as regards the manner in which we associate ideas in a state of excitement" is reminiscent of a claim made by Flaubert, Joyce's more obvious precursor. Writing to Louise Colet in 1852, Flaubert demanded that the work of a great artist should always make one "aware of a secret impassiveness in every atom and at every angle of vision; the effect on the spectator should be a kind of astonishment."[21] This kind of artistic impassiveness, combined with astonishment, plays an important role in the modern epiphany.

Joyce's goal, like Wordsworth's, is the production of Flaubert's kind of astonishment in his readers. The object is suddenly revealed as an interaction between the world and the mind: "Its soul, its whatness, leaps to us from the vestments of its appearance. The soul of the commonest object, the structure of which is so adjusted, seems to us radiant. The object achieves its epiphany." The world provides the objects; the sensitive imagination adjusts them to the radiant point of epiphany. Central to Joyce's idea, as to the Wordsworthian idea from which it derives, is the suggestion that epiphany occurs in the mind. A theological concept takes on a psychological application in Joyce's definition. Aquinas, to whom Joyce refers in his definition of epiphany, argued that beauty was composed of three parts: integrity, symmetry, and radiance (*claritas*). Stephen accepts this division. The first quality of the beautiful object—integrity—allows us to perceive it as "one integral thing." The second quality—symmetry—allows us to consider it as a whole composed of a relationship of parts, "an organized composite structure." The third quality causes Stephen the most difficulty:

> Now for the third quality. For a long time I couldn't make out what Aquinas meant. He uses a figurative word (a very unusual thing for him) but I have solved it. *Claritas* is *quidditas*. After the analysis which discovers the second quality the mind makes the only logically possible synthesis and discovers the third quality. This is the moment which I call epiphany.[22]

For Stephen, epiphany is the moment when the mind discovers the *claritas* (brilliance or radiance) of a thing to be identifiable with its *quidditas* (whatness), its essence as that which it is and no other thing. In the process the object achieves a significance in the mind which elevates it beyond its status as *an* object to its status as *this* particular object. In the mind of the artist this new significance gives rise to the desire to recreate this perceived essence in a work of art. Such an analysis helps to explain how the Joycean epiphany involves the reader. Any reader of a literary epiphany becomes a potential participant in the experience, who can likewise undergo the passage from an awareness of integrity through a sense of symmetry to a recognition of the significance of an experience. The claritas/quidditas of the object or image is available to the reader of an epiphanic poem or prose narrative in much the same way that it was to the author. The reader, in effect, is always able to complete the epiphany in his or her own mind.

As an aesthetic theory, Joyce's adoption of Aquinas's tripartite division is intentionally vague. We must remember that, however autobiographical *Stephen Hero* may be, the theory is put into the mind of a literary character, not Joyce himself. Our central concern should not be with the validity of the aesthetic theory but with the way the epiphany produces a new kind of literary representation of experience. Joyce systematizes a means of bestowing significance on objects and mental states that would have previously been considered trivial. The modern literary epiphany is the logical culmination of the celebration of the ordinary which began in English poetry with Wordsworth.

The New Epiphany

Now we must examine the historical forms of inspiration with which the modern epiphany is often confused, in order to understand what separates the literary epiphany from its theological counterpart. This examination will reveal a fundamental change in the notion of inspiration, a change that affected not only the form but also the content of poetry.

From Inspiration to Interpretation

> [Among the ancients] there were as many Religions almost as men; for every man's religion was his phansy; and they had most credit and authority, that could best invent, and make best shew . . . . There was no talk among men, but of dreams, revelations, and apparitions: and they that could so easily phansy god in whatsoever they did phansy, had no reason to mistrust or to question the relations of others.
> —Meric Causabon, *A Treatise concerning Enthusiasme* (1655)

In traditional visionary experience, revelation is described as a moment when the soul of the recipient is filled with something from outside the self. A literal inspiration occurs. Consciousness finds itself flooded, or breathed into, or simply filled, by a force it ascribes to an external agency. The metaphoric agent may be a wind, a flash of light, or a disembodied voice. Divine grace descends; the voice of God is heard in the whirlwind; a spirit inspires the prophet or poet with a truth that comes from outside the self and is incorporated into the soul of the recipient. The total meaning of the event is contained in its telling. We are not left to interpret what has happened. Interpretation in such cases is always the province of the teller. The coal that touches the lips of Isaiah is described by the prophet as the direct agency of his ability to speak truth. The recipient of divine visitation is always the one who reports the meaning of the event. This interpretive aspect of revelation will change in the modern literary epiphany.

The Old Testament prophets Ezekiel and Jeremiah each attribute their inspiration to direct physical agency. Ezekiel hears a sound that becomes part of himself: "And the spirit entered into me when he spake unto me" (2.2). In Jeremiah's case the active principle is no less direct—"Then the Lord put forth his hand, and touched my mouth. And the Lord said unto me, Behold, I have put my words in thy mouth" (1.9). The seer is a vessel, a passive recipient who becomes active only when the word enters his flesh. In the biblical account, events large and small have a direct connection to the divine will. In such instances, God's intervention has a direct relevance to the story being told or the individual being described. God is thus interpreted as the cause of untold natural and supernatural occurrences. This tendency was noted in the nineteenth century by the biblical scholar D. F. Strauss:

> There prevails in the biblical writers a ready disposition to derive all things down to the minutest details, as soon as they appear *particularly important*, immediately from God. He it is who gives the rain and sunshine; he sends the east wind and the storm; he dispenses war, famine, pestilence; he hardens hearts and softens them, suggests thoughts and resolutions. . . . In the history of the Israelites we find traces of his immediate agency at every step: through Moses, Elias, Jesus, he performs things which *never would have happened* in the ordinary course of nature.[23]

My italics indicate the source of the change represented by the modern literary epiphany. Though deriving from "particularly important" details of specific lives, the epiphanies of the nineteenth century emphasize not the interpretation of the ultimate meaning of the event but the emotional importance attached to certain transformed perceptions. Instead of revealing moments of supernatural manifestation, the new epiphany discloses a process of mind.

In religious experience, the impulse is always inward, which necessarily leads the individual to judge the final meaning of the experience as divine. Religious experience always relies on a specific interpretation of the meaning of a perceptual event. Jeremiah cannot say, "I think it is the voice of the Lord." He must say, "It *is* the voice of the Lord." Isaiah is not free to interpret his experience by saying, "It felt *like* a coal." He must say that it was a coal and that it came from God; otherwise the validity of his utterance is compromised. The recipient must say *what* power has entered him and changed him. Without this kind of certainty, the prophet's enterprise is no different from the poet's.

In a similar way, the power of revelation in a work like Augustine's *Confessions* rests on the role of the self as interpreter of the revelatory experience. Augustine's conversion hinges on an interpretation of perception based on the authority of Christian dog-

The New Epiphany

ma; as such it becomes the prototype for countless similar conversions. Its details reveal that traditional inspiration always involves an interpretive act on the part of the recipient. Augustine's description of his despair is well known. After allying himself with a number of intellectually sound positions, he is still racked with doubt. He accepts the arguments of Nebridius against the Manichaean heresy, embraces the doctrines of Simplicianus, and hears the story of Victorinus's powerful conversion. Yet his intellectual struggle with the concept of evil and his estrangement from direct divine mediation have left him alone and without solace.

Finally one afternoon in a garden with his friend, Alypius, Augustine hears a voice. He assumes that the voice is human, but he gives its message divine importance:

> So I was speaking, and weeping in the most bitter contrition of my heart, when, lo! I heard from a neighboring house a voice, as of boy or girl, I know not, chanting, and oft repeating, "Take up and read; Take up and read." Instantly, my countenance altered, I began to think most intently, whether children were wont in any kind of play to sing such words: nor could I remember ever to have heard the like. So checking the torrent of my tears, I arose; *interpreting it to be no other than a command from God* to open the book, and read the first chapter I should find.[24]

My italics emphasize Augustine's role in interpreting the meaning of this experience. This process is ultimately not perceptual but intellectual; Augustine hears a voice which he interprets as the voice of God. He has never heard children singing these words before; he knows no game to which they correspond. On this basis, and because of a powerful personal disposition to such an interpretation, he concludes that this overheard singing must be a message from God. Augustine's perception and his interpretation actually contradict each other; he relies on his interpretation and disregards his perception. He immediately takes up the volume of Paul he has been reading and opens to the passage "Not in rioting and drunkenness, not in chambering and wantonness, not in strife and envying: but put ye on the Lord Jesus Christ, and make not provision for the flesh." Augustine interprets this passage as having a particular relevance to his own past. As he finishes reading he describes a change in himself: "No further would I read; nor needed I: for instantly at the end of this sentence, by a light as it were of serenity infused into my heart, all the darkness of doubt vanished away."[25]

Augustine describes the revelation in purely intellectual terms. It involves no direct perception beyond the voice he interprets as sent from God. After he has decided that this voice cannot be a children's game, he takes up the Scripture. The Pauline passage is directly responsible for the resolution of his doubts and despair. The memory of his own past combines with the thought of serving Christ to cure Augustine's despair. He is put at ease, not by an experience of this world, but by a *thought* which reconciles the conflicting tendencies within him. The perceptual experience is merely the raw material of an interpretation. In the modern literary epiphany this process is reversed; revelation is found in the perceptual experience itself. The new epiphany reveals not an otherworldly spirit but the imaginative essence of experience, an essence which does not demand any particular interpretation.

Augustine's change of heart sets a pattern for numerous conversions that indicate how traditional religious experience differs from the imaginative literary epiphany. In the Puritan autobiographical writings of the seventeenth and eighteenth centuries, for example, revelatory conversion concentrates on the attempt to rid the soul of its sinful aspect. Among the Puritans, an external influence—always interpreted as divine intervention—becomes the means of casting off an old self (often called a husk or shell) and embracing a new self reborn in the light of divine grace and favor. In the literary epiphany that begins in the nineteenth century, this idea of one self replacing another gives way to the notion of a self formed out of the successive sensations in which it participates. While Puritan conversion produces intellectual satisfaction in the sudden discovery of a hitherto unrealized coherence—usually by means of Scripture—the Romantic epiphany seeks only the self-validating awareness of experience. The Puritan autobiographer awaits an experience that can be interpreted as the voice or hand of God. When it comes, an old identity is shed and a new one created. For the post-Enlightenment poet, by contrast, identity is forged out of countless experiences, large and small, which reveal the power of the mind to make experience meaningful. Unlike their traditional counterparts, the epiphanies that begin with Wordsworth leave their ultimate meaning unstated. When a meaning is stated, the interpretation is always distinct from the experience. The literary

The New Epiphany

epiphany, as a form of revelation, is suggestive rather than definitive, connotative rather than denotative.

Whenever the traditional means of describing revelation threatens to separate experience and interpretation, the author is careful to stress the integral connection between the experience and one specific interpretation. Thomas Traherne, for example, although sounding like Wordsworth when he says, "It did not so much concern us what Objects were before us, as with what Eys we beheld them," maintains that he regains the innocent eyes of a child solely so that he "may enter into the Kingdom of God." Jonathan Edwards, similarly, finds himself infused with a sense of the "divine glory" that is "in almost every thing" only at the moment when he is accepting the justice of God's preelection of saved souls.[26] No similar fusion of experience and interpretation is necessary for the Romantics and their followers. From the time of Rousseau and Wordsworth, the powerful perceptual experience becomes primary and self-sustaining. Interpretation of the event may be important, but it is always subject to an indefiniteness that does not characterize the powerful moment itself.

An examination of several examples of traditional revelation sharpens the difference between traditional religious experience and the imaginative revelations of the Romantics and their successors. In 1666, John Bunyan recorded what he called "the merciful working of God upon my soul," in *Grace Abounding to the Chief of Sinners*. Bunyan's work is a masterpiece of self-scrutiny, analyzing every passage of Scripture and every autobiographical event that contributed to his eventual commitment to a life of ministry. Like those of Augustine, Bunyan's revelations are intellectual rather than perceptual: "One day, as I was passing in the field, and that too with some dashes on my conscience, fearing lest yet all was not right, suddenly this sentence fell upon my soul, Thy righteousness is in heaven; and methought withal, I saw with the eyes of my soul, Jesus Christ at God's right hand."[27]

Bunyan's vision rests not on any perceptual event but on his having understood a particular passage and then interpreted this understanding as the work of God. "Now did my chains fall off my legs indeed, I was loosed from my affliction and irons, my temptations also fled away." The old self drops away to reveal a new self free from sin. Bunyan's spiritual autobiography goes on to recount the continual backslidings and struggles of the new self. It con-

The Poetics of Epiphany

cludes with an affirmation of the endless tension between doubt and faith as represented by the Puritan doctrine of election: "I have sometimes seen more in a line of the Bible than I could well tell how to stand under, and yet at another time the whole Bible hath been to me as dry as a stick."[28] Bunyan suggests that the Bible's efficacy as a religious tool bears a direct relationship to his state of mind, which is one reason he can never be sure of the state of his soul in the eyes of God—"I find to this day seven abominations in my heart." For the Puritan there is no fulfillment until death. Until then, only the individual's judgment, or interpretation of the meaning of events, can guide action.

George Trosse, in his *Life*, records a series of incidents which interpret ordinary perceptual events in religious terms. During the first such instance Trosse has reached the limits of despair because of a continued life of drunkenness and debauchery. "While I was thus walking up and down," he writes, "hurried with these worldly disquieting Thoughts, I perceiv'd a *Voice*, (*I heard it plainly*) saying unto me, *Who art thou?* Which, knowing it could be the Voice of *no Mortal*, I concluded was the *Voice of God*."[29] Trosse's religious experience rests entirely on his assumption that this voice must be the voice of God, although he never explains the necessity for this conclusion. The voice tells Trosse to be more humble, and he obliges—first by falling to his knees and then by removing his kneeler, his hose, and his doublet. The figurative sloughing off of an old self is accompanied in Trosse's case by a literal shedding of his garments. Like Augustine, an intellectual conclusion leads Trosse to action.

This humbling process continues with another physical alteration of his identity: "At length, standing before the *Window,* I either *heard a Voice,* which bid me, or *had a strong Impulse,* which excited me to *cut off my Hair.*" Trosse offers two interpretations: either he has heard a voice or he has had a strong impulse. In either event, he is "excited." His final "vision," the only part of the experience that is visual, finds him once again interpreting the meaning of his perceptions in religious terms:

> Immediately, in a Corner of the Room, towards which my Eyes were directed, I saw, as it were, *Breath* coming down from the Roof, about the Bigness of a Man's Thigh, and to look to was somewhat like the *Beams of the Sun* shining into a Window; and by and by, from that *Breath,* I (*seemingly*) heard a Voice. . . . This *Breath* I then believ'd to have been the *Holy-Ghost.*[30]

The New Epiphany

Trosse's diction indicates his awareness of his own role as the interpreter of the value he claims for this experience. A shaft of sunlight looks to him *like* a breath; he *seems* to hear a voice; he *believes* this voice to be the Holy Ghost. Once again the language suggests the central role of interpretation in such revelatory occurrences. Milton, in one of his most often quoted sonnets, is similarly careful to say, "Methought I saw my late espoused saint" (not "I know I saw"), and then to describe, not an actual experience, but a dream. To interpret the form of meaning present in Augustine, Bunyan, and Trosse in terms of the modern literary epiphany, we would have to describe experiences that could stand alone without theological claims. If we removed the theological interpretations from these experiences, however, we would be left with events that were essentially meaningless.

One final example will clarify the essential difference between the literature of religious revelation and the literary epiphany. Of the British Protestants, no single reformer had a wider influence than John Wesley. Like Bunyan, Trosse, and others, Wesley's personal religious history rests on several significant autobiographical events. By Wesley's own account, the most important of these was the Aldersgate Street meeting of May 24, 1738. Here, while listening to a reading from Luther's preface to Romans, Wesley first claimed to have felt God's touch: "About a quarter before nine, while he [the reader] was describing the change which God works in the heart through faith in Christ, I felt my heart strangely warmed. I felt I did trust in Christ."[31] This event has always been described as the central conversion of Wesley's life. As one biographer has said, "Methodists and non-Methodists alike have seen in this event the evangelical conversion of Wesley. But of late years more and more scholars have classified this as a mystical rather than an evangelical conversion."[32] The important issue here is not the distinction between evangelical and mystical conversions but the way that Wesley interprets the warming of his heart in religious terms.

Wesley describes this feeling as a direct intervention of divinity into his life; he feels the presence of a redeemer in himself. We might think the experience would be absolute. As interpretation alters, however, so can the meaning of the event. In a letter written twenty-eight years after the Aldersgate experience, Wesley places the final meaning of any such revelation in a new and surprising context:

> I do not feel the wrath of God abiding in me; nor can I believe it does. And yet (this is the mystery) [I do not love God. I never did]. Therefore [I never] believed in the Christian sense of the word. Therefore [I am only an] honest heathen, a proselyte of the Temple, one of the [God-fearers]. And yet to be so employed of God! and so hedged in that I can neither get forward nor backward! Surely there never was such an instance since the beginning of the world. If I ever [have had] *that faith*, it would not be so strange. But [I never had any] other [evidence] of the eternal or invisible world than [I have] now; and that is [none at all], unless such as fairly shines from reason's glimmering ray. [I have no] direct witness.[33]

Wesley recognized so well the controversial tone and subject of this letter that he concealed essential passages in Greek and a form of private shorthand. At this point, the last great Protestant reformer reveals himself to be a victim of the prevailing empiricist current of thought. He is lamenting the lack of a more immediate confirmation for his faith than he has hitherto received. Wesley even suggests that the most likely evidence of an invisible world is reason, the same human faculty which so threatens his faith and will give a name to the historical age.

Wesley is anticipating the leap Wordsworth will make within three decades. Wesley has had no direct witness or incontrovertible evidence of the "eternal or invisible world." But perhaps the mind does not need direct, incontrovertible evidence or, as medieval scholastics had assumed, an absolute, intellectual interpretation of experience. The mind may be able to leave certain questions unanswered or unasked and in the process develop a more immediate response to experience. As Keats points out, defining negative capability, a mind should "be capable of being in uncertainties, Mysteries, doubts, without any irritable reaching after fact & reason."[34]

From Interpretation to Epiphany

> The shock-receiving capacity is what makes me a writer. I hazard the explanation that a shock is at once in my case followed by the desire to explain it. I feel that I have had a blow; but it is not, as I thought as a child, simply a blow from an enemy hidden behind the cotton wool of daily life; it is or will become a revelation of

The New Epiphany

some order; it is a token of some real thing behind appearances; and I make it real by putting it into words.
—Virginia Woolf, "A Sketch of the Past"

In all traditional religious inspiration certain experiences are interpreted as external influences of the divine on the mundane. In the literary epiphany ushered in by the Romantics, this traditional order is reversed; the ordinary is rendered remarkable by an imaginative transformation of experience. The visible reveals *something* invisible, but the status of the invisible component is left unstated. Its mystery becomes part of the value of the experience. For the Romantic, the imagination produces significance out of the mundane. In the new form of epiphany inaugurated by Wordsworth, the perceiving self flows into the world. It then sees in the world its own powers, reflected in the processes of nature, manifested in particularly intense imaginative perceptions, and preserved by memory.

The literary epiphany leaves open the ultimate meaning of the experience. Gone is the sense that an event has only one interpretation. This view is replaced by a belief that experience is a function of a mind that "half perceives and half creates." The new epiphany occurs both in the mind of the poet and in the poem. The literary epiphany emphasizes the ability of the mind to assign significance to events. At the same time, this new form of inspiration is not weakened by an absolute subjectivism; it reflects a world which is, in one sense, shared by all those who recognize its significance. The epiphany is private and subjective insofar as it originates in the emotional state of one individual. But its power, its tone, and its ability to radiate significance are not limited by its origins in a particular mind.

The possibility of such a new form of revelation emerges, in part, from the profound changes that were occurring in early nineteenth-century conceptions of time. The very possibility of the Wordsworthian spot of time is bound up with these changes. For centuries, time had been seen as an unbroken linear flow, sustained in its continuity by the mind of God and moving progressively from the beginning of the universe to a final apocalyptic end. According to this view, the mind of an individual enters into the "river" of time at birth and passes out of chronological time into a timeless "ocean" of eternity at death. During most of human history, time conceived as limitless duration had not been distinguished from time conceived as successive moments. God's mind, as Berkeley suggested, assured the continuity between all time and the limited time of a single human life.

Georges Poulet has argued that this idea underwent a radical change in the eighteenth century, when the notion of God as the sustainer of time from instant to instant was replaced by the idea that "feelings, sensations and whatever causes sensations" were the only guarantors of continuity over time. In psychological terms, an emphasis on continuous time was replaced by an emphasis on time conceived in momentary terms. "It is the greatness of the eighteenth century to have conceived the prime moment of consciousness as a generating moment and generative not only of other moments but also of a self which takes shape by and through the means of these very moments."[35] This same self will become the self of Romanticism, a self that desires to give "the moment all the profundity, all the infinity of duration of which man feels capable." Browning's infinite moment likewise emerges from this idea that a moment can suggest limitless duration.

New emphasis on the moment was facilitated by the radical empiricism of Locke and his followers. Locke describes sensations that are individual mental events which succeed one another with great rapidity and give rise to ideas. The concept of such mental events emphasizes the fragmentary nature of consciousness and the momentary succession of one perception by another. Hume expands the logical consequences of Locke's view and concludes that "every moment must be distinct from, and posterior or antecedent to another . . . each moment, as it succeeds another, [is] perfectly single and indivisible."[36] Hume's account assures the independence and uniqueness of each successive instant. The result is an emphasis, not on the continuity between these moments, but on the content and importance of each moment considered individually.

Hume reflects this view most directly in his account of personal identity. Locke had argued that all our ideas derive from impressions. Hume adds that all such impressions "must either be some sensations deriv'd from the sight, or some internal impressions arising from these sensations. Our internal impressions are our passions, emotions, desires and aversions." While searching for the unity behind these momentary mental events, the individual is presented, not with a unity, but with a collection of fragments. "When I enter most intimately into what I call *myself*, I always stumble on some particular perception or other." If there is a self beyond these particular perceptions, it can only be described as "a bundle or collection of different perceptions, which succeed each other with an inconceivable rapidity." In Hume's skeptical account, the notion of time as a continuous flow gives way to a view of time as an invisibly rapid succession of "still" moments. These singular moments provide continuity only as the frames of a movie film provide the illusion of motion. "The mind is a kind of theatre," he writes, "where several perceptions successively make their appearance; pass, re-pass, glide away, and mingle in an infinite variety of postures and situations."[37] Hume's thoroughgoing skepticism about time likewise challenges the traditional conception of the soul when he concludes, "Nor is there any single power of soul, which remains unalterably the same, perhaps for one moment." Human experience becomes a series of distinct moments.

This increased emphasis on experience as a series of independent moments is one of the root intuitions behind the new literary epiphany. In traditional revelation, rare instances of divine intervention into temporal life were seen as the cause of inspiration. Religious visions were described in fleeting terms because they were seen as interruptions in the normal flow of linear time. A soul in touch with God was a soul suddenly removed from the limitations imposed by earthly time. Divinity was described as having spoken or appeared in whirlwinds, flashes, thunderclaps, or bolts of lightning—all startling breaks in the normally unbroken stream of linear time. Milton suggests just such a break in the flow of time in "On the Morning of Christ's Nativity," when the stars "will not take their flight" and the "Sun himself withheld his wonted speed." Divine power, in Milton's description, affects the means by which mankind measures time.

As experience is seen in increasingly fragmentary terms, however, the role of time is reversed. All experience comes to be founded on momentary mental events. Metaphors once used only to describe divine occurrences are used to refer to ordinary events. The Romantic who adopts the fragmentary view implied by the empiricist critique must find a new way of validating the meaning of short-lived mental events. The literary epiphany becomes one way of elevating the status of certain of these experiences. In Locke, momentary sensation leads to reflection. In Hume, sense impressions give rise to internal mental impressions. The two aspects of this form of empiricism become the prototype for the Wordsworthian relationship between perception and the emotions that arise as a result of perception. The new imaginative epiphany suggests that the mind itself, aided by emotion, can make the kinds of momentary leaps of understanding that were once ascribed only to an external, divine agency.

Romanticism distinguishes two senses of time, one which chronologically orders events, the other which evaluates an experience on the basis of its ability to possess atemporal significance. Frank Kermode has adopted two theological terms to call these senses of time *chronos*, or chronological time, and *kairos*, or imaginative time. The former describes the time in which experience occurs, while the latter refers to time as it is conceived in the mind, with emphasis given to moments of significance. Chronos can be seen as clock time, while kairos is a psychologically determined sense of time. Chronos is dreaded, says Kermode, because of the realization that, once it has passed, it is gone forever. In kairos, by contrast, there is a possibility for the retention of value through emphasis and memory. In this regard Kermode comments perceptively on Wordsworth when he says,

> The hiding places of power, for Wordsworth as well as for Proust, are the agents of time's defeat, discovered by involuntary memory, pure of discursive significance like the girl with the pitcher, they provide the structure and meaning and pleasure which constitute our deliverance from the long meaningless attrition of time.[38]

In the new literary epiphany, likewise, kairos will defeat chronos and replace the fear of temporal physical decay with the possibility of momentary mental redemption.

In *Wordsworth in Time*, John Beer adopts Kermode's distinction and indicates even more clearly how kairos is a distinguishing characteristic of Romanticism. He notes that the poets of the eighteenth century always spoke of time without a sense of crisis. Beginning with the Romantics, however, "The moment of judgment, the moment of decision, the sudden illumination, the sudden despair"—all examples of kairos—become increasingly significant organizing principles in poems. Kairos, says Beer, depicts "time as offering repeated opportunities—which in turn call for an agile readiness that can turn them to account." Memory is central to the process because it suggests the possibility of "constant intervention of acts of renewal" within a consciousness that can draw on the creative (imaginative) aspect of mind. In Coleridge as in Wordsworth, we are offered "new ways of thinking about memory . . . through its power of restoring instantly to the human consciousness moments revived from years before."[39] One of the most common forms of epiphany involves just such restorative acts of memory. Memory combines with a present perception to produce a heightened sense of the significance of a specific image. The impulse toward kairos leads directly to the new epiphany as it is first expressed in the Wordsworthian spot of time.

Beer also expands Kermode's use of kairos by contrasting it with another Greek word—*aiōn*—which helps to illuminate the origins of the nineteenth-century literary epiphany. He quotes Panofsky, who points out that, in classical art, time was not identified with Chronos, but rather "was depicted only as either fleeting Opportunity ('Kairos') or creative Eternity ('Aion')." Aiōn often appears as an Orphic divinity called Phanes, standing for an eternity available to mortals in life. Beer writes that Kairos

> depicted time as offering repeated opportunities—which in turn called for an agile readiness that could turn them to account. The Orphic Aion, similarly, offered a view of eternity as an ever-resurgent youthfulness, a sense which had later come to be sapped, as eternity was increasingly identified with an unending sequence of time, stretching limitlessly into the future.[40]

Beer does not point out, however, that Phanes, the hypostatized embodiment of aiōn, derives from the root of the term "epiphany," meaning simply a showing forth. I suggest that Wordsworth and his followers have developed a literary technique that derives from just such a concept of creative eternity. The "moment" becomes a way of defeating chronological time by emphasizing kairotic instants and recognizing an aionic timelessness that can be felt in experience.

Coleridge makes just such a distinction in a footnote to an 1817 poem entitled "Time, Real and Imaginary." Explaining the title, Coleridge says, "By imaginary Time, I meant the state of a school boy's mind when on his return to school he projects his being on his day dreams, and lives in the next holidays, six months hence: and this I contrasted with real Time." Time as real and time as felt, he continues, exist in "two different states of being."[41] The idea of such projection becomes central to many of Coleridge's epiphanies. The importance to subsequent literature of this distinction between two sorts of time is evident in a passage from Virginia Woolf's *Orlando*, which mistakenly suggests the concern as a new one:

> An hour, once it lodges in the queer element of the human spirit, may be stretched to fifty or a hundred times its clock length; on the other hand, an hour may be accurately represented on the timepiece of the mind by one second. This extraordinary discrepancy between time on the clock and time in the mind is less known than it should be and deserves fuller investigation.[42]

Abrams has noted the nineteenth-century German origins of this new sense of the value of the moment. He cites Schelling's mental state that "sets absolute eternity into the middle of time," Hölderlin's "Moments in which the imperishable is present in us," and Goethe's "flash of a now." Particularly revealing is Novalis's Joycean-sounding emphasis on experiences that "are especially striking at the glimpse of many a human form and face . . . at the hearing of certain words, at the reading of particular passages" and "at sight of 'many incidents and occurrences in the natural scene.' "[43] This tradition is imported into England by way of Coleridge and later Carlyle, whose own brand of secular spirituality sets forth a variation on this new means of valuing the ordinary.

Shelley also suggests that there may be more to a moment than temporal chronology allows. As early as *Queen Mab*, he senses the limitations imposed by the linearity of time. In a note to the poem, he writes,

> If, therefore, the human mind, by any future improvement of its sensibility, should become conscious of an infinite number of ideas in a minute, that minute would be eternity. I do not hence infer that the actual space between the birth and death of a man will ever be prolonged; but that his sensibility is perfectible, and that the number of ideas which his mind is capable of receiving is indefinite.[44]

This perfection of sensibility allows aionic moments to possess more than normal significance because of the powerful feelings with which they are invested. Such feelings, in turn, derive from the large number of associations—Shelley suggests "infinite"—that are focused in a single instant. Keats, in *Endymion*, assumes that one sense of immortality may derive from a similarly psychological source:

> O what a wild and harmonized tune
> My spirit struck from all the beautiful!
> On some bright essence could I lean, and
>   lull
> Myself to immortality.
> [3.170–74]

Under such circumstances, ordinary perceptions are transformed into archetypes of everlastingness. Keats's "bright essence" is like the perceptual experience that gives rise to Wordsworth's spot of time or Joyce's epiphany; it is the raw datum of consciousness that finds its manifestation and significance in the mind.

The difference between the Romantic epiphanic moment and the tradition of Puritan conversion has already been noted. The questing follower of Wesley feels that the world is devoid of meaning in the absence of an indwelling spirit of divine grace. The Romantic longs for a literal re-formation of a dead Newtonian universe. Both move from doubts and uncertainties to declarations based on specific momentary events. In the Puritan's case, the soul undergoes an instantaneous conversion to faith in a revealed redeemer. For the Romantic, the self is renovated, in fact created, through the perception of the world in particularly intense moments of experience. In both cases, the short-lived significant event possesses intense personal importance. In both cases, the experience tends to follow on the heels of a period of despair and to occur at the close of a particular sequence of events. It then becomes a source of continuing renovation. The critical difference is in the attribution of the source and the significance of the experience. The religious convert or religiously inspired poet always ascribes a specific source and meaning to the event. For the Romantic, the experience itself is more important than any particular interpretation of its meaning. In fact, the multiplicity of possible interpretations increases the potential value of the modern epiphanic moment.

While the emotional intensity and autobiographical aspect of Puritan conversions form a bridge between traditional inspiration and the Romantic renovation of the self in experience, the literary epiphany ushered in by Wordsworth, Coleridge, and others represents a radical departure from previous experiences of significance. The Romantics and their followers are not looking for a single, blinding, all-encompassing insight into the nature of reality and the self's place in the world. Instead they are building up a self defined by its relations, a self created out of its own awareness of its responses to experience. Epiphany becomes a key to this achievement by imaginatively describing moments when the perceiving self sees its own imaginative and associative powers helping to create the world. I do not mean to suggest that every momentary or extraordinary experience is potentially epiphanic. Indeed, the epiphanies I will be discussing originate in commonplace events. The extraordinary aspect is the mind's role in receiving, organizing, and creating a new vision of the experience. The emphasis is not on seeing a new thing but on seeing a familiar thing in a new way. These are the sights, as Wordsworth says, "of common day," invested with new and lasting significance by a sensitive mind. The feeling of the experience—its expansiveness, its atemporality, its mysteriousness—always seems greater than any interpretation placed on its objects. The ordinary is rendered remarkable by a heightened awareness, a sense of the potential value and profundity of the mundane. Nor is the momentariness of the literary epiphany its sole defining characteristic. Epiphany defies chronological time in favor of a psychological time based on emphasis and vividness, not duration of the clock. It achieves aiōn, a sense of eternity, when time becomes a function of the mind's ability to achieve peaks of intensity in defiance of chronology.

The new literary epiphany that begins in the nineteenth century is also separated from traditional forms of inspiration by its frequency. Epiphanies are neither visionary nor mystical nor rare. They are, in Wordsworth's phrase, scattered everywhere. They are vivid transformations of perception that intrude on the poet's ordinary perceptual consciousness as a result of the poet's willingness to feel deeply about the details of ordinary experience. The poet often does not do so consciously, which accounts for the extrasensory quality that may be attributed to these moments. The emotion attached to the epiphany presents a value that is left to the reader to interpret. The recipient may suggest, but never delimits, the meaning of the experience. The mind in epiphany assumes that organic role so well defined by Coleridge; it becomes like the plant that grows by absorbing the very atmosphere it helps to create. We cannot say exactly why Wordsworth's leech-gatherer is important, but we can say that he *is* important at that moment. The process of explanation opens out from the powerful image, rather than closing in on it. We identify epiphanies by their tone. The described experience always seems more significant than any moral or didactic interpretation to which it gives rise. The expansiveness of the feeling helps to make the epiphany memorable. The process exemplifies that disequilibrium between events and the meaning of events that is a unique characteristic of modern literature.

When the seventeenth-century poet Henry Vaughan claims to have seen "eternity the other night," his experience involves nothing perceptual. The vision is an intellectual achievement; the poem accordingly is not epiphanic. For the same reason, the metaphysical poets, whose language is easily confused with the language of epiphany, are not describing epiphanies. In all such cases inspiration is the result of interpretation rather than of a powerful perception. Such experience is just the reverse of Wordsworth's, whose vision, no matter how much it may be imaginatively elaborated, is absolutely grounded in the world of sense. Wordsworth's epiphanies reveal heightened perceptions, but they are perceptions nonetheless. Wordsworth asks only for an intensified imaginative perception of this world.[45] The meaning of such experiences is open ended; in a sense it is endless. We go on interpreting epiphanies because they do not completely contain or restrict meaning within themselves. In Coleridge's "Frost at Midnight," for example, icicles as a part of ordinary experience are transformed into imaginative icicles—"quietly shining to the quiet moon"—which reflect the processes of nature described in the poem. We are not told what the imagined icicles mean; we are *shown* that they are significant. Epiphany, in this sense, reveals the essence of a mental event.

Traditional inspiration tends to be theophanic, not epiphanic. This distinction is crucial to an understanding of the new literary epiphany, which replaces theophany as the dominant form of literary inspiration during the nineteenth century. Traditional inspiration claims that a specific theological entity is contained in the experience it records. But the literal and original meaning of "epiphany" carries only the sense of a manifestation, without specifying a particular content. This sense of the term is applicable to the Romantics and their followers, from Tennyson and Browning to Wallace Stevens and Seamus Heaney. Theophanies, like earlier forms of epiphany, record appearances of God, while epiphanies record the mind caught in the act of valuing particularly vivid images. Any interpretation of the epiphany is derivative, originating first in the powerful feeling that accompanies the illumination. The biblical prophets, Augustine, and the Puritan divines always attribute their inspiration to a specifically named manifestation of divinity: God, Christ, the Holy Ghost.[46] Wordsworth and Coleridge—like Tennyson, Browning, Yeats, and Stevens—record a form of non-theophanic inspiration in which the source of the revelation is internal and the results of the revelation are unspecified. This lack of specificity, however, does not mean that the experience cannot be significant or life altering.

It is not coincidental that the forms in which poetry is written change during this period. Romantic attempts at continuous narrative fail in part because the experiences they seek to describe cannot be sustained over time. Keats abandoned "Hyperion," Coleridge never completed "Christabel," Shelley struggled with "The Triumph of Life," and Byron rendered Don Juan's epic episodically. *The Prelude* includes numerous interconnected lyrics that are worked into a narrative sequence. In much the same way, the self these works seek to describe is the product of a series of experiences that form a coherent body of memory and create unity over time. *The Prelude,* as early drafts of the poem indicate, evolved out of a series of lyrical fragments, almost all of which can be described as epiphanic. Carol T. Christ reminds us that Frank Kermode has located "the continuity between nineteenth- and twentieth-century poetry in a belief in the image as a radiant truth out of space and time." This Romantic emphasis on the radiant image is central to "Pound's imagism, Eliot's objective correlative, and Yeats's concept of the symbol."[47] Christ links Tennyson, Browning, and Arnold to Yeats, Eliot, and Pound in terms of what we now see as their shared Romantic assumptions. J. Hillis Miller suggests another continuity over the past two centuries in terms of what he calls the "linguistic moment," those points "in poems from Wordsworth to Stevens in which the intrinsic equivocations of ordinary language interfere with the expression of a univocal meaning."[48] Both Christ's emphasis on the "radiant image" and Miller's on the "linguistic moment" can be connected to the development of the literary epiphany.

In a structural sense, epiphany becomes an organizing narrative principle for much of the poetry that comes after *Lyrical Ballads,* just as it serves later in the twentieth-century novel. This tendency is clearest in Browning, whose dramatic monologues begin the transition from lyric to narrative that gives rise to the modern novel.

The New Epiphany

Victorian poetry is crucial in this development because of the ways epiphany is transformed, particularly by Browning, from a primarily lyrical poetic form—associated with the poet's own voice—into a means of expressing character in the dramatic monologue. Much work remains to be done on the shift from socially grounded lyric to episodic long poem, dramatic monologue, and self-revelatory lyric from the eighteenth to the twentieth century. We must grasp the role played by epiphanies in this shift in order to understand the way in which poetry was written during this period. The process charts, in one sense, a history of modern poetry. By the time D. H. Lawrence and Virginia Woolf are writing their avowedly poetic novels, epiphanies have become a new means of organizing prose narratives. Traditional narrative emphasis on linear time gradually gives way to an emphasis on heightened psychological moments of perceptual intensity.

This book does not offer a restrictive definition or narrowly selected illustrations of epiphany. Nor do I want to overextend the notion of epiphany to encompass every noteworthy event. In discussing the epiphanic we are dealing with a cluster of ideas related by family resemblance, not a single concept that can be discursively articulated. The epiphany takes a variety of forms and displays varying tendencies within these forms. Wordsworth's spots of time are by no means identical to Browning's infinite moments; Shelley's fleeting upward flights are not equivalent to Coleridge's flashes. But the similarities that unite these forms of epiphany are greater than the differences that separate them. All involve a new way of evaluating experience, and all relate in similar ways to immediate perception, the role of self-consciousness in poetry, and the importance of the affective memory. The open-ended nature of the concept derives from the fact that a central aspect of epiphany occurs in the reader. In every instance I will examine, the poet is trying to make something happen in the reader. There is no need to demand any absolute truth or falsity from the experience. Our judgment is suspended while we receive a description of a mental event. The literary epiphany becomes one way of deriving meaning from experience in the modern world. The process is similar to that which occurs every time new myths are created. In epiphany, words manifest the power of language to reify experience.

Jung has called such coalescences of thought and feeling "synchronistic." They constitute "meaningful coincidences of external and internal events." In synchronistic events, the correlation of a preexisting mental disposition and a corresponding experience in the present produces powerful feelings of connection between the two. These "patterns of mental behavior contain not only an imaginative but a cognitive element which can influence the conscious mind in the form of sudden 'flashes of insight.'" Jung, echoing what Joyce calls the "radiance" of epiphany, labels the cognitive element of the synchronistic disposition "luminosity." This luminosity is distinguished from ordinary consciousness because it leads to particularly strong emotional responses. Among the responses produced by this luminous aspect of mind, Jung cites conversions, religious convictions, fanaticism, obstinate thoughts, and the "passionate and creative pursuit of a theme." Jung's concept of synchronicity derived from his study of dreams, in which he "again and again encountered cases where rare outer chance events tended to coincide meaningfully with archetypal dream images."[49] These tendencies apply to literature at the point where the writer records synchronistic experiences of "luminous" correspondence between an internal predisposition and a powerfully felt external perception. This connection between the accidental and the meaningful, however, is not new. De Quincey commented on the mind's ability to bestow value on coincidence when he said:

> The fleeting accidents of a man's life, and its external shows, may indeed be irrelate and incongruous; but the organising principles which fuse into harmony, and gather about fixed, predetermined centres, whatever heterogeneous elements life may have accumulated from without, will not permit the grandeur of human unity greatly to be violated.[50]

Human unity for De Quincey, as for Jung, derives from the "organizing principles" of the mind which fuse accidental, incongruous elements into a luminous harmony. Exactly this process occurs in modern literary epiphanies.

Ricoeur provides a model that can be modified to explain further the relationship between experience and its literary representation in the poetic epiphany. In his criteriology of symbols he suggests that in "poetry the symbol is caught at that moment when it is a welling up of language, 'when it puts language in a state of emergence,' instead of being regarded in its hieratic stability under the protection of rites and myths."[51] Language breaks free in poetic images to suggest new forms of meaning. But, of course, "poetic images themselves are essentially words." The epiphany, in this sense, takes place in the poem. It is a verbal manifestation of significance that emerges from the poem. Experiences become epiphanies, as Ricoeur says of symbols, when they "gather together at one point a mass of significations which, before giving rise to thought, give rise to speech. The symbolic *manifestation* as a *thing* is a matrix of symbolic meanings as words."[52] The emphasis is Ricoeur's and suggests a connection between his "poetic symbols" and literary epiphanies.

Language, in all of the epiphanies I will be examining, is the means of intensifying an experience. The valuable experience cannot be declared to be significant until it assumes verbal form. In the process of this transformation the perceptual experience itself becomes more significant. In traditional revelation, the ineffable aspect of the experience—the supposedly unreachable essence—was primary. In the modern literary epiphany, by contrast, the perceptual experience and its transformation into language is primary. The new epiphany does not try to point beyond language as much as it reveals the ways in which language can manifest the essence of experience. The literary text is able to heighten, exalt, confirm, or reveal one kind of mental event. In the process, the literary epiphany transmits mental power through language. The modern epiphany emphasizes the perception of significance rather than the interpreted meaning of the significant moment.

For this reason Wordsworth's spots of time defy final interpretation and Romantic poetry generally has given rise to numerous—often conflicting—interpretations. Epiphany places the burden of interpretation on the reader. It records an individual experience, which passes into the realm of the symbolic when the reader relates the epiphany to the wider details of experience. Arnold thus can claim that Wordsworth makes us feel, and John Stuart Mill can ascribe therapeutic properties to *Lyrical Ballads*. Epiphany records a moment when the human potential for ordering consciousness finds its object in experience. In the process the world achieves a new, open-ended significance. If the author who seeks to escape the ordinary limits of consciousness through language is driven by a complex set of factors, then so is the interpreter of such a text. As a result, the literary epiphany contributes to the multifarious interpretations that characterize contemporary discourse about literature. The richness and complexity—and even confusion—produced by diverse interpretations of epiphanies suggest that this new form of meaning contributes to critical pluralism. Numerous

The Poetics of Epiphany

interpretations—historicist, psychoanalytic, feminist, deconstructive—can thus be grounded in the circumstances behind the text (historical, biographical, experiential, critical) but at the same time anchored in the text itself. In many cases the epiphany is reproducible in the process of interpreting such texts.

The modern epiphany is produced by a wise man of sorts, a magus who strives to make a new truth manifest. In epiphany, the phenomena of experience are described as at once high and low, sacred and profane, mundane and transcendent. The mundane element is the individual's perception. The transcendent feature is the self's ability to recognize the value both of the experience and of the mind as an interpreter of the experience; to say as Wordsworth does, "To my soul I say, I recognize thy glory." As Joyce makes clear, the theophanies of the past will no longer serve to describe the essence of life made manifest. The creator, for Joyce, is identified with the total creation:

>—The ways of the Creator are not our ways, Mr Deasy said. All history moves toward one great goal, the manifestation of God.
> Stephen jerked his thumb toward the window, saying:
>—That is God.
> Hooray! Ay! Whrrwhee!
>—What? Mr Deasy asked.
>—A shout in the street, Stephen answered, shrugging his shoulders.[53]

As this transcript of an epiphany suggests, a shout in the street can reveal the essence of life if it is remarked upon and transformed in the mind of the creative artist. "Imagination," as Shelley said, "is as the immortal God which should assume flesh for the redemption of mortal passion." This imagination can always be incarnated in language. In the instances I will be examining, the epiphanic imagination is always literary; its products are expressed as poems or prose narratives. The new dispensation represented by the literary epiphany is based on the ability of the experiencing self to recognize its powers and limitations and to recreate imaginatively the sources of its strength. In the literary epiphany, the isolated moment of one individual's immediate experience becomes a potential source of value in the minds of others. Wordsworth and his followers sense the extent and the limitations of the new epiphany; these modern magi bear a message only as valid as their ability to tell its truth.

2

Wordsworth and the Origins of Epiphany

Wordsworth's Originality

> Human creatures are swarming in the enclosure, moving backwards and forwards through the thick ooze. Some ask if the race is going on; they are answered "Yes" and "No." A band begins to play. . . . A beautiful brown horse, with a yellow rider upon him, flashes far away in the sunlight.
> —Joyce, *Epiphanies*

SHELLEY is perhaps the first to connect the accidental and the oracular in Wordsworth when he says:

> he never could
> Fancy another situation
> From which to dart his contemplation,
> Than that wherein he stood.
> [*Peter Bell the Third*, 4.299–302]

To an ideal imagination like Shelley's, this inability to extrapolate from immediate experience is clearly a weakness. Yet even amid the blistering satire of "Peter Bell the Third," Shelley indicates that Wordsworth is able to transform the situations "wherein he stood" into substantial and significant poetry:

> Yet his was individual mind,
> And new created all he saw
> In a new manner, and refined

35

> Those new creations, and combined
> Them, by a master-spirit's law.
> [4.303–7]

The master spirit is Wordsworth, whose particular genius, according to Shelley, lies in recreating his own experience poetically. The individual mind refines and then recombines the materials on which it operates. This ability to create "all he saw / In a new manner" is also the source of the Wordsworthian epiphany.

In this stanza and the one immediately following, Shelley shows himself to be one of the most perceptive of Wordsworth's early critics:

> Thus—though unimaginative,
>   An apprehension clear, intense,
> Of his mind's work, had made alive
> The things it wrought on; I believe
>   Wakening a sort of thought in sense.
> [4.308–12]

While Coleridge, Hazlitt, and others are calling Wordsworth the most imaginative poet in English, Shelley is claiming that any poet who derives so much from his own personal experience cannot be said to be using his imagination: "He had as much imagination / As a pint-pot" (298–99). Although this comment sounds like merely another criticism of Wordsworth's egotism, Shelley's critique is actually more subtle. Wordsworth is using a faculty which Shelley is willing to call only the mind, a faculty that gives rise to thoughts derived from the objects of sense. In the process, a clear apprehension of the poet's own mind enlivens these same objects. Yet Coleridge, in his praise of Wordsworth's imagination, makes a related point. Wordsworth "does indeed," says Coleridge, quoting from the poet, "to all thoughts and to all objects 'add the gleam, / The light that never was, on sea or land.' "[1] For Coleridge, this gleam is identified with imagination itself, the "prime agent of all human perception." While others are praising Wordsworth for his self-avowed ability to "see into the life of things," Shelley is claiming the opposite. If the mind of the poet makes "alive / The things it wrought on," then it is giving them life, not recognizing a life that already exists in them. Wordsworth's "gleam . . . that never was on sea or land" is in the mind, not in things.

The central experience in Wordsworth's poetry will come to

serve all of the Romantic poets: the suggestion that certain short-lived perceptual occurrences can be invested with significance by a sensitive soul. As a result, these experiences can give ordinary events a quality that can only be described as revelatory. The process also gives rise to powerful new images in the mind. Wordsworth shows how receptiveness to the raw data of consciousness can lead to a manifestation of the essence of the object perceived. At the same time, this receptivity has the potential to reveal something essential about the nature of the perceiver as well. De Quincey connects this relationship between subject and object in Wordsworth with the accidental when he says:

> It is astonishing how large a harvest of new truths would be reaped simply through the accident of a man's feelings, or being made to feel, more *deeply* than other men. He sees the same objects, neither more nor fewer, but he sees them engraved in lines far stronger and more determinate: and the difference in strength makes the whole difference between consciousness and subconsciousness.[2]

In 1845, De Quincey hints that the power of Wordsworth's epiphanies lies somehow below or beneath consciousness. Coleridge's verses in praise of the poem that later became *The Prelude* make a similar claim. Wordsworth's theme, Coleridge says in "To William Wordsworth," is of "moments awful," of "currents self-determined . . . by some inner Power." Coleridge likewise came to rely on the power of a creative imagination that could infuse otherwise ordinary moments with awe and wonder.

Many attempts to "explain" Wordsworth fail to acknowledge the extent to which his most far-reaching contribution to poetry, and perhaps to cultural history, is his most basic. In his formative period and during his most creative decade, 1798–1807, Wordsworth establishes a new means of organizing experience by focusing on commonplace events, subjects that would never before have warranted poetic concern. As a result, the imagination—however it is defined—has new materials on which to operate. Countless individuals, both readers and writers of poetry, suddenly find themselves with a new way of validating the emotions they attach to events by creating a mental image that makes the experience valuable. We should note here that *Lyrical Ballads* created the climate in which it was to be appreciated and imitated. Wordsworth is not telling the whole truth when he claims in 1815 in the "Essay, Supplementary to the Preface" that "every author, as far as he is great and at the same time *original,* has had the task of *creating* the taste by which he is to be enjoyed." Wordsworth attributes the remark to Coleridge. This claim is, in fact, the theoretical opposite of Pope's "what oft was thought, but n'er so well expressed." Wordsworth and Coleridge are perhaps the first poets in English to form at once a body of poetry and the taste by which it was to be appreciated; they originate the notion, which has far-reaching consequences for literary history, that poetic innovation is praiseworthy.

Wordsworth's poetry often says nothing more complex than "this is what I saw—this is how it affected me." Such a simple claim differs from the premise that generally underlay earlier poetry: "this is what is important—this is what it means." Much of Wordsworth's finest poetry makes surprisingly few claims about the meaning of the experiences it describes. Instead it merely relates an event and attributes to it a particular emotional response. The poem then produces a new sense of the experience transformed: an image of daffodils, leech-gatherer, drowned man, or moonrise which can radiate significance. Wordsworth's ability to hold certain tensions and balance opposing philosophical viewpoints derives from the fact that his intentions are often cloaked in nuances of meaning, in a pervasive sense of mystery. Such multiple and problematic meanings originate with Wordsworth and Coleridge precisely because they sensed that creativity was partly, as we would now say, unconscious: irrational, coincidental, and ultimately inexplicable.

Wordsworth's notes and letters record numerous conversations and numerous lines of poetry written "exactly" as their original speaker spoke them to Wordsworth. The untitled poem "on my own life" was subsequently subtitled "Growth of a Poet's Mind: An Autobiographical Poem." Keats's attribution of the phrase "egotistical sublime" is a legitimate insight into poems that focus on the poet's own experience. One of the earliest reviewers of *The Prelude* called it "the first *regular versified* autobiography we remember in our language."[3] More revealing, however, are other early critical comments which suggest how a recounting of mundane autobiographical details could have poetic value. The *Eclectic Review* noted that the moods "of such a mind will be ranked with the dramas, lyrics, and epics of inferior poets. . . . His fragments will be valued as if they were bits of the ark. . . . Wordsworth can extract poetry from anything. . . . His eye anoints every object it encounters." The reviewer for *Tait's Edinburgh Magazine* remarked that "the external imageries of the visible are but accessories deriving their interest only from their relation to the sentient soul of man," while *Graham's Magazine* said that Wordsworth's "topics, therefore, though trite in themselves, all are made original from the peculiarities of the person conceiving them." The poem is not so much about the external world as it is about the "mind of man"; "*The Prelude* conveys more real available knowledge of the facts and laws of man's internal constitution, than can be found in Hume or Kant." The *British Quarterly Review* concluded that the book-length poem is "not so much a complete autobiography of the poet up to his thirtieth year, as a theoretic retrospect of what the poet himself considered significant in that portion of his life."[4] All of these critics recognize the heart of Wordsworth's originality: his ability, as Wordsworth himself says, "to choose incidents and situations from common life . . . and . . . throw over them a certain colouring of imagination, whereby ordinary things should be presented in an unusual aspect." The mind elevates the ordinary; the "gleam, / The light that never was, on sea or land," produces literary epiphanies.

The radical aspect of this notion is the range of experience that the poet can treat. Wordsworth thus created a revolution not only in poetic style and subject but also in the circumstances surrounding the writing of poetry. Dorothy's comments about her brother's techniques of composition are revealing: March 18, 1798—"The withered leaves danced with the hailstones. William wrote a description of the storm" ("A whirl-blast from behind the hill"). March 19— "William and Basil and I walked to the hill-tops, a very cold bleak day. We were met on our return by a severe hailstorm. William wrote some lines describing a stunted thorn" ("The Thorn"). October 11, 1800—"After dinner we walked up Greenhead Gill in search of a sheepfold. . . . The Sheepfold is falling away it is built nearly in the form of a heart unequally divided." October 12— "William went into the Wood to compose" ("Michael"). April 16, 1802—"When we came to the foot of Brothers water I left William sitting on the Bridge. . . . When I returned I found William writing a poem descriptive of the sights and sounds we saw and heard" ("The Cock is crowing," published as "Written in March, while resting on the bridge at the foot of Brother's Water"). Wordsworth's own comments on the process of composition also reveal the potential immediacy of the transformation of experience into poetry: "The little girl who is the heroine I met within the area of Goodrich Castle in the year 1793" ("We Are Seven"); "composed October 3rd or 4th, 1802, after a journey over the Hambleton Hills, on a day memorable to me—the day of my marriage" ("Composed after a Journey across the Hambleton Hills"); "felt and in great measure composed upon the little mount in front of our abode at Rydal" ("Composed upon an Evening of Extraordinary Splendour and Beauty"); "composed on the road between Nether Stowey and Alfoxden, extempore. I distinctly recollect the very moment when I was struck, as described— 'He looks up—the clouds are split'" ("A Night-Piece"); "actually composed while I was sitting by the side of the brook" ("Lines Written in Early Spring").[5]

These references all describe instances when Wordsworth immediately appropriated his experience as the raw material for poetry. The importance of this connection is often lost on modern readers, for whom the immediate utilization of personal experience has become a staple of poetic expression. For Wordsworth, transformation occurs when the imagination—seen in Romantic terms as essentially a creative faculty—operates on these experiences to recreate them by giving them a new form in language: But why should this particular sheepfold more than any other become the germ of a poem? Why stop on this particular bridge and begin composing a poem? Why record one experience rather than any other? Wordsworth's term "memorialize" suggests an answer. Subjects are chosen because they are memorable; they are memorable, in turn, because certain emotions accompany them. The subject matter of poetry arises out of experience in those moments when a powerful feeling is attached to a perception. Reversing the traditional notion of inspiration, Wordsworth claims that the feeling "gives importance to the action and situation, and not the action and situation to the feeling." If we try to imagine Augustine claiming that his personal feeling gives importance to the moment of his inspiration, we will sense the extent to which Wordsworth's epiphany reverses traditional notions of divine afflatus.

Wordsworth is not the first to pay close attention to powerful moments that can elevate consciousness. As early as 1765, Rousseau pointed out that "our existence is nothing but a succession of moments perceived by the senses." But Rousseau goes beyond this Humean emphasis on the momentary character of experience. In his definition of reverie he hints at that aspect of the mind that later produces Wordsworth's epiphanic spots of time. In reverie Rousseau is able to return to those powerfully felt moments from the past:

> In dreaming that I am there, do I not do the same thing? I do even more: to the allure of an abstract and monotonous reverie, I join charming images which make it more intense. In my ecstasies, their objects often eluded my senses. Now the deeper my reverie is, the more intensely it depicts them to me. I am often more in the midst of them and even more pleasantly so than when I was really there.[6]

An aspect of mind—Rousseau calls it "the wings of imagination"—elevates common events when it returns to them via memory. The elevation applies to even the most trivial occurrences:

> I feel these remembrances revive and imprint themselves on my heart, with a force and charm that every day acquires fresh strength; as if, feeling life flee from me, I endeavored to catch it again. . . . The most trifling incidents of those happy days delight me, for no other reason than being of those days.[7]

Rousseau does not elaborate the connection between these moments and his creative powers, but he is willing to see these reveries as productive of moments when "like God one is sufficient into oneself."[8] Thus the autobiographical St. Preux, in *Julie, ou la nouvelle Héloïse*, can describe a vision transformed by memory. Seeing Lake Geneva "from the heights of the Jura . . . aroused *again* all the sentiments I had enjoyed—all *threw me into ecstasies* which I cannot describe and seemed to infuse me with all the joy of my whole life at once." The emphasis is mine and suggests how the moment becomes more than a fleeting perception because it is allied with a powerful emotion. Judith H. McDowell points out that the moments of intense emotion in St. Preux are important because, "as Rousseau emphasizes throughout the novel, such states are revelatory of new truths, always vague but significant."[9] In *The Poetics of Reverie*, Gaston Bachelard clarifies this connection between the affective memory and revelation. "Certain poetic reveries," he says, "are hypothetical lives which enlarge our lives."[10] He cites Shelley's dictum that imagination enables us to create what we see and notes that reveries in this sense help us to escape time. Bachelard's discussion returns us to Wordsworth when he describes moments in childhood when every child "is an astonished being, the being who realizes the *astonishment of being*."[11] Wordsworth records this astonishment in his spots of time. Ordinary events astonish the young sensibility and are then meditated on over time until they gain significance. Rousseau senses the mind's power to elevate events; Wordsworth analyzes this process and uses this power to produce a new kind of poetry.

The "Preface" to *Lyrical Ballads* is a defense of this connection between ordinary events and the emotions they engender. The poet, Wordsworth says, looks upon this "complex scene of ideas and sensations" and finds "everywhere objects that immediately excite in him sympathies." He is not merely a recipient of Lockean ideas, nor is he moved to "thought" in its traditional sense. He is moved to sympathy. Wordsworth then defines our thoughts as "the representation of our past feelings." Emotion is recollected in tranquility not so that composition can begin in tranquility but in order that the recollected emotion can replace the tranquility: "The emotion is contemplated 'till, by a species of re-action, the tranquility gradually disappears, and an emotion, kindred to that which was before the subject of contemplation, is gradually produced, and does itself actually exist in the mind." At this point, poetic composition can begin. The poet works, not in a state of tranquility, but in a state of emotional excitement created by the recollection of an earlier feeling. In the process, the object which gave rise to the feeling achieves a significance it did not originally possess.

The poet's job, says Wordsworth, is to trace the "primary laws of our nature," chiefly "as far as regards the manner in which we associate ideas in a state of excitement." This excited state is not the ordinary state of the mind; in Wordsworth's new poetry "ordinary things should be presented to the mind in an unusual aspect." We associate ideas in a different way when we are "excited." The emotions surrounding certain experiences allow them to be colored by an "auxiliar light" of the mind that can bestow a radiance on otherwise trivial circumstances.

The ability to elevate events based on the emotions they produce underlies Wordsworth's own poetic development. In an important note to "An Evening Walk" (1793), Wordsworth explains the autobiographical sources of this early poem. "There is not an image in it which I have not observed," he says. Who can imagine Denham or Pope noting, as Wordsworth does, that he was an "eye-witness" to an event, as if thereby to confirm its validity? "I recollect distinctly the very spot where this first struck me," Wordsworth adds, describing an image of oak boughs and leaves intertwining. "It was in the way between Hawkshead and Ambleside, and gave me extreme pleasure." The ordinary sight of a tree illuminated by the western sun gives rise to an "extreme" feeling. The eyewitness then records the long-range significance of this seemingly trivial image: "The moment was important in my poetical history: for I date from it my consciousness of the infinite variety of natural appearances which had been unnoticed by the poets of any age or country. . . . I made a resolution to supply, in some degree, the deficiency."[12] Other poets have missed the significance of such simple sights because they have experienced no corresponding emotion which would render the event significant. Poets had traditionally claimed a special sight; they saw things unseen by others. For Wordsworth the emphasis is shifted so that poets experience feelings unfelt by others in the presence of objects that all people see. Because they are moved by their ordinary experience, poets possess what Joyce calls the "spiritual eye," an eye which not only sees an object but which can also bring the object into revelatory focus.

Wordsworth analyzes this process when he describes the "first Poetic spirit of our human life." The young mind in *The Prelude* is

> eager to combine
> In one appearance all the elements
> And parts of the same object, else detached
> And loth to coalesce.
> [1799, 2.277–80]

Locke's fragmentary sensations are defeated by the mind's ability to coalesce the various parts of a perception into a single image that is often indefinite in its contents but never vague in its intensity. Our emotions are aroused, in part, by our ability to combine disparate phenomena into one intense image. We are able to fit individual objects into a framework of other ideas, all within a web of complex relationships. The mind, as the associationist psychologists had suggested, connects objects because of their perceived contiguity in space and time. For Hume and his followers, we can claim nothing else. For Wordsworth, by contrast, the mind's role involves an imaginative connection of inner feelings with the outward objects of sense. The Wordsworthian epiphany declares an otherness outside of the self, while at the same time acknowledging a self-conscious self aware of this otherness and open to connections with the world.

This connection between perceptions and the feelings they produce is an outgrowth of eighteenth-century ideas about the imagination. As James Engell has shown, the Romantic idea of the imagination was not so much a new development as it was the outgrowth of eighteenth-century speculations about the creative aspect of mind. Leibniz had argued that self-consciousness is itself an imaginative act and that, once self-consciousness is acknowledged, an identity emerges from the need to produce an image of the self-conscious Cartesian "cogito." The sense of personal identity stems, according to Engell, "from experience that is not merely receptive, but also allows the self-aware individual to act and suffer and become." Only through individual experiences and the emotions they create does such action, suffering, and self-becoming occur. Wordsworth is a prime exemplar of the characteristics Engell claims are necessary to any poet operating under this new imaginative dispensation: "Good memory, passion, and strong imagination—which a poet ideally has—permit us to conceive of things and feelings with electrifying strength. This enthusiasm, or fire—similar to the ancient's belief in the divine fire and inspiration of the poet—signifies the divinity in us."[13]

Wordsworth's originality lies in his ability to turn these experiences to advantage by describing them as atemporal through memory and by giving them the potential to become valid for others. Rousseau had recorded the powerful, almost excruciating, intensity of his own feelings, but it was left to Wordsworth to expose those same feelings to scrutiny after the fact. The feelings may be ambiguous or vague, and their message may be unclear, but the feelings themselves are absolute. "Each poet," Donald H. Reiman has noted of the Romantics, "realized that he himself was more alive to the higher values during a few inspired moments than during the ordinary, routine pattern of life." Reiman adds that Wordsworth relied on spots of time, "many of them experiences remembered from his childhood, to illuminate the rest of his life."[14] These spots are valued not only when they occur but, more important, after the fact. At first they are significant enough to be remembered, but only when they "flash upon the inward eye" does their true value become apparent. Wordsworth eventually came to believe that these moments which increase in significance over time are more than aesthetically satisfying; they contain a generally applicable sense of what is good for people. Initially, however, such "spots" tend to be ambiguous and destabilizing.

Wordsworth's success in grounding revelation in the ordinary was pointed out by numerous early readers of *Lyrical Ballads*. John Stuart Mill praised Wordsworth's ability to make the empirical world seem meaningful. William Hale White (Mark Rutherford) likewise testified to this power to ennoble the ordinary.

> Instead of an object of worship which was altogether artificial, remote, never coming into genuine contact with me, I had now one which I thought to be real, one in which literally I could live and move and have my being, an actual fact present before my eyes. God was brought down from that heaven of the books, and resided on the downs visible in the far-away distances seen from the top of a hill and in every cloud shadow which wandered across the valley. Wordsworth unconsciously did for me what every religious reformer has done,—he recreated my Supreme Divinity, substituting a new and living spirit for the old deity, once alive but gradually hardened into an idol.[15]

This ability to produce inspiration out of commonplace hills and clouds has theological significance for White. But White's theological interpretation is only one among many possible ways of valuing Wordsworth's elevated facts. Hazlitt, for example, derives a purely aesthetic, nontheological, significance from the same quality in Wordsworth. Commenting on "The Thorn," Hazlitt compares Wordsworth to Rembrandt.

> In the way in which that artist works something out of nothing, and transforms the stump of a tree, a common figure into an *ideal* object, by the gorgeous light and shade thrown upon it, he perceives an analogy to his own mode of investing the minute details of nature with an atmosphere of sentiment.[16]

The stump, the cloud, the thorn: these objects in the world are used by the creative artist to produce an epiphany. Powerful sensations in the life of the poet can then be powerfully felt by the poet's readers. As Poulet has noted, "To escape nothingness means to be aware of one's own sensations. The more intense they are the more one will feel his present existence; and the more numerous they are the more one will sense a duration in his existence."[17] Wordsworth infuses the cult of Romantic sensibility with the desire to find meaning in experience.

Wordsworth is the first poet in the language who consciously and consistently turns the details of his life into art. The need to organize the randomness of experience into a unity had never been greater. In the paradoxically satisfying and troubling memories of emotionally significant events, Wordsworth found a way of creating and sustaining not only images but also an identity. As James Olney says in his account of the historical rise of autobiography, it appeals to those "looking for an order and meaning in life not always to be found in experience itself." If not in experience, then in experience made meaningful by a subjective, creative consciousness. "That one should be transformed and different with passing time, yet be continuing and the same, is a phenomenon of obvious and singular importance for the autobiographer and the poet of personal experience." Wordsworth fills both of Olney's categories well; the Enlightenment fear of a deadness out there is overcome by a sense of an inner life that can infuse the world in moments of intensified perception. Olney also offers a definition of the kinds of experience that give rise to the autobiographical impulse. They are moments "when the universe is mine, organized and infused with meaning by my creative act and when paradoxically I have surrendered to a pattern that is not me."[18] Language provides the pattern demanded by experience that often seems patternless.

The literary epiphany, likewise, includes a sense of the ennobling interchange from without and within. The objective world makes no guarantee beyond the fact that it exists in perception. The subjective consciousness makes no promise beyond a declaration of the way it feels. The result, however, is a formal, artistic relationship later defined by Yeats: "We artists . . . are the servants not of any cause but of mere naked life, and above all of that life in its nobler forms, where joy and sorrow are one, Artificers of the Great Moment."[19] The epiphanies that begin with Wordsworth are derived from just such great moments; they serve those noblest forms of life where joy and sorrow meet in experience. Unlike traditional revelation, they never lead to a change in ideology; instead, they reveal the mind's ability to value its experience and to record that valuation in language.

In "Rural Architecture," a poem composed in 1800, Wordsworth describes three boys who create a statue of a man out of stones they find on a hilltop. The statue is formed "without mortar or lime" and is christened "Ralph Jones . . . the Magog of Legberth-

Wordsworth and the Origins of Epiphany

waite dale." Several days later a wind blows the giant stone man down. On the next day the boys return and build up another "Man on the peak of the crag." In the final stanza Wordsworth calls on these boys to continue their building and rebuilding in the face of all the threats to their creations. "I'll build up a giant with you," he concludes.[20] More than being a lighthearted tribute to the diligence of rural schoolboys, this poem reflects Wordsworth's view of the function of poetry. The sensitive, creative imagination transforms the stones of experience into a verbal statue of the self. *The Prelude* records the development of this process in Wordsworth's own life.

Wordsworth's desire to build up a self out of fragmentary perceptual details was noticed by his early critics. The liberal theologian Frederick Denison Maurice criticized this aspect of Wordsworth when he called *The Prelude* a "self-building process," one which Maurice claimed was also employed by Byron and Goethe and by certain evangelicals, who turned God into a derivative agent employed to help produce men of genius, artists, and saints in a new secular age.[21] Likewise, the critic in the *Examiner* for July 27, 1850, who said that Wordsworth "contracted a habit of exaggerating the importance of every day incidents and situations," did not realize the full implication of this comment. Epiphanies are just such exaggerations; they record those moments when a sensitive mind values the bare details of phenomena not for what they contain but for the way they affect the sensibility.

The sense of building up an identity out of the raw data of experience is the Romantic solution to the historical problem of personal identity. The self is built up by experiencing not only the "life of things" but also the lives of other selves. The process was well described by Keats in his analysis of "soul making": "Nothing startles me beyond the Moment. The setting sun will always set me to rights—or if a Sparrow come before my Window I take part in its existence and pick about the Gravel."[22] Souls are made, Keats suggests, in moments of particularly intense and revealing perception, intense in their emotion, revealing the reality outside a single consciousness:

> There may be intelligences or sparks of the divinity in millions—but they are not Souls till they acquire identities. . . . Intelligences are atoms of perception—they know and they see and they are pure, in short they are God—how then are Souls to be made? . . . How, but by the medium of a world like this? . . . A Place where the heart must feel and suffer in a

thousand diverse ways! Not merely is the Heart a Hornbook, It is the Minds Bible, it is the Minds experience, it is the teat from which the Mind or intelligence sucks its identity—As various as the Lives of Men are—so various become their souls.[23]

Keats's "intelligences," the atoms of perception, are valueless. They take on value only when they are allied with a "heart" that is able to feel. For Keats, meaning emerges from the interaction between heart and mind, between feeling and intelligence. "This point I sincerely wish to consider," he adds, "because I think it a grander system of salvation than the chrystain religion—or rather it is a system of Spirit-creation." The Romantic epiphanies that find their first formulation in Wordsworth's spots of time are all a form of imaginative "Spirit-creation." In defining negative capability, Keats suggests that the poetic mind can achieve "a fine isolated verisimilitude caught from the Penetralium of mystery."[24] The power of Keats's sonnets and odes often derives from this achievement of such "isolated" yet "fine" verisimilitudes, which value experience as experience, not as a representation of another realm. The Romantic epiphany describes a moment that is privileged because in it a sensitive mind has elevated an otherwise ordinary event into the status of an archetype.

The building blocks of the new Romantic self are, to a large extent, epiphanies. They are characterized by their perceptual intensity, their power to bring about feelings, and their ability to provide a radiating sense of significance over time. A. D. Nuttall has noted that the Romantic tradition has a "distaste" for

> the sequential, the developing, the discursive, and [a] predeliction for an atomised experience, separated out into chunks or moments of perception. One moment may be especially important but never because of what it leads to or discloses at the level of ordinary plot, only because it tastes stronger than the others. The only important characteristics of any moment of perception (leaving aside the philosophic *use* of such moments) will be those intrinsic to it. The informed reader will easily supply analogues—*haecceitates* or epiphanies—from other writers in the same tradition, beginning with Wordsworth.[25]

This passage, perhaps not surprisingly, comes from a discussion of Sartre. If we continue looking for the source of Wordsworth's modernity, we will eventually find it not in theories of the imagination nor in a radically new poetic diction but in an approach to experience that elevates biographical events to the status of verbal archetypes. We turn now to those epiphanic building blocks in their first form—spots of time.

"Spots of Time": From Dread to Benediction

I only know that many of these exceptional moments brought with them a peculiar horror and a physical collapse; they seemed dominant; myself passive. This suggests that as one gets older one has a greater power through reason to provide an explanation; and that this explanation blunts the sledge-hammer force of the blow. I think this is true, because though I still have the peculiarity that I receive these sudden shocks, they are now always welcome; after the first surprise, I always feel instantly that they are particularly valuable.
—Virginia Woolf, "A Sketch of the Past"

The earliest manuscript drafts of Wordsworth's *Prelude* are, in effect, simply descriptions of events from the poet's childhood. In a letter to Coleridge, written in December 1798, Dorothy included three short, self-contained lyrics taken directly from a manuscript on which Wordsworth had been working that fall. These three poems appear almost unaltered in the 1805 edition of the work Wordsworth was then calling "the poem to Coleridge." *The Prelude* began as a series of such poems, stanzaic verses under forty lines long describing autobiographical events from Wordsworth's youth. When Wordsworth collected these fragments into the so-called Two-Part Prelude in 1799, the first four hundred lines included distinct recollections of a dozen such incidents. This opening section concluded with a description of the importance of certain moments in an individual's life:

> There are in our existence spots of time
> Which with distinct preeminence retain
> A fructifying virtue, whence, depressed
> By trivial occupations and the round
> Of ordinary intercourse, our minds—
> Especially the imaginative power—
> Are nourished and invisibly repaired;

The Poetics of Epiphany

> Such moments chiefly seem to have their date
> In our first childhood.
> [1799, 1.288–96]

The childhood incidents recorded in this early manuscript are all, in the broadest sense, epiphanies. Although the phrase "spots of time" is directly used to describe only two incidents in the 1805 edition, Wordsworth clearly relies on all of these childhood recollections to support the "spots of time" passage, which appears as the theoretical conclusion to the first part of the 1799 version.

All of these events are autobiographical and essentially lyrical: short, self-contained records of powerful experiences that became significant with the passage of time. Many were composed as shorter poems which Wordsworth later collected thematically into a sequence. A number were published individually under separate titles in periodicals. Why did Wordsworth incorporate these poems into *The Prelude*, moving from short poems to a book-length epic on his own experience? Although he never addresses these questions directly, Wordsworth, in a letter to George Beaumont on May 1, 1805, indicates how humility and not self-conceit led to a nine-thousand-line poem on his own life:

> I began the work because I was unprepared to treat any more arduous subject and diffident of my own powers. Here at least I hoped that to a certain degree I should be sure of succeeding, as I had nothing to do but describe what I had felt and thought, therefore could not easily be bewildered.

The fear of being bewildered by more expansive projects leads Wordsworth to approach a task in which he is confident of success—the description of his own thoughts and feelings. If he cannot poetically render his philosophical views on "Man, Nature and Society"—the avowed aim of *The Recluse*—at least he can make a record of his own experience that reveals the source of these broader ideas. A month later he writes to Beaumont again, hoping he lives long enough to complete not only this autobiographical work but also *The Recluse* and a "narrative Poem of the Epic Kind."[26] *The Recluse* began as *Home at Grasmere* and evolved into *The Excursion*. The narrative epic was never heard of again. The autobiographical poem—*The Prelude*—went on to become the most influential long poem of the century. Modern poetry begins, in one sense, when the greatest poet of the age can succeed as a poet only by making descriptive claims about his own experience.

Wordsworth and the Origins of Epiphany

The publication of the 1799 version of *The Prelude* has increased our understanding of the poem because, as J. R. MacGillivray has noted, in this earliest draft "one observes a much more unified theme and a much stronger sense of structure than in the poem completed first in 1805, and published in 1850."[27] The 1799 version clearly reveals the relationship between the early childhood incidents and Wordsworth's theoretical discussion of spots of time. Three incidents are specifically allied with the "spots of time" passage in 1799: the drowned man on Esthwaite, the wind-blown girl with the pitcher on her head, and the misty highway outside Hawkshead. In addition, however, all of the incidents recorded in part one of the two-part version lead to an understanding of the way these childhood experiences, "albeit lifeless then," are transformed by the mind into manifestations of significance when "maturer seasons call them forth / To impregnate and elevate the mind."

The earliest temporal "spots" hint at the source of the epiphany but make no explicit statement about the power that can elevate consciousness. Wordsworth, the snare robber, is full of guilt and "expectation" when he imagines "low breathings" and footsteps pursuing him, undistinguishable from his own hurrying feet. As he hangs from the cliff, the wind in his ears seems strangely like a voice, yet Wordsworth explicitly says that he is alone. The moving clouds transform the sky that is actually seen into a new image, a sky that is not "of earth." In all of these instances, the diction suggests that the young boy himself is responsible for these elevations of consciousness. Jonathan Wordsworth has recently pointed out that the spot of time is simply a "progression from detailed and quite ordinary description, through the poet's heightened and heightening response, to a new, odder, and more general vision."[28] The oddity—the sense of strangeness and mystery—is produced when the mind reveals the invisible in the perceptual details of experience. As Jonathan Wordsworth notes, the vision is both strange and personal.

"They guided me," Wordsworth says of these interventions into normal consciousness; "one evening led by them / I went alone into a shepherd's boat" (1.81–82). He rows the stolen boat away from the shore, and a distant mountain, "As if with voluntary power instinct," suddenly appears and blots out the stars. Once again the agency of power is identified with the natural object, which, "With measured motion, like a living thing / Strode after

51

me." But the true power becomes evident as time passes. He returns the stolen boat only to find himself unable to shake the spectacle of the cliff from his mind. Instead, the memory of the scene causes a series of dim and indeterminate thoughts—unrelated to the objects of sense—to enter his mind by day and also to become "the trouble" of his dreams.

In the boat-stealing incident the pattern of the Wordsworthian epiphany is established. A period of time during which the mind is relatively quiet and unoccupied ("I fixed a steady view . . . twenty times / I dipped my oars into the silent lake") gives way to a sudden, startling perception ("a huge cliff . . . Upreared its head"). The phenomenon is actually an optical illusion. The immediate effect of this sudden appearance is emotional: "trembling hands" and "grave / And serious thoughts." A simple perceptual event which involves an optical illusion—the sudden appearance of one mountain behind another—leads to a powerful emotion, so powerful that it produces a mood that cannot be overcome, "a darkness—call it solitude, / Or blank desertion." Unlike the earlier incidents, where the mood ends once the event is over, in the boat stealing we see for the first time the pattern that will become central to all subsequent epiphanies. The mountain only seems to rise up; in fact, the sensitive mind of the young boy makes the otherwise ordinary experience memorable. The power of the incident does not end with the passage of time. A message in the transformed perception of the mountain scares the young child; this message is, in one sense, untranslatable. It will nevertheless last in the mind, allied with the powerful memory of a feeling. "The surface of the universal earth" can "Work like a sea," but only when the objects of sense are allied with "meanings of delight, of hope and fear."

Wordsworth makes a stock, eighteenth-century appeal to

> Ye powers of earth, ye genii of the springs,
> And ye that have your voices in the clouds,
> And ye that are familiars of the lakes
> And of the standing pools.
> [1799, 1.186–89]

This appeal, however, is eventually replaced by a sense that the genius loci is actually in the mind of the observer. Emotions connected with a particular scene are recollected upon return to that scene or a scene like it, resulting in an uncanny feeling that is associated with, and actually brought into, the present scene by the mind. This spirit of place is actually a spirit of the perceiver. Although Wordsworth's diction often confuses the subjective and objective aspects of this phenomenon, he is not rejecting one theory for another; he is structuring language to fit the complexity of his own experience.

The ice-skating incident in the 1799 version of *The Prelude* develops the role of the mind in epiphany even further by suggesting that the mind's most powerful images often have little to do with veridical perception. Unlike Coleridge's epiphanies, which are more strictly imaginative experiences, Wordsworth's "spots" are almost always associated with objectified physical activity. Yet this physical activity can confuse the mind. The young Wordsworth stops short, and in his dizziness the cliffs continue to move "even *as if* the earth had rolled / With visible motion her diurnal round" (1.181–82, my italics). No eyes ever see the earth turning. The epiphany, however, records just such a vision; the imagination heightens experience, as it does in the epiphany that describes the dead Lucy, "Rolled round in earth's diurnal course, / With rocks, and stones, and trees." For the ice skater, the epiphany transforms an actual stillness into motion, an icy winter lake becomes an image that leaves the mind as "tranquil as a summer sea." But this same mind has also learned that the earth *is* moving, even if this motion is not evident in ordinary perception.

In just this way Wordsworth later comments to De Quincey that, when "the attention is energetically braced up to an act of steady expectation, then, if this intense condition of vigilance should suddenly relax, at that moment, any beautiful, any impressive visual object, or collection of objects, falling upon the eye is carried to the heart with a power not known under other circumstances." The result, in this instance when Wordsworth suddenly sees a star after he has been listening for carriages on the Keswick road, is that "the bright star hanging in the air above those outlines of massy blackness fell suddenly upon my eye, and penetrated my capacity of apprehension with a pathos and a sense of the infinite, that would not have arrested me under other circumstances."[29] This pattern of the interrupted concentration which gives way to sudden revelation characterizes the ice skating, boat stealing, horse waiting, water-carrier, and Snowdon incidents in *The Prelude*. "A Night-Piece" likewise describes the "instantaneous gleam" of the moon, which "Startles the pensive traveller" as he walks along under a cloudy sky. The result is a "Vision" and a "mind, / Not undisturbed by the delight it feels."[30] Any question about the source of this power is answered by a letter in which Wordsworth defined poetry:

> Objects . . . derive their influence not from properties inherent in them, . . . but from such as are bestowed upon them by the minds of those who are conversant with or affected by those objects. Thus the Poetry, if there be any in the work, proceeds whence it ought to do, from the soul of Man, communicating its creative energies to the images of the external world.[31]

The "soul" turns mundane experiences into meaningful epiphanies.

The spots of time passage itself appears in the 1799 two-part version of *The Prelude* between two epiphanies. In the first, the young boy comes upon a pile of clothes by Esthwaite Water and proceeds to watch the lake steadily for half an hour. On the following day, the body of the drowned man to whom the clothes belonged is recovered. The corpse,

> 'mid that beauteous scene
> Of trees and hills and water, bolt upright
> Rose with his ghastly face.
> [1.277–79]

It is revealing that Wordsworth never admits to having actually seen the drowned man. The boy gazes long on the quiet lake and pile of clothes, but the body rising bolt upright on the next day may simply be an image that impresses his mind, not necessarily an event he has actually witnessed. The power of "accidents in flood or field," of "tragic facts / Of rural history," is conveyed not in perception but in an epiphany. This incident, Wordsworth affirms, is but one of many such accidents that occur as a normal part of rural life. Nothing more, but that this particular circumstance

> impressed my mind
> With images to which in following years
> Far other feelings were attached—with forms
> That yet exist with independent life,
> And, like their archetypes, know no decay.
> [1799, 1.283–87]

"Higher minds," Wordsworth suggests in a later version of the poem, "build up greatest things / From least suggestions" (1805, 13.98–99).

Early in his poetic career, Wordsworth defined imagination as "the faculty which produces impressive effects out of simple elements."[32] The moments which trigger this faculty are "scatter'd everywhere." The mind of the child acts on the objects of its fear and the results are positive emotions. The young Wordsworth grows older and learns of his own power to elevate consciousness to a point where the objects of sight appear "like something in myself, a dream, / A prospect in my mind" (1805, 2.370–71). Finally he realizes the completely independent life of these forms in the mind:

> An auxiliar light
> Came from my mind, which on the setting sun
> Bestowed new splendor; the melodious birds,
> The gentle breezes, fountains that ran on
> Murmuring so sweetly in themselves, obeyed
> A like dominion, and the midnight storm
> Grew darker in the presence of my eye.
> Hence my obeisance, my devotion hence,
> And hence my transport.
> [1805, 2.387–95]

The poet devotes himself to his own power, to the auxiliar light that heightens the natural light of sunset and the natural darkness of the storm. When the incident of the drowned man appears in later versions of *The Prelude*, Wordsworth is thus able to analyze the way fear is transformed in the epiphany. As a boy of nine years old, Wordsworth argues, he was not possessed by a "vulgar fear,"

> for my inner eye had seen
> Such sights before among the shining streams
> Of fairyland, the forests of romance—
> Thence came a spirit hallowing what I saw
> With decoration and ideal grace,
> A dignity, a smoothness, like the words
> Of Grecian art and purest poesy.
> [1805, 5.475–81]

Epiphany as a mode of heightened perception in life can be rendered verbally in a work of art. The associative powers of mind reconcile the child's fear into a "grace" that derives from an inner "spirit" and can be described in aesthetic terms, "like . . . art and purest poesy," with emphasis on "the words."

Although the transitional passage—"forms / That yet exist with independent life"—does not appear in later versions of *The Prelude*, it is important in the genesis of the "spots of time" passage, which immediately follows in the two-part version of 1799. The forms existing with an independent life in the mind are like those forms produced earlier by the fear of the upreared cliff. An imaginative vision of the dead man's face likewise has power in the mind to produce feelings that can be sustained over time. These feelings change in later years from their original, fearful aspect to take on a positive quality. Dread, the emotion strong enough in the child to preserve the memory of the original scene, is "fructified" (a term changed later to "renovated"). Emotion revivified by memory can continue to bear new fruit as a result of the "imaginative power." What was once dreadful becomes a source of benediction.

The mind does not go looking for the Wordsworthian spot of time, nor does it call on it to appear. Unlike traditional inspiration, the Wordsworthian revelation does not result from a longing for fulfillment. It can emerge from a particular expectation but end up reversing that expectation. Indeed, the modern literary epiphany often describes an effect totally unlike the one that is expected. Ordinary occurrences take on a radiant quality when suddenly associated with a new image powerful enough to assure their continued life in the mind. The new image is epiphanic when it manifests the essence of the original experience, whose value and meaning may change over time.

Thus, when Wordsworth passes the spot where a murderer had been hanged and sees the girl with the pitcher on her head, he must explain why the scene is significant:

> It was in truth
> An ordinary sight, but I should need
> Colours and words that are unknown to man
> To paint the visionary dreariness
> Which, while I looked all round for my lost guide,
> Did at that time invest the naked pool,
> The beacon on the lonely eminence,
> The woman and her garments vexed and tossed
> By the strong wind.
> [1799, 1.319–27]

It is not immediately evident why this girl should be so important, until we understand the circumstances. The young boy has lost his guide; he sees a piece of turf shaped like a grave near the spot where a man was once hanged. Next his eyes light on a stone beacon like the one built by the boys in "Rural Architecture," and suddenly a girl appears, carrying a pitcher on her head and forcing her way against a strong wind. There is no suggestion that the conjunction of events is anything more than coincidental. But the emotions that result are caused by this particular ordering of events. A conjunction of visual images gives rise to powerful "visionary" feelings of dreariness and loneliness. The woman as we now understand her, presented in the light of the poet's former emotions, becomes an epiphany in the boy's mind. She is transformed in the poet's mind, and in ours. The ordinary is rendered remarkable by its role in establishing meaning.

Such scenes, as Wordsworth says, always implant in the mind the power to use these memories in later years. In just this way, one set of images comes to remind Wordsworth of his father's death:

> the wind and sleety rain,
> And all the business of the elements,
> The single sheep, and the one blasted tree,
> And the bleak music of that old stone wall,
> The noise of wood and water, and the mist. . . .
> [1799, 1.361–65]

When Wordsworth first experienced the rainy day, he did not know that his father would die. The epiphany occurs only later when his "anxiety of hope" about the horses is connected with guilty sorrow about his father's death. This powerful association is ultimately remembered, not as something unpleasant or dreadful, but as "spectacles and sounds" to which Wordsworth "would often repair, and thence would drink / As at a fountain." In the future, when subsequent storms remind him of that earlier wind and rain, he suddenly finds himself aware, through no act of will, of the workings of his spirit. The child learns gradually how to fit his own existence and his emotional life to existing things, the bare objects of his perceptions. Wordsworth claims to have the capacity to create a "bond of union betwixt life and joy," between perceptual experience (life) and the human value placed on that experience (joy).

The Poetics of Epiphany

This fitting of our existence to existing things bears comparison to modern theories of child development. Wordsworth's poetics is, in one sense, a theory of psychic growth. Piaget has argued that the egocentricity of children, who identify the "I" with the world, is finally challenged, paradoxically, by self-consciousness. Infants, who identify themselves with the world, learn that there is a world beyond their consciousness only as they become aware of that which is uniquely and intrinsically themselves. Approaching adolescence, children gradually learn to distinguish between an ego with capacities for relation and a "social or cosmic universe" to which these capacities will be applied and related. The self learns what it is by learning what it is not. Memories, according to Piaget, are not merely copies of previous experience. They always involve an active "construction" during the initial experience and a "reconstruction" when the memory is recalled. We do not have memories; we *make* memories.[33]

Likewise, Edward Edinger analyzes the way positive value can emerge from negative experiences as a result of the child's transformational consciousness. Edinger's description of the process is strikingly Wordsworthian:

> The inadequacies of the childhood environment or the child's adaptational difficulties, or both, generate a loneliness and dissatisfaction that throw him back on himself . . . . the unconscious . . . proceeds to produce symbols and value-images which help consolidate the child's threatened individuality. Often secret places or private activities are involved which the child feels are uniquely his and which strengthen his sense of worth in the face of an apparently hostile environment. Such experiences, although not consciously understood or even misunderstood and considered abnormal, leave a sense that one's personal identity has a transpersonal source of support. They thus may sow the seeds of gratitude and devotion to the source of one's being which emerge in full consciousness only much later in life.

Rudolf Otto, writing earlier in the century, notes that, in primitive societies and in children, dread is always associated first with fascination and later with awe, leading eventually to veneration of certain physical locations, or "spots," which are associated with the original feelings of awe and the uncanny. A similar analysis is offered by G. van der Leeuw, who concludes that "the experience of the potency of things or persons can occur at any time," in "even the most ordinary of events."[34]

The child in Wordsworth's autobiographical poem creates a self out of the ways in which the personal, privileged consciousness responds to and recreates the objects of experience. Poetic epiphanies are the standard form in which this change occurs. The epiphanic "gleams" come like the "flashing of a shield." The "common face of Nature" speaks to the growing child "Rememberable things." But the scenes assume their full importance only later. The "common range of visible things / Grew dear" to Wordsworth because it could be invested by his developing mind with feelings. The simplest fact of experience—"The calm / And dead still water" of a lake at dusk—had the power to

> lay upon my mind
> Even with a weight of pleasure, and the sky,
> Never before so beautiful, sank down
> Into my heart and held me like a dream.
> [1799, 2.211–14]

The visual sight is so intense as to be almost tactile; the pleasure has "weight." Epiphanies often employ synesthesia because they strive to go beyond the categories imposed by the five senses. The feeling is like a dream, not because dreams are epiphanies, but because epiphanies, in their imaginative intensity, remind the poet of dreams. This connection becomes particularly important to Coleridge, who will exploit ambiguous dream logic in complex ways.

Where does such a powerful ability to relate to past experience in these vivid extrasensory terms originate? Wordsworth provides both a developmental theory and an account of the moment when he recognized this power in himself. In the passage that begins "Blest the infant babe," Wordsworth argues, in terms that bear a striking similarity to modern developmental psychology, that the child, whose life is initially emotionless, derives its power to feel emotion directly from its mother. "Nursed in his mother's arms," the child is able to claim "manifest kindred with an earthly soul" by the simple act of gazing into the mother's eyes. The gaze is important because through this exchange the child gathers "passion from his mother's eye" (1799, 2.268–75). Emotions, first seen in the eyes of another, pass into the child's otherwise "torpid" existence and awaken an emotional life. The mother's love is a powerful presence that becomes a source of value.

Gradually this ability to feel emotions is transformed into the adult's ability to connect value with the facts of existence. In

> those sensations which have been derived
> From this beloved presence—there exists
> A virtue which irradiates and exalts
> All objects through all intercourse of sense.
> [1799, 2.287–90]

"Irradiation" exalts objects; that is, epiphany elevates the ordinary. Objects, the empiricist's "things," are rendered radiant and exalted by the association of simple perceptual sensations with the beloved presence of the mother. The child, learning to feel, is no longer the bewildered outcast of a post-Newtonian world. Instead, emotions provide the child with bonds of "filial" love that "connect him with the world." The relationship established between infant and mother becomes, in adult life, the potential to have emotions evoked, not by the mother's gaze, but by certain objects in the visible world. These objects seem to return something to the eye of the beholder, just as the mother's gaze returned "passion." A literal child of woman becomes a metaphoric child of earth:

> Emphatically such a being lives
> An inmate of this *active* universe
> From Nature largely he receives, nor so
> Is satisfied, but largely gives again;
> For feeling has to him imparted strength.
> [1799, 2.295–99]

The artistic impulse derives from this dissatisfaction with pure reception of phenomena. The creative mind is not satisfied until it receives and gives again. Wordsworth's strength derives from his ability to give back to the world, via emotion, a sense of its value. The universe is "active" because it acts on the mind to give rise to the "sentiments of grief, / Of exultation, fear and joy."

Having had such feelings about experience, the child of *The Prelude* is able to become a creator. The developing soul is not satisfied until it has connected perceptual sensations with an equivalent mental action that employs imagination and leads to poetry. The mind of such a soul

> Creates, creator and receiver both,
> Working but in alliance with the works
> Which it beholds. Such, verily, is the first
> Poetic spirit of our human life.
> [1799, 2.303–6]

Poetry begins during those moments when the mind connects powerful emotions—grief, exultation, fear, joy—with the perceptual data of consciousness. In defining epiphany, Joyce's Stephen Dedalus explains how the voices he overhears in the streets of Dublin can "afflict his sensitiveness very severely."[35] The emotional content of the experience, its radiance, leads to epiphany. In Wordsworth, a keen awareness of phenomena also gives rise to emotional sentiments that allow the mind to create. The result is often an epiphany. "Yet what is an epiphany," says Carlos Baker, "but a visionary overstatement which one hopes time will prove to have been approximately right."[36]

Wordsworth records the exact moment when he first understood the power of certain experiences to infuse life with meaning. He was fourteen years old, sitting one evening in a boat on Lake Coniston.

> It was a joy
> Worthy the heart of one who is full grown
> To rest beneath those horizontal boughs
> And mark the radiance of the setting sun,
> Himself unseen, reposing on the top
> Of the high eastern hills. And there I said,
> That beauteous sight before me, there I said
> (Then first beginning in my thoughts to mark
> That sense of dim similitude which links
> Our moral feelings with external forms)
> That in whatever region I should close
> My mortal life I would remember you
> Fair scenes.
> [1799, 2.156–68]

The sun, bestowing a radiance on the scene, is literally out of sight. In the view before Wordsworth, the light is reflected as a memorial gleam; the sun illuminates the "mountain-tops where first he rose." Likewise, the soul of the child will, in later years, illuminate the scenes of childhood with memory. But the adult mind recalls not only a visual field but a link between "moral feelings" and "external forms."

Wordsworth is not concerned to offer a coherent theory of mind as much as he is to describe the sources of his own poetic power. Spots of time provide a form of nourishment for the imagination. Elsewhere Wordsworth calls them "food" for later years. The two-part *Prelude* ends with a description of the origins of Wordsworth's poetic career. Three years have passed since the evening on Lake Coniston when he vowed to remember the fair scenes of youth for a lifetime. During those three years the sense of a "dim similitude which links / Our moral feelings with external forms" has become a powerful sense of the creative aspect of mind, variously described as a "plastic power" and a "forming hand." Recalling his seventeenth year, he admits, "To unorganic natures I transferred / My own enjoyments." In the 1805 draft he is even more specific and revealing. There he says that to every natural form—rock, fruit, or flower—"I gave a moral life—I saw them feel, / Or linked them to some feeling" (3.126–27). Synesthesia also becomes a crucial aspect of the Wordsworthian epiphany, for it can mingle senses that are ordinarily distinct. The poet "inspires" the world; the world then "respires" with "inward meaning" (1805, 3.129).

To the young child who steals the boat and birds, fear gives rise only to a sense of dim shapes, unknown modes of being, huge imaginative forms with no relation to human life. The epiphany, in these cases, is an epiphany of fear. By the time of the epiphany of the drowned man, however, an important development has occurred. The image of the man's face should invoke terror, but instead it produces "a spirit hallowing what I saw / With decoration and ideal grace." The spirit that hallows the otherwise fearful scene is in the mind of a nine-year-old child who has imagined dead bodies by reading fairy tales and romances. Instead of an infant's dread of the unknown comes a sense of recognition; the inner eye has seen, or imagined, this event many times, which now gives it a "decorated" aspect. Wordsworth describes this elevation as the recognition of an earlier state of mind related to fantasy. Instead of fear, the child feels a dignity; instead of harsh mental strain, a smoothness. The mind is prepared for the experience by having seen such sights before, not in the world, but in imagination. Like "Grecian art or purest poesy," the thought of the dead man rising from the lake takes on an aesthetic quality in the developing consciousness. This experience typifies all of Wordsworth's memory epiphanies.

Wordsworth and the Origins of Epiphany

T. S. Eliot's theory of the "objective correlative" derives from a similar idea. An object of experience described in a poem has the power to evoke an emotion in the reader, even when the emotion itself is not described. Thus the "only way of expressing emotion in the form of art is by finding an 'objective correlative'; in other words, a set of objects, a situation, a chain of events which shall be the formula of that *particular* emotion; such that when the external facts, which must terminate in sensory experience, are given, the emotion is immediately evoked."[37] For Eliot, Wordsworth should have recorded merely the objects of his experience and left out the analysis of his feelings. Eliot's own epiphanies will emerge from just such a valuation of ordinary experience. Without it, no experience could ever be described as superior to any other.

Wordsworth is moving toward an awareness of the mind's role in turning sensations into meaning. When the twenty-year-old poet learns, toward the end of *The Prelude,* that he has crossed the Alps and is already descending, he understands that the source of epiphany is within consciousness itself. The Alpine crossing is a description of that moment when Wordsworth sees clearly, for the first time, why spots of time are so valuable. The realization in this case is not of completion or fulfillment but of the process whereby these goals are sought. The glory of the soul is praised, that is, its ability to hope, inspire effort, and act on its expectations and desires. Flashes of epiphanic recognition reveal an "invisible" world distinct from the world of sense. The mind, in its ability to move beyond the objects it perceives, is able to imagine "something evermore about to be" (1805, 6.542). Such a mind does not need "spoils" or "trophies"; it does not need to achieve any state beyond the one it possesses. Its blessedness derives from thoughts which, through the power of the feelings they evoke, are their own "perfection and reward."

The apocalyptic close of this famous passage is revealing in the way it relies heavily on similes to conditionalize its claims:

> The rocks that muttered close upon our ears—
> Black drizzling crags that spake by the wayside
> As if a voice were in them—the sick sight
> And giddy prospect of the raving stream,
> The unfettered clouds and region of the heavens,
> Tumult and peace, the darkness and the light,
> Were all like workings of one mind, the features
> Of the same face, blossoms upon one tree,

Characters of the great apocalypse,
The types and symbols of eternity,
Of first, and last, and midst, and without end.
                    [1805, 6.562–72]

The passage produces a moving eschatology out of the otherwise ordinary experience of descent from a mountaintop. The rocks mutter and the crags speak, not because a voice is in them, but *as if* a voice were in them. The mind is doing its work. It is not hearing a voice; it is creating one. The stream, the clouds, the dark, and the light are not the workings of one mind but are *like* the workings of one mind—*like* the features of one face, *like* the blossoms of one tree, *like* apocalyptic characters signifying eternity. In an extremely powerful extended simile, Wordsworth suggests the mind's greatest strength: it can transform an experience of walking down a rainy mountainside into a typology of eternal existence. We note that all of the objects described here as lasting forever are inanimate—rocks, stream, clouds—while all the vehicles of the simile are animate—mind, face, blossoms. Here we see clearly Wordsworth's tendency in epiphanies, which he later describes in discussing "Resolution and Independence," to make the animate inanimate and the inanimate animate.

Hartman says of the Alpine crossing that "Wordsworth's experience, like Petrarch's or Augustine's, is a conversion: a turning about of the mind from one belief to its opposite, and a turning *ad se ipsum.*" But the experience is not a conversion in any traditional sense; it is a confirmation. The passage actually confirms all that Wordsworth has suggested about the powers of the mind to produce an epiphany. "The light of sense / Goes out in flashes" that reveal the "invisible world." The power that comes "athwart" Wordsworth in this scene is nothing new; it is "Imagination!" The glory is not of the world but of a mind that is "lord and master." A conversion always recognizes the glory of something outside the self. Wordsworth says the reverse: "To my soul I say / 'I recognise thy glory'" (1805, 6.531–32). Hartman reveals that he is using "conversion" in a limited and nontraditional sense, however, when he quotes from Petrarch's "conversion." Petrarch says that he could have learned from pagan philosophers "that nothing is great but the soul, which, when great itself, finds nothing great outside itself."[38]

The most recent editors of *The Prelude* suggest in a note that the claims made in the Alps crossing are "less extravagant than they seem." They cite early nineteenth-century geologists, who argued that the Alpine peaks were created when the waters of the Flood retreated. Thus the landscape Wordsworth was describing would have been literally "charactered" or engraved by the first apocalyptic event. These objects would likewise stand as typological symbols for the last apocalypse. The scene two books later when Wordsworth describes his feelings upon entering London indicates even more clearly the unextravagant nature of the Alps-crossing passage. The diction of his arrival in London almost parodies the Alpine crossing, suggesting that the mountain descent is meant to be less exceptional than we might at first assume.

Wordsworth entering London offers, not an epiphany, but a critique of the way epiphanies are derived from the ordinary. The carriage in which he is riding has passed through the villages leading up to the city when he is suddenly struck by the thought of the moment during which he entered the city, a moment he says he will never forget. It was the "very moment" when Wordsworth first knew that "the threshold now is overpast," a clear echo of the earlier "we had crossed the Alps." In both cases the crossover occurs without Wordsworth's knowledge. Indeed, the important moment is not when he actually crosses but when he realizes that the crossing has occurred. In both cases

> Twas a moment's pause:
> All that took place within me came and went
> As in a moment, and I only now
> Remember that it was a thing divine.
> [1805, 8.707–10]

The "thing divine," which was nothing external, was not clear at the moment; it became clear only later in memory.

Wordsworth next analyzes this capacity for creating meaning when he describes a visitor to a limestone cave. At first, the visitor can distinguish only light and darkness, undefined shapes and forms that "shift and vanish, change and interchange." These unspecific shapes gradually give way to an unalloyed perception of the physical details on the wall of the cave;

> every effort, every motion gone,
> The scene before him lies in perfect view
> Exposed, and lifeless as a written book.
> [1805, 8.725–27]

Coleridge describes the mental anticipation that precedes epiphany as an "awful idealess watching." But such pure perception does not last for long. The creative aspect of the mind goes to work almost immediately.

> But let him pause awhile and look again,
> And a new quickening shall succeed, at first
> Beginning timidly, then creeping fast
> Through all which he beholds: the senseless mass,
> In its projections, wrinkles, cavities,
> Through all its surface, with all colours streaming,
> Like a magician's airy pageant, parts,
> Unites, embodying everywhere some pressure
> Or image, recognized or new, some type
> Or picture of the world—forests and lakes,
> Ships, rivers, towers, the warrior clad in mail,
> The prancing steed, the pilgrim with his staff,
> The mitred bishop and the throned king—
> A spectacle to which there is no end.
> [1805, 8.728–41]

The senseless mass of shapes and shadows on the limestone wall suddenly becomes, in the mind, a picture of the world. A rough stone surface, meaningless in itself, conveys recognizable images: forests, lakes, ships, rivers, and towers. A warrior, a horse, a pilgrim, and a bishop all appear amid the uneven light and shadow of the wall. These objects are not there, but the mind acts on the objects of experience, imposing a meaning by filling in the gaps left by perception. The eye sees a pattern of light and dark; the mind calls it a face. The creative act produces what Wordsworth calls a "swell of feeling." Just as a cloud can look like a dragon or a profile, so the cave wall can take on recognizable features. The result, as in the apocalyptic Alpine scene, is a "spectacle" without end. To such a mind the world of perception is an infinite stockpile of potential meanings and symbols. Earlier in this passage (8.727) Wordsworth suggests that a "written book" is likewise "lifeless" until a reader's response produces meaning from words on a page.

Past emotions can always alter the description of a present scene. When Wordsworth returns to the site where he first saw the water-carrying girl, he is accompanied by his future wife, Mary Hutchinson, and his sister, Dorothy. Walking with them daily in the presence of the same dreary crags, and the same naked pool, he finds the "spirit of pleasure and youth's golden gleam" falling on the beacon which once had seemed so melancholy,

> And think ye not with radiance more divine
> From these remembrances, and from the power
> They left behind? So feeling comes in aid
> Of feeling, and diversity of strength
> Attends us, if but once we have been strong.
> [1805, 11.323–27]

If we have once possessed a strong feeling, our memory allows that emotion to form the germ of subsequent feelings. In this case, the radiance of the epiphany is divine because it is remembered; the retrospective quality heightens the emotion. Likewise, the sensitive soul must give feelings to the world, otherwise it can never receive feelings in return. The imagination must give a "substance and a life" to disembodied emotions by employing specific memories of time and place which enable the individual to "enshrine the past for future restoration." The affective events of the past are literal memorials, that is, memory savers. Even in the dismal circumstances surrounding his wait for the horses—blasted tree, bleak stone wall, and mist—the poet finds epiphanic "spectacles and sounds" to which he can in later years "repair" and "drink / As at a fountain."

The final spot of time in *The Prelude* indicates the extent to which Wordsworth identifies epiphanies with the human mind. As he approaches the top of Snowdon, he has no particular perceptual awareness, a state which often characterizes the advent of the Wordsworthian epiphany. For almost an hour he has walked with his head bent, like the old Cumberland beggar, seeing only the ground directly beneath his feet. Suddenly, the light falls "upon the turf . . . like a flash," and the startling change prepares the mind for epiphany. The light that falls at his feet is the light of the moon, hanging above his head and illuminating the sea of mist that lies at his feet. In this instantaneous appearance of the moon, we find the sudden change in perception that triggers the epiphany. He is startled by the light. The flash makes him keenly aware of the objects now in view: the "hundred hills" that appear as islands in the ocean of vapor, the shining moon, and, in the distance, the crack in the mist through which the sound of inland waters can be heard, a sound which confirms the optical illusion of the sea of mist. This experience is clearly analogous to the moment described in the "Immortality Ode" when the mind returns to its source and hears "the mighty waters rolling evermore." The imaginative sea of mist is made manifest in the moonlight which works the transformation. It carries the mind out to the "real sea" which dwindles and gives "up its majesty." The epiphany replaces the natural world with imaginative vision. The chasm in the clouds of mist can then be described as the place where nature has lodged the "soul, the imagination of the whole" (1805, 13.65). The imagination is the soul; it reveals the essence of the experience.

As the scene passes away, Wordsworth meditates on what he has just seen and describes it as the "perfect image of a mighty mind, / Of one that feeds upon infinity" (1805, 13.69–70). Images of this kind are products of the imaginative faculty. Central to my argument is that aspect of this power which is capable of exerting "dominion . . . upon the outward face of things." This is a power which by

> abrupt and unhabitual influence
> Doth make one object so impress itself
> Upon all others, and pervades them so,
> That even the grossest minds must see and hear,
> And cannot chuse but feel.
> [1805, 13.80–84]

Abrupt and unhabitual action by the mind highlights one object and transforms it to reveal the essence of experience. The epiphany is also valuable because it has the potential to evoke similar feelings in others. The mind that once stood in utter fear of an upreared mountain stands on top of Snowdon, exalted by its own power to imagine creatively. The spirit of place gives way to "the perfect image of a mighty mind," the mind of a poet that feeds on unseen infinity. This mind comes to recognize its own powers; it is no longer a passive recipient of fear but the subject of an ennobling interchange. This mind finally becomes the agent of wonder, able to feel in experience the sources of its own power.

Spots of time serve to renovate experience. Wordsworth finally settled on "renovate" after first employing "fructifying" (1799) and "revivifying" (1805). Just as Joyce's epiphanies artistically transform experience, so Wordsworth's epiphanic spots of time "build up greatest things / From least suggestions" (1805, 13.98–99). They allow the poet to create the past anew, not only in feelings, but in poems. The past does not simply become present; it finds itself remade. It is transformed into a new experience no longer directly related to perception. Imagination, in epiphany, becomes the "spirit" which higher minds use to "deal / With all the objects of the universe." Such minds, subject to such moments, do not require intervention from another world. Wordsworth is explicit on this point. The sensitive consciousness needs no "extraordinary calls." It holds communion with an "invisible world," not by virtue of external inspiration, but by virtue of its own ability to be "quickened" and "rouzed" by ordinary "sensible impressions." The mind is "lord and master" because it is the source of the power without which sense impressions are accidental and meaningless. The answer to the dead universe of the Enlightenment rationalists lies in the ability of "higher minds" to "send abroad / Like transformation" from themselves and thereby "for themselves create / A like existence."

3

Flashes of Internal Inspiration

"Resolution and Independence": The Ordinary Transformed

> A white mist is falling in slow flakes. The path leads me down to an obscure pool. Something is moving in the pool; it is an arctic beast with a rough yellow coat. I thrust in my stick and as he rises out of the water I see that his back slopes towards the croup and that he is very sluggish. I am not afraid but, thrusting at him often with my stick drive him before me. He moves his paws heavily and mutters words of some language which I do not understand.
> —Joyce, *Epiphanies*

The Prelude, as we have seen, evolved out of a series of fragmentary incidents in Wordsworth's life, most of which were first written down as short lyrics and, in a number of cases, published in lyric form. When, in "Ode: Intimations of Immortality," Wordsworth describes the "season of calm weather" during which we can travel "in a moment" to an immortal sea, he is formalizing a poetics of the kind of experiences recorded in *The Prelude*. These moments can be identified with spots of time and with the imagination I have been describing, which gathers diverse mental impressions into a single epiphanic image. For Wordsworth, the child is progenitor of the adult because epiphanies have their origin primarily in childhood experiences. But the Wordsworthian memory epiphany in these

Flashes of Internal Inspiration

cases is an adult phenomenon in which the adult invests powerfully felt childhood experiences with a new significance.

For Wordsworth, our ability to recall the joy we possessed in childhood is not a limitation but a source of strength, a means to what Keats calls soul-making, or self-creation. Memory, intensified and modified over time, can become redemptive rather than restrictive. The child described in *The Excursion* develops through great but perplexing ideas:

> So the foundations of his mind were laid.
> In such communion, not from terror free,
> While yet a child, and long before his time,
> Had he perceived the presence and the power
> Of greatness; and deep feelings had impressed
> So vividly great objects that they lay
> Upon his mind like substances, whose presence
> Perplexed the bodily sense.
> [1.132–39]

Coleridge, who relates his own epiphanies directly to the mind's ability to create images distinct from the objects of sense, also suggests the word "perplexed" to describe the heightened "fancy" that leads to epiphany:

> Oft o'er my brain does that strange fancy roll
> Which makes the present (while the flash doth last)
> Seem a mere semblance of some unknown past,
> Mixed with such feelings, as perplex the soul
> Self-questioned in her sleep.[1]

Like Wordsworth's archetypal "great objects," Coleridge's "fancy" has its origins in sense perception but comes to live in the mind with such an intensity that it seems substantial. Epiphany likewise perplexes the sense because it does not seem like ordinary perception; it possesses a mysterious power.

> He had received
> A precious gift; for, as he grew in years,
> With these impressions would he still compare
> All his remembrances, thoughts, shapes, and forms;
> And, being still unsatisfied with aught
> Of dimmer character, he thence attained
> An active power to fasten images

> Upon his brain; and on their pictured lines
> Intensely brooded, even till they acquired
> The liveliness of dreams.
> [1.139–48]

The associative powers of the mind are central to such epiphanies. The comparison of powerful childhood impressions with "remembrances, thoughts, shapes, and forms" gives rise to an intense feeling. This feeling is then attached to the immediate perception that has triggered the powerful association. Epiphany occurs when an immediate perception is associated with "perplexing" ideas in the mind until the imaginative perception achieves the "liveliness" of a dream. The experience is more like a dream than like ordinary perception.

Powerful recollections from childhood can erase years in an instant and provide a way of seeming to live for a moment "outside" of time. The memories that possess this quality can become epiphanic, possessing a sense not of durational eternity but of kairotic timelessness. Certain images are associated with ideas already in the mind, producing a transformed image of the past. The very vividness of these heightened recollections allows them to take on a life of their own. Basil Willey says that Wordsworth's spots of time are renovating precisely because they involve intense "self-activity." They reveal a mind "in its native dignity, creating significance in alliance with external events."[2] These moments, for Wordsworth, are not isolated. Unlike many of the other poets who employ epiphany, Wordsworth uses this state of imaginative perception as a ground for belief. Spots of time do not depend on any system of belief, but as Willey notes, "It was out of the repetition of these imaginative moments that the belief arose; the belief itself was the intellectual formulation of what they seemed to mean." Without the possibility of deriving a more consistent belief from these independent moments of elevated consciousness, "Wordsworth would probably not have conducted his *recherche du temps perdu* with such eagerness."[3]

Just such a theory is set forth in "Tintern Abbey." The poem does not contain an epiphanic moment, but it does provide Wordsworth's clearest description of the kind of mind that produces epiphanies. The poet returns to the Wye valley after an absence of five years and describes the effects of this return on his awareness of his own mental powers:

> O sylvan Wye! thou wanderer thro' the woods,
> How often has my spirit turned to thee!
> And now, with gleams of half-extinguished thought,
> With many recognitions dim and faint,
> And somewhat of a sad perplexity,
> The picture of the mind revives again:
> While here I stand, not only with the sense
> Of present pleasure, but with pleasing thoughts
> That in this moment there is life and food
> For future years.
>
> [56–65]

The moment in which the mind revives—by associating a present scene with faint memories—intensifies the emotion that accompanies the present perception and the memory of the past. Such an elevation has the potential to reveal or manifest something that can be described only as "a motion and a spirit," an invisible quality, a harmony, the "life of things." The revelation has no specific significance, for the predominant feature is the powerful feeling produced by the experience. The mind is "perplexed"; the recognition is "dim and faint"; the thought is "half-extinguished" during such "gleams." "Pleasure" and a "serene and blessed mood" control the experience; the eye is made "quiet" while the poet feels a presence, "a sense sublime / Of something far more deeply interfused." Amid the critical discussion of the Romantics' use of the term "sublime," we should remember that the word originally meant simply "to elevate by an internal force." Edmund Burke suggests that the sublime is "the strongest emotion which the mind is capable of feeling."[4] The internally elevated sensation Wordsworth describes is felt "in the blood, and felt along the heart." Interpretations of the meaning of the experience are secondary and are made primarily in an effort to account for the otherwise unaccountable richness of the sensation.

There is no "moment" in "Tintern Abbey." Instead, the poem describes a search for compensation, for "abundant recompense," that can replace the powerful immediacy of childhood experience. This hope may be a "vain belief," but there are times when we feel that the senses stop, when "we are laid asleep / In body." At these moments the eye is "made quiet," and another aspect of mind takes over, the aspect that can produce epiphanic elevations of the ordinary. The eye that half-creates is described in "Tintern Abbey,"

The Poetics of Epiphany

but it never acts to elevate consciousness. For this reason the poem lacks an epiphany.

Wordsworthian memory epiphanies emerge from moments that take on an independent life in the mind. As a result they can be recollected in the future without direct reference to an immediate perception. In the dead of winter, reclining indoors, the poet can retrieve a long-vanished image of daffodils:

> For oft, when on my couch I lie
> In vacant or in pensive mood,
> They flash upon that inward eye
> Which is the bliss of solitude;
> And then my heart with pleasure fills,
> And dances with the daffodils.
> [19–24]

The power of the moment is not realized in the immediate perception but only later, in the imagination. The epiphanic imagination fills in the details that memory neglects and creates a unity out of fragmentary "dead" details from the past. The epiphany is the "flash upon the inward eye" that finally reveals the potential wealth in the initial experience of the daffodils. Wordsworthian memory epiphanies reveal that tendency of the adult mind to enhance the details of memory. The imagination completes memories by producing order and coherence where none existed in the bare details of the past.[5] Stephen Prickett notes that, for Wordsworth, "recollection has the power of converting aimless drifting into moments of insight and joy as he remembers his own change of mood under this revelation."[6] More recently, Hillis Miller has noted that the "early stages" of Wordsworth's experience "are not transcended in the climax of his poems. They are held suspended in a vibration among alternative ways of thinking that is impossible to fix in a single unequivocal formulation."[7]

We may borrow terms from Epicurean philosophy to distinguish two different forms of epiphany in Wordsworth: one based on memories that gain strength and yield up their significance over time, the other derived from powerful perceptions that are transformed immediately by the associative powers of the imagination. Epicurus used the term *prolēpsis* for the anticipation produced by repeated experiences preserved by memory. A *proleptic epiphany*, then, is one in which the mind, in response to a present predisposition, transforms a past experience to produce a new sense of significance. Examples include the flash of daffodils in "I wandered lonely as a cloud" and a number of the spots of time in *The Prelude:* the fearful image of the drowned man that comes to be invested with "far other feelings," the mist on the road outside of Hawkshead that advances in "indisputable shapes" and yet leads to various "workings of [the] spirit," and the visionary dreariness brought on by the solitary water carrier that turns into a blessing when Wordsworth returns to the spot with Mary and Dorothy. The proleptic epiphany is characteristically Wordsworthian.

Wordsworth also employs what we can call the *adelonic epiphany.* Epicurus used the term *adēlon* to refer to the unobservable component of experience that was nevertheless confirmed by reference to empirical data. An adelonic epiphany refers to a nonperceptual—Joyce will say "spiritual"—manifestation produced immediately by a powerful perceptual experience. This form of epiphany is employed most often by the other poets I will be discussing. Wordsworthian examples include those moments when the "light of sense goes out" in flashes that reveal an "invisible world": the characters of the "great apocalypse" Wordsworth imagines while descending the Alps, the illusory sea of mist that "usurps" the real sea when seen from the top of Snowdon, the spectacle of the blind man with his story on his chest, whose "fixed face and sightless eyes" admonish Wordsworth "as if . . . from another world." Many of the childhood experiences in *The Prelude* possess the immediacy of the adelonic epiphany. The snare-robbing child is overcome immediately by epiphanic "low breathings." While rock-climbing he finds the sky instantly transformed into a sky that is not "of earth." The illusory moving mountain of the boat-stealing incident strides after the young boy with "measured motion, like a living thing," as soon as he flees. These adelonic epiphanies, whether of fear or benediction, testify to the mind's ability to move beyond the perceptual details of consciousness while in the grip of a powerful experience.

Both kinds of epiphany are records of "such structures as the mind / Builds for itself" (1805, 7.625–26). Whether based on a specific memory (proleptic) or on a powerful immediate experience (adelonic), Wordsworth's epiphanies always describe an altered state of consciousness when

>   the shapes before my eyes became
> A second-sight procession, such as glides
> Over still mountains, or appears in dreams,
> And all the ballast of familiar life—

> The present, and the past, hope, fear, all stays,
> All laws of acting, thinking, speaking man—
> Went from me, neither knowing me, nor known.
>   [1805, 7.601–7]

Such a mood, says Wordsworth, is "beyond / The reach of common indications." Wordsworth's early drafts of these epiphanies retain their often fearful aspect. Later Wordsworth tended to use these experiences to justify a system of belief. This tendency to moralize epiphanies accounts in large measure for the change of tone from the 1805 to the 1850 version of *The Prelude*. In both versions, however, Wordsworthian epiphanies always reveal an experience with an ultimately vague or partial meaning.

"Resolution and Independence" is important to a discussion of the Wordsworthian epiphany because it is one of those rare occasions when the poet describes the passage into the epiphanic mood as it is occurring. As a result, the reader is able to leave behind the "ballast of familiar life" and see with the poet's "second sight." The poem opens with a calm morning. The early stanzas trace the poet's emotional state:

> I heard the woods and distant waters roar;
> Or heard them not, as happy as a boy:
> The pleasant season did my heart employ.
>   [17–19]

Into this relatively calm scene, however, comes a mood of doubt and uncertainty:

> But, as it sometimes chanceth, from the might
> Of joy in minds that can no further go,
> As high as we have mounted in delight
> In our dejection do we sink as low;
> To me that morning did it happen so;
> And fears and fancies thick upon me came;
> Dim sadness—and blind thoughts, I knew not, nor could
>   name.
>   [22–29]

Wordsworth here hints at the state of mind that often characterizes the advent of epiphany. A tension is established between the carelessness and happiness of this particular morning and "another day," a time in the future which may bring "solitude, pain of heart, distress, and poverty." Wordsworth calls these thoughts "untoward" because they are only awkwardly associated with his dominant emotion of happiness. He does not understand why such a pleasant morning should give rise to fears and "dim sadness."

Suddenly he sees an old man, a leech-gatherer, whose head and feet are drawn close together. The man is "bent double," as though he labored under some invisible weight. He is neither fully sentient nor "all asleep." He seems "not all alive nor dead." He is at once like a stone and a sea creature. The poet is at first drawn out of his own dilemma by the mere force of the leech-gatherer's presence. The epiphany is prepared for, as always, by a powerful perceptual trigger. The leech-gatherer first startles the poet and then begins a chain of associations that draw the poet out of ordinary consciousness into epiphany:

> The old Man still stood talking by my side;
> But now his voice to me was like a stream
> Scarce heard; nor word from word could I divide;
> And the whole body of the Man did seem
> Like one whom I had met with in a dream;
> Or like a man from some far region sent,
> To give me human strength, by apt admonishment.
> [106–112]

Sense perception fades as the old man is replaced in the mind by the dreamlike epiphany. The leech-gatherer's actual words, like the words of the solitary reaper, do not matter; what matters is his effect on the poet.

The epiphany is adelonic because no time passes between the perception of the old man and his transformation into a dreamlike, ghostly presence. Though the leech-gatherer now seems like someone sent to Wordsworth, the poet offers no interpretive suggestion that such is actually the case. The epiphany is not divine; instead, a purely "human strength" is being offered to Wordsworth. The comparison to the dream state is revealing. This actual occurrence seems like a dream because of the unusual associations it produces in Wordsworth's mind. These mysterious mental connections lead him to compare the leech-gatherer to a dream or a spirit sent from another world. But it is a world of Wordsworth's own making. Whether Wordsworth actually met the leech-gatherer is irrelevant to the epiphany; its power occurs in the poem. The details of ordinary experience undergo a startling transformation in the poet's sensitized mind.

Understanding fails at this point. Wordsworth passes out of his state of altered consciousness, and "former thoughts" of cold, pain, and "fleshly ills" return. To ward them off he once again questions the leech-gatherer: "How is it that you live, and what is it you do?" The old man claims to be a victim of "slow decay" who nevertheless perseveres. The thought of this endurance then reveals the power of the epiphany to Wordsworth:

> While he was talking thus, the lonely place,
> The old Man's shape, and speech—all troubled me:
> In my mind's eye I seemed to see him pace
> About the weary moors continually,
> Wandering about alone and silently.
> [127–31]

The leech-gatherer has been preserved in Wordsworth's mind as an image of endurance. The mind's eye—Joyce will call it "the spiritual eye"—reveals the invisible. This old man is no longer ordinary, for the mind transforms him into an image. Epiphany has allowed this image making to occur. The ordinary becomes extraordinary in an imaginative vision that resolves the tension between decay and perseverence.

As Wordsworth begins the poem he is caught between thoughts of youthful gladness and the "despondency and madness" of old age. The tension between joy and dejection leaves the mind uncertain and unsatisfied. The mind's associative capacity is unable to resolve these disparate ideas into a unity. Into this scene comes an old man who tells his tale "cheerfully" and with "demeanor kind." The association of this decrepit human frame with such a firm mind startles Wordsworth into recognition. The image of the old man, wandering alone and silently across the moors, becomes the associative link between joy and dejection, perseverance and despondency. The epiphany occurs when Wordsworth feels admonished from "another world." This heightened state allows him to transform the old man into a symbol of human endurance. The tension between youthful happiness and future sorrow is resolved in Wordsworth's epiphany of an almost lifeless old man who nevertheless continues his search for bloodsucking leeches, the lowliest creatures imaginable.

What connection could an old leech-gatherer have with a young poet meditating on the fate of Chatterton and Burns? Seemingly, none; but the old man enters directly into the associative pattern of

Wordsworth's mind at a precipitous moment and leads to a poem that claims to solve the poet's problem. The revelation of the leech-gatherer cannot be specifically articulated; it can only be felt. Expressed as an epiphany, however, the experience gains meaning. The epiphany does not convey knowledge; it produces a feeling that gradually becomes a conviction and leads to knowledge. Beyond the memorable image of the old man there remains only the feeling of the importance of the experience, the recognition that, for months, years, even decades, the mind will return to "think of the Leech-gatherer on the lonely moor!" We sense here one of the most direct ways in which a mental image passes from consciousness into the realm of the symbolic.

Wordsworth's prose description of the poem locates the epiphany and suggests the source of its continuing power:

> A young Poet in the midst of the happiness of Nature is described as overwhelmed by the thought of the miserable reverses which have befallen the happiest of all men, viz Poets—I think of this till I am so deeply impressed by it, that I consider the manner in which I was rescued from my dejection and despair almost as an interposition of Providence. . . . A person reading this Poem with feelings like mine will have been awed and controuled, expecting almost something spiritual or supernatural—What is brought forward? "A lonely place, a Pond" "by which an old man *was,* far from all house or home"—not stood, not sat, but *was*—the figure presented in the most naked simplicity possible. This feeling of spirituality or supernaturalness is again referred to as being strong in my mind in this passage—"*How came he here* Thought I, or what can he be doing?" I then describe him, whether ill or well is not for me to judge with perfect confidence, but this I can *confidently* affirm, that, though I believe God has given me a strong imagination, I cannot conceive a figure more impressive than that of an old man like this.[8]

The epiphany occurs at that point in the poem when the "feeling of spirituality or supernaturalness" is "strong" in the poet's mind. Epiphany is not synonymous with imagination; it begins in a feeling on which the imagination works. Wordsworth defines the poet as one who is "pleased with his own passions and volitions, and who rejoices more than other men in the spirit of life that is in him; delighting to contemplate similar volitions and passions as man-

The Poetics of Epiphany

ifested in the goings-on of the Universe, and habitually impelled to create them where he does not find them."[9] The leech-gatherer solves the poet's problem by providing a subject that can become significant, via epiphany, in a poem. When the poet does not find meaning, he makes meaning.

More than any other poet of the century, Wordsworth strives to retain objective validity for his epiphanies. He seeks always to maintain a connection between the external world that triggers the epiphany and the sense of significance that results. Coleridge, as we will see, is much more willing to let the epiphany stand on its own. Wordsworth wants to testify to transcendence, to claim that his fearful epiphanies—drowned man, water carrier, upreared mountain—are redeemed by a process that transforms them, via memory, into something beneficent. His benedictional epiphanies—leech-gatherer, Snowdon, Alps crossing—demand that ordinary experience be seen as an extraordinary means of moving beyond self into relationship with an objective, external world. But the role of the mind is never denied. To the wanderer in *The Excursion*,

> the least of things
> Seemed infinite; and there his spirit shaped
> Her prospects, nor did he believe,—he *saw*.
> [1.230–32]

Epiphany in Wordsworth records a special form of imaginative seeing. As a way of producing meaning, Wordsworth's poetic epiphanies become the prototype for poems by all of the major poets of the century.

COLERIDGE: "PHANTASY" IN "FROST AT MIDNIGHT"

> The whole tide of all life and all time suddenly heaves, and appears before us as an apparition, a revelation. We look at the very white quick of nascent creation. A water-lily heaves herself from the flood, looks around, gleams, and is gone.
> —D. H. Lawrence

No Romantic understood better than Coleridge the mind's ability to intensify the effects of experience. His definition of the imagination—the ability of the mind to apprehend an objective world and at the same time imaginatively to create external reality—defends

Flashes of Internal Inspiration

just such an intensification. In the revealingly titled "Apologia Pro Vita Sua," he details the process of visual creation:

> The poet in his lone yet genial hour
> Gives to his eyes a magnifying power:
> Or rather he emancipates his eyes
> From the black shapeless accidents of size—
> In unctuous cones of kindling coal,
> Or smoke upwreathing from the pipe's trim bole,
>   His gifted ken can see
>   Phantoms of sublimity.

This short lyric analyzes the aspect of the mind that produces a certain kind of poetry. The size and form of objects are described by Coleridge as "shapeless accidents." The mind however, sees sublime phantoms in the fireplace coals and curling pipesmoke. In much the same way, a child sees monsters and animals in puffs of cloud. This emancipation of the eyes is a function of the imagination. It is a special form of imaginative knowing, a "gifted" kenning. These fanciful images are not simply illusions, however, because they record the mind in the act of turning "accidents" into meaning.

Coleridge's works are filled with illuminations of the ordinary which can best be described as epiphanies. For Coleridge, "All truth is a species of revelation." Any perception can be revelatory when transformed by a sensitive mind. In the most well-known revelation in Coleridge's poetry, the sea snakes seen by the ancient mariner undergo a startling transformation in an agitated mind. They begin as "a thousand thousand slimy things" and end as "happy living things" whose beauty is indescribable. The transformation is brought about not by an external force but by a simple, powerfully moving perception in the moonlight that leads to the epiphanization of these lowly creatures:

> Beyond the shadow of the ship,
> I watched the water snakes:
> They moved in tracks of shining white,
> And when they reared, the elfish light
> Fell off in hoary flakes.
>
> Within the shadow of the ship
> I watched their rich attire:
> Blue, glossy green, and velvet black,

The Poetics of Epiphany

> They coiled and swam; and every track
> Was a flash of golden fire.
> [272–81]

An image of eerie moonlight ushers in the radiant perception. The epiphanic flash of the coiling snakes becomes the means to the mariner's moral transformation. The epiphany of the shining snakes allows the cursed sailor to bless these living creatures. He blesses them "unaware"; that is, he does not know why he suddenly feels so differently about the snakes. As always in epiphany, interpretation *follows* an experience of altered perception. Unlike Wordsworth's epiphanies, which are usually grounded in autobiography, Coleridge's can often be completely imaginative. Coleridge does not need to have seen water snakes or been on a ship in the moonlight in order to work this powerful transformation of experience through the character of the ancient mariner. Such character revelation becomes the defining characteristic of Browning's epiphanic infinite moments.

On two occasions, phantoms in Coleridge's poems are called by name. The poem "Phantom" records the manifestation of the essence of a self:

> All look and likeness caught from earth
> All accident of kin and birth,
> Had pass'd away. There was no trace
> Of aught on that illumined face,
> Uprais'd beneath the rifted stone
> But of one spirit all her own;—
> She, she herself, and only she,
> Shone through her body visibly.

The invisible is made visible by the poet's mind, a mind that is able to divest a particular woman of the accidents of time and place in order to reveal an essential identity that shines through her physical body. The manifestation is nonsensible, but it can be described in perceptual terms. As Joyce argues, quidditas is revealed in a moment of this kind. There is "no trace" on the visage of this image because the ultimate self is finally inscrutable, although it can be made manifest in an epiphany. The revelatory quality of the experience is confirmed by the description of the face as "illumined." In a note to the poem Coleridge says that the image is intended to "illustrate the idea that the love-sense can be abstracted from the accidents of form or person." The poet employs epiphany to reveal the woman's essential nature.

This poem and another entitled "Phantom or Fact: A Dialogue in Verse" were described by Coleridge as "fragments from the life of dreams." As Ernest Hartley Coleridge notes however, "It was the reality which lay behind both 'phantom' and 'fact' of which the poet dreamt, having his eyes open."[10] Epiphany in Coleridge is almost always like a dream. Unlike Wordsworth's epiphanies, which usually derive from physical activity and undertake to realize the objective validity of an object or event, Coleridge's epiphanies are more strictly psychological. Coleridge is willing simply to ally himself with the supersensible tone of certain experiences. As in Wordsworth, this alliance helps him to produce poetry. But while Wordsworth most often uses epiphany as a means to a wider vision, Coleridge enjoys the altered state of consciousness for its own sake, like a dream. Indeed, his fondness for such heightened receptivity may help to account for his use of drugs to induce a similar state. As he suggests in a variant of "Sonnet: Composed on a Journey Homeward,"

> Oft of some unknown Past such Fancies roll
> Swift o'er my brain as make the Present seem
> For a brief moment like a most strange dream.[11]

In this agitated state, the facts of experience conjure up an imaginative world beyond sense.

"Phantom or Fact" records a fearful epiphany which Coleridge calls "a moment's work." In this poem the soul sees a vision of itself, a sort of doppelgänger based on a real person by Coleridge's bedside, transformed by the mind. As always in epiphany, the experience begins in a particularly vivid perception—"A lovely form there sate beside my bed, / And such a feeding calm its presence shed"—and ends in transformation:

> But ah! the change—It had not stirr'd, and yet—
> Alas! That change how fain would I forget!
> The shrinking back, like one that had mistook!
> That weary, wandering, disavowing look!

The calm and gentle mood gives way suddenly to an unforgettably fearful aspect of this visitor. As Hartley suggests, the "vision" was inspired by an actual visitor to Coleridge's bedside. But only in Coleridge's imagination is this flesh-and-blood visitor tranformed into an image of terror, an image of Coleridge's own soul "newly come from heaven."

The friend in the dialogue is perplexed and asks if this "riddling tale" is "history? vision? or an idle song?" The poet replies that it is none of these, but an imaginative creation intensified by the emotions: "a moment's work, a fragment from the life of dreams . . . a record from the dream of life." In his greatest poems—"The Rime of the Ancient Mariner," "Kubla Khan," "Christabel," and "Frost at Midnight"—Coleridge explores the complex relationship between the "life of dreams" and the "dream of life." These phrases suggest much more than phantasmagoria. Coleridge's verbal fantasies arise out of such moments of epiphanic intensity, the "awful idealess" state in which wonder overwhelms rationality and gives a flashlike intensity to experience: "All is vanity that does not lead to Quietness and Unity of Heart, and to the awful idealess watching of that living Spirit, of the Life within us, which is the motion of that Spirit—that Life, which passeth all understanding."[12] The state is "idealess" because the mind is not in its ordinary rational mode; a living "spirit" has dispersed normal consciousness. To perceive life in the universe the mind must be open to connections, to Coleridge's sense of organic unity. Epiphany catches the mind in a moment of awareness, not only of the continual flux, but of the ultimate elusiveness of experience.

In the sonnet "To Nature," Coleridge anticipates his critics and defends the soul's ability to intensify its experience emotionally:

> It may indeed be phantasy, when I
> Essay to draw from all created things
> Deep, heartfelt, inward joy that closely clings.[13]

Such a notion reminds us of Wallace Stevens's "necessary fictions," imaginative creations which, because of their connection to our experience, allow us to live. Such creations may be fantasy, but they are not useless. As fantasy, such mental creations are related to the original Greek term "phainein"—"to cause to appear," or "to bring to light." The poet brings to light certain connections between seemingly unrelated objects of experience, in the process forming hitherto unconnected associations in the minds of readers. The epiphanic poem gives the experience a new tone and projects a new sense of power. "At times I dwell on man with such reverence," Coleridge wrote to William Godwin, "that the Llama's dung pellet, or the cowtail which the dying Brahmin clutches convulsively become sanctified and sublime by the feelings which cluster round them."[14] This notion of feelings clustering around a single image directly describes the epiphanies I have been discussing. The image is elevated by the impressions and emotions with which it is associated. Value then adheres not only to the image but to the object itself—not only to the association but to the objects that triggered this powerful mental state. In this way Wordsworth can sanctify a degraded leech-gatherer, and Coleridge's mariner can similarly transform slimy water snakes into blessed objects of beauty.

Wordsworth likewise saw the poet as the source of the epiphany, though he always closely related the mental process to some external object. As Oscar Campbell has noted, for Wordsworth, "Every object that meets the mature eye or ear assumes its place in an intricate pattern of sensations, memories, and ideas. Sensation thus becomes transmuted into insight and past experiences into vision. The meanest flower that blows . . . radiates passion."[15] The Wordsworthian epiphany originates in the intensity of an individual's immediate response to experience. It leads to a sharply focused image of an object or process. In Coleridge, by contrast, the emphasis is on what Lowes has called "a fusing flash of imaginative energy through chaos." Coleridge leaves the objective world behind, goes to work on the "chaos of elements and shattered fragments of memory," and produces an imaginative structure in which "every shattered fragment has been new-minted—sharp, and clear, and salient." The result, Lowes claims, is the "unification of a clutter of details" into "one breathless instant."[16]

Coleridge's poem "Frost at Midnight" most clearly describes this process. The poem begins with a perfectly ordinary experience and ends in a powerful epiphany that records a mysterious transformation of nature as reflected in the processes of mind. In the image of frost reflecting moonlight, Coleridge offers a perfect representation of the process that occurs in the Romantic epiphany. The frost, condensed into ice from an unseen vapor in the air, is like the human mind that can render the invisible visible. Frost also symbolizes the processes of transformation in nature, the subject of the poem. In Coleridge the sense of the unity of the "One Life" is most clearly felt in the image of "silent icicles, / Quietly shining to the quiet Moon."[17] How does Coleridge move from the commonplace scene of a man by the fireside to this powerfully focused epiphany?

The poem opens with the bare autobiographical details which so

The Poetics of Epiphany

often prepare the way for epiphany. The poet is alone with his sleeping infant by the fire. The night is still, but the frost, like the poet's mind, continues to work, unassisted by any wind. In the same way, the mind of the poet does not require external inspiration. Only the sound of a lone owl startles Coleridge out of this silence into awareness. Otherwise, the calm is overwhelming,

> so calm, that it disturbs
> And vexes meditation with its strange
> And extreme silentness.
> [8–10]

Ordinary thought is upset, disturbed by a calm so calm it is strange. The normal associative pattern of thought is interrupted. This stillness contrasts sharply with the active life around it:

> Sea, hill, and wood,
> This populous village! Sea, and hill, and wood,
> With all the numberless goings-on of life,
> Inaudible as dreams!
> [10–13]

The last line suggests that the numberless activities are unheard as a dream is unheard and also that the surrounding stillness is like a dream. The only disturbance Coleridge senses is one ordinarily so trivial as not to be noticed:

> the thin blue flame
> Lies on my low-burnt fire, and quivers not;
> Only that film, which fluttered on the grate,
> Still flutters there, the sole unquiet thing.
> [13–16]

But this fluttering film is deceptive. It is the sole unquiet thing except for the poet, who immediately draws a parallel between himself and this dancing light against the coals:

> Methinks, its motion in this hush of nature
> Gives it dim sympathies with me who live,
> Making it a companionable form,
> Whose puny flaps and freaks the idling Spirit
> By its own moods interprets, every where
> Echo or mirror seeking of itself,
> And makes a toy of Thought.
> [17–23]

The role of the poet as interpreter is evident here. Nature seems lifeless; the poet is the only active agent in the scene, similar to the film of firelight in being unquiet. His mind—"the idling Spirit"—is subject to "its own moods." In this mood the mind studies the world, seeking an echo, a mirror image of itself. In the process, thought becomes a toy, something to be manipulated in an effort to find sympathy between the inner world of thought and the outer world of things.

A canceled passage of the poem elaborates this process of self-projection:

> the living spirit in our frame,
> That loves not to behold a lifeless thing,
> Transfuses into all its own delights,
> Its own volition, sometimes with deep faith
> And sometimes with fantastic playfulness.

Coleridge here connects faith and play, echoing Schiller's correlation between the aesthetic impulse and playfulness. Wordsworth likewise senses the connection between pleasure and self-projection—"to inorganic natures I transferr'd / My own enjoyments." The mind, as a prelude to epiphany, transforms the objects of experience by infusing them with "its own delights," its own will. A sense of external lifelessness leads an active intellect to fill the seeming void with its own contents.

The fluttering "stranger" on the grate triggers just such a series of associations, by calling up the memory of similar firelights seen in the past. It is not coincidental that these films of light—as Coleridge's note points out—are "called *strangers* and supposed to portend the arrival of some absent friend." Coleridge is in a state of receptivity comparable to Wordsworth's just prior to meeting the leech-gatherer. While Wordsworth meets a flesh-and-blood stranger who becomes the trigger to his epiphanic imagination, Coleridge's stranger portends the arrival of a series of mental associations that culminates in an epiphany. The fluttering film on the grate in front of Coleridge thus carries his mind back suddenly to an earlier, similar feeling:

> How oft, at school, with most believing mind,
> Presageful, have I gazed upon the bars,
> To watch that fluttering *stranger!* and as oft

> With unclosed lids, already had I dreamt
> Of my sweet birth-place.
> [24–28]

In an earlier time, as in the present, the stranger has triggered memories so powerful they take on the heightened intensity of a daydream. The image of Coleridge as schoolboy reminds us of the young Wordsworth of *The Prelude*, "stirred and haunted" by the memories on which he broods. This brooding causes a blending of the waking and sleeping worlds: "So gazed I, till the soothing things, I dreamt, / Lulled me to sleep, and sleep prolonged my dreams!" (34–35). This daydream is about dreaming. Whenever the dreamworld is evoked in Coleridge, it suggests a form of mental activity ordinarily unavailable to human consciousness. In this case, the young boy daydreams that he has fallen asleep. The memorable aspect is the subtle and complex interplay, the blending of memory and daydream with sleep and dream. The description suggests that daydreams are to powerful memories what dreams are to sleep. In both cases the mind draws on previously existing contents to produce a heightened sense of the power of the present.

This mental state is not permanent, however; at any moment it can be interrupted by the power of youthful expectation. Because the stranger on the grate is meant to signal the arrival of an absent friend, the child is in a constant state of anticipation, a mental predisposition that is particularly likely to lead to epiphany. When the door to the schoolroom opens, the child's heart leaps up in expectation of seeing the stranger's face. The use of the term "stranger" here reminds us of the earlier stranger on the grate, though its application is confusing. Those listed as strangers include a "townsman, or aunt, or sister," all of whom are more or less known or beloved. "Stranger" in this context suggests not the unknown person but the unexpected one. This sense of unexpectedness hints at the epiphany that is about to occur.

The full effect of this passage depends on a complex series of associative connections. The present perception of the fluttering film on the grate has carried the mind back to a similar grate in the childhood schoolroom. The stranger in childhood carries the mind back to even earlier memories—the birthplace, church tower, and bells—and provokes an eerily vivid daydream. Even in this state of mind the child remains susceptible to the sudden shock, the arrival of the unexpected face at the door that will return the mind to normal consciousness. Coleridge chronicles here the means by which hidden contents of the mind can be unexpectedly dredged to the surface, coming into focus in a present perception as a result of a mental predisposition. Such a process occurs in Coleridge's mind as he sits by the otherwise insignificant fluttering on the fireplace grate. This stranger prepares the way for the arrival of a closely parallel chain of thought.

One link in this chain is the image of his sister. Though recently dead she is not mourned; rather, she is recalled as part of a pleasing memory—"My play-mate when we both were clothed alike!" With this satisfying memory the mind returns suddenly to the present. We learn that there is one other unquiet thing by the fire amid the silence and solitude: beside the poet lies the "dear Babe," whose gentle breathings amid this

>   deep calm,
> Fill up the interspersed vacancies
> And momentary pauses of the thought!
>   [45–47]

The Hartlean-Humean language of sensation is always implicit in Romantic descriptions of mental process. Thoughts are momentary and distinct, separated by pauses and vacancies. The mind's motion is represented as a rapid succession rather than a continuous stream. The child's breathing interrupts the sequence of memories and gives rise to a wish stated in the present tense.

Coleridge then claims that the loveliness of the world is more apparent amid rustic natural scenes than in the city's "cloisters dim." The specific value of the natural world results, not from anything intrinsic to nature, but rather from the effect these particular scenes have on the mind. The growing child will find imaginative powers brought to life in

>   the clouds,
> Which image in their bulk both lakes and shores
> And mountain crags.
>   [56–58]

The child creates images that betoken an "eternal" language from the raw materials of perception. The ability of the clouds to look like lakes and shores and mountains is like the power of a mind that can imagine. The mind projects its contents onto the world, and the creations that result are, Coleridge suggests, signs of a truly godlike power. This section of the poem closes with the suggestion that mental integrity lies in the ability to reconcile internal tendencies with external objects in "lovely shapes and sounds intelligible." Not just shapes and sounds are at issue here, but all sensations that can be rendered meaningful by their aesthetic ("lovely") and rational ("intelligible") components.

The power to bestow value on nature leads directly to the object that will become epiphanized in "Frost at Midnight." A series of images of natural process culminates in a powerfully focused mental image of the frost with which the poem opened, but now a new frost, felt almost supernaturally in light of its associations. Three natural processes are first described: the invisible seasonal rhythm of summer, which will clothe the visible earth in green; the unseen heat of the sun, which will cause the damp thatched roof to smoke; and the frost, which will act on the drops of water hanging in the eaves. The secret ministry of an invisible natural force then "Shall hang them up in silent icicles, / Quietly shining to the quiet Moon" (73–74).

The epiphany is finally achieved in this vivid image. These icicles are seen only in Coleridge's mind. The powerful emotions that move throughout the poem are crystallized in the description of a natural process that corresponds to the mental process described in the poem. Like the frost, the mind has the capacity to solidify certain moments in time. Such moments, caught for an instant amid the otherwise transitory flow of consciousness, take on powerful feelings of significance. Out of such illuminated instants we draw "lovely shapes and sounds" that mold the spirit. Traces of past and present in the mind are like the unseen vapor that produces the frost. In an epiphanic imagination, these mental contents coalesce in secret into powerfully felt verbal images. Ordinary icicles assume significance as an image of the mind's ability to perform a secret operation on the eavesdrops of experience. Instead of allowing these drops to fall in the onrush of passing time, the mind hangs them up, through language, as momentarily solid icicles of powerfully realized experience. Like the actual icicles, these vivid moments shine with a light of their own to the moon, which is seen as an image of the mind from which their light is actually derived. This insight is revealed in the literary epiphany.

Coleridge's identification of the icicles with this aspect of mind is not evident in the text of the poem as it is usually printed. The original poem included an interpretation of the experience that

Flashes of Internal Inspiration

weakened its impact as epiphany. This 1798 version included six additional lines following the epiphanic image of silent icicles. The removal of these lines occurred ten years after the poem was first published and left the interpretation of the icicle's significance unstated. The poem originally concluded:

> the secret ministery of cold
> Shall hang them up in silent icicles,
> Quietly shining to the quiet moon,
> Like those, my babe! which ere tomorrow's warmth
> Have capp'd their sharp keen points with pendulous drops,
> Will catch thine eye, and with their novelty
> Suspend thy little soul; then make thee shout,
> And stretch and flutter from thy mother's arms
> As thou wouldst fly for very eagerness.

Bloom has suggested that the usual close of the poem indicates an analogy between the frost and memory.[18] But as the original ending of the poem indicates, the frost recapitulates not memory but the emotionally projective aspect of mind. This difference is fundamental. Romantic criticism has tended to overemphasize the role of memory per se, without realizing that, not memory itself, but the relationship between memory and present experience defines much that is unique in the poetry that begins to be written around 1800. The mind has the capacity to freeze disparate aspects of experience into a unity by using the raw material of memory. But a process of association—culminating in a present moment—actually creates this unity. Memory, in and of itself, is restrictive, trapping the mind in an unchangeable past. Only when combined with the power of the present does the past recorded in memory have the potential to be redemptive. Language reforms the past to solidify the present.

In the case of the infant Hartley Coleridge, the sight of the icicles will be a moving experience, literally and figuratively. The icicles will catch his eye, and their novelty will cause him to reach out, to "flutter" toward the sight. From such experiences the soul will take shape; the hitherto passive receptor of sense will come to life. The Romantic is always concerned to turn the world described by Locke and Hume to meaningful account. The equivalent experience for the adult is one which focuses disparate ideas, feelings, and memories into a seemingly unified whole. Such powerfully focused unity may last only for an instant before its "keen points" melt back into the normal disruptive flow of mind. While the epiphany lasts, however, it provides the same emotional impact as the intense perceptions of childhood. In a similar way, the schoolboy's heart "leapt up" when the fluttering stranger on the grate in the classroom promised the arrival of an absent friend. Likewise, the mature poet focuses the mixed associations of past and present in an image, an image that begins in the ministering frost that opens the poem and ends in the epiphanic vision of icicles. The poem itself produces the illusion that time has stopped.

The epiphanic imagination creates images that connect external events and internal dispositions, but the emphasis on outer and inner can vary. Donald A. Stauffer has noted that Coleridge was particularly susceptible to the mental state in which "thoughts are seen as things." Coleridge describes these states as moments when "the somnial magic (is) superinduced on, without suspending, the active powers of mind."[19] This state of mind produces Coleridge's epiphanies, which are much more subjective and dreamlike than Wordsworth's. Wordsworth always grounds his epiphanies in the external object or event that triggers the heightened mental state. At the same time, Coleridge's epiphanies tend to be adelonic rather than proleptic; that is, they record an immediate imaginative transformation of experience, rather than revitalizing the past in light of a present disposition. One other way of classifying epiphanies is by considering their emphasis on the subjective or the objective aspect of experience. Joyce's epiphanies, as I have suggested, are even more objective than Wordsworth's. Coleridge, by contrast, is willing to move from epiphany into a realm of subjective phantoms which confirm his experience. His increasing fears about the validity of these phantoms helps to explain the dread described in poems like "Limbo" and "The Pains of Sleep."

Coleridge may have altered the ending of "Frost at Midnight" because the original interpreted too completely the suggestive power of the "secret" ministries of frost and mind. The canceled lines actually detract from the epiphany. The epiphanic imagination tends always to allow the powerful image to demonstrate its power rather than to articulate its meaning, to "flash" or "shine" rather than to speak. Unlike traditional inspiration, which typically relies on specific sacred words or texts for the power of its message, the Romantic epiphany rests on inarticulate figures, pregnant silences, and ineffable images. Mist, snow, cloud, rainbow, flame, smoke, shadow, and reflection all play a new role in poetry because of their power to suggest the indefinite nature of experience. When the epiphany records a conversation, as in Joyce's overheard Dublin dialogues or Wordsworth's exchange with the leech-gatherer, the significance of the spoken words differs from their literal meaning. They unfold as their power is contemplated. The leech-gatherer conveys nothing specific; his power lies in his mysterious suggestiveness and affects us before any interpretation of his meaning is attempted. The icicles which close "Frost at Midnight" are unforgettable for the same reason. Coleridge has found in nature the perfect analogue for the aspect of mind that the poem attempts to describe. The image of shining icicles is a symbol of the mental process which allows epiphany to occur.

SHELLEYAN "MOMENTS": A DEFENSE OF THE EPIPHANIC IMAGINATION

> The sun is hot. I see the river. I see the trees specked and burnt in autumn sunlight. Boats float past, through the red, through the green. . . . Oh, I am in love with life. . . . Now begins to rise in me the familiar rhythm; words that have lain dormant now lift, now toss their crests, and fall and rise and fall and rise again. I am a poet, yes. Surely I am a great poet. Boats and youth passing in the distant trees, "the falling fountains of the pendent trees." I see it all. I feel it all. I am inspired. My eyes fill with tears.
> —Virginia Woolf, *The Waves*

Romanticism characteristically intensifies certain moments. Shelley, while not relying on autobiographical material to the same extent as does Wordsworth or on the dream world of Coleridge, nevertheless suggests, in a number of poems, that he has experienced fleeting moments of fusion between emotion and immediate perception. Like Wordsworth and Coleridge, Shelley claims that these experiences are related not to an external aspect of nature or to the supernatural but to an internal aspect of mind. In "A Defence of Poetry," Shelley analyzes the origins and effects of these short-lived instants and relates them directly to the process of poetic creation. In this discussion he anticipates the outlines and the details of Joyce's subsequent definition of epiphany.

In the dedication to *Laon and Cythna* (later *The Revolt of Islam*),

Shelley recounts an experience which occurred in his youth and came to have immense personal and artistic importance:

> I do remember well the hour which burst
>   My spirit's sleep: a fresh May-dawn it was,
>   When I walked forth upon the glittering grass,
> And wept, I knew not why; until there rose
>   From the near school-room, voices, that, alas!
> Were but one echo from a world of woes—
> The harsh and grating strife of tyrants and of foes.
>   [21–27]

> 5
> And from that hour did I with earnest thought
> Heap knowledge from forbidden mines of lore. . . .
>   [37–38][20]

This carefully described moment of dedication, though it sounds like traditional inspiration and is unusually abstract, is actually an epiphany. Its power would not be apparent, however, if it did not appear in an earlier and more important form in "Hymn to Intellectual Beauty." In the earlier poem, as in the later one, the moment of crisis is preceded by a period of anxiety and followed by a personal dedication. The important difference between the two versions appears in Shelley's claim in "Hymn to Intellectual Beauty" that this experience is life's only source of "grace and truth." The hymn praises a nonmaterial force which allows the poet to ascribe beauty to the sensible world. This spiritual component of beauty derives from an "unseen Power" and is revealed to consciousness only with a mysterious and fleeting inconstancy.

The poem records Shelley's youthful—and unsuccessful—search for traditional forms of divine inspiration. The failure of this search for "God and ghosts and Heaven" leads Shelley instead to assert a new form of revelation based on the individual's ability to feel deeply about experience. An inability to find a divine sanction for his thoughts or for poetry leads the poet to conclude that "No voice from some sublimer world hath ever / To sage or poet these responses given" (25–26). Instead, the light of intellectual beauty most closely approximates such a visitation. The experience fills the mind like mist, aeolian music, or moonlight, bringing with it a benediction of grace and truth. The nonmaterial beauty apprehended by the mind is the direct source of poetic inspiration. These moments are "uncertain" not because they are vague but because they do not last. On the contrary, such moments provide feelings of immortality and omnipotence. The moments depart, and with them these feelings, because intellectual beauty is not able to keep a "firm state" in the heart. The epiphany is not an object of perception but a state of mind. Nevertheless, while such moments last they provide a deep sense of fulfillment, of "Love, Hope, and Self-esteem."

Having described the operation of this power of mind, Shelley recounts the exact moment when he first felt this force, clearly the same moment described in the dedication to *Laon and Cythna,* an autobiographical occurrence which powerfully united emotion and sensation in an instantaneous perception. Having called on "poisonous names" ("God and ghosts and Heaven"), the young poet received no reply—"I was not heard—I saw them not." In the original manuscript of the poem, Shelley personalized this absence as God—"He heard me not, I saw him not." But the personified divinity does not respond. The failure of this search leads to a state of mind that gives way to a sudden revelation and an emphatic dedication to the spirit of a new form of inspiration:

> When musing deeply on the lot
> Of life, at that sweet time when winds are wooing
>   All vital things that wake to bring
>   News of buds and blossoming,—
>   Sudden, thy shadow fell on me;
> I shrieked, and clasped my hands in extacy!
>
> 6
> I vowed that I would dedicate my powers
>   To thee and thine—have I not kept the vow?
>   With beating heart and streaming eyes, even now
> I call the phantoms of a thousand hours. . . .

Like Coleridge, Shelley invokes timeless phantoms in his attempt to describe the heightened feeling. This spirit is clearly internal and depersonalized. It emerges not from some unseen external power but from a musing mood of mind galvanized by a spring wind that blows amid "buds and blossoming." The perceptual details are vague, as always in Shelley, but they are still the proximate cause of the revelatory shock.

As Bloom notes, the "Hymn to Intellectual Beauty" is a response

The Poetics of Epiphany

to Wordsworth's "Intimations Ode." Shelley's poem suggests that the reality revealed in sensation is intimated in such moments. The sense of coherence and order is not an ever-present reality; instead, it is "fleetingly manifested in any phenomenon that moves us by its grace and mystery."[21] Shelley's epiphanies originate in an attempt to describe the kinds of experiences that possess this grace and mystery. Although it can move the emotions, the powerful moment subordinates judgments about meaning to the felt experience. Shelley suggests that the result of such internal visitations is a powerful conviction of a truth that cannot be completely articulated, or even certainly avowed, once it has passed. He also believes that these states are more often sought than achieved.

Earl Wasserman has reprinted the text of the earliest draft of Shelley's dedicatory moment. Appearing in a rejected introduction to *The Revolt of Islam,* the passage connects the heightened moment of awareness with "phantasy" and with the mind's desire to put powerful feelings into words:

> It is not then presumption if I watch
> In expectations mute & breathless mood
> Till it descend—may not the fountain catch
> Hues from the green leaves & the daylight wood
> Even if blank darkness must descend & brood
> Upon its waves?—each human phantasy
> Hath such sweet visions in the solitude
> Of thought, that human life (this drear world) like
>   heaven wd. be
> Could words invest such dreams with immortality.[22]

The dreamlike solitude of thought is epiphanic when it transforms the "drear world" into sweet vision. Like Wordsworth, who describes that "blessed mood" in which the "burthen of the mystery . . . is lightened," Shelley seeks a mood that will transform human "phantasy" into hypothetical visions of immortality.

For Shelley the mood that gives rise to poetry is often more significant than the resulting words. He even suggests that words fail in their attempt to reveal the essence of experience. In "On Life," he describes the moment when language fails: "We are on that verge where words abandon us, and what wonder if we grow dizzy to look down the dark abyss of—how little we know." In "On Love," he is more precise, saying of his own attempt to describe the epipsyche, "These words are inefficient and metaphorical—Most words so—No help—."[23] In "Epipsychidion," he finally calls words "chains of lead" which hold the soul to earth. For Shelley, however, the moment of epiphany—described as a feeling—can give the soul "whate'er these words cannot express." The meaning of the epiphany is secondary; the epiphany as psychic experience is primary. In "A Defence of Poetry," he clarifies the inability of words to interpret the original richness of the experience that gives rise to epiphany. During moments which lead to poetic creation, the mind is awakened to "transitory brightness." The source of the power is internal: "This power arises from within." There is always a loss between the initial conception and the poetic result: "When composition begins, inspiration is already on the decline, and the most glorious poetry that has ever been communicated to the world is probably a feeble shadow of the original conception of the poet."[24] The poet, attempting to recapture the complex associations of thought and feeling that characterized the initial sense of revelation, calls on phantoms—manifested appearances—to reproduce the sensations of an original autobiographical event.

Shelley's epiphanies are more strictly intellectual than those of either Wordsworth or Coleridge. They resolve the tension often found in his poems between idealism and skeptical empiricism. The mind possesses ideas which can imaginatively fuse with the objects of sense. In the process, inanimate things are animated, and the mind is able to anchor its own intellectual reality in the sensible world. This strain in Shelley's poetry always threatens to turn experience into pure idea. He often idealizes epiphany to the point where it becomes almost unattainable. The poetic result is a lack of concrete imagery, which is the reverse of the epiphanic tendency in Coleridge and Wordsworth. Wordsworth infuses the leech-gatherer with a dreamlike power that transforms him into an admonition from another world. Coleridge lets the phantom of illuminated icicles arise in his mind to associate diverse thoughts into an image of natural process. Shelley, however, achieves an intellectual vision and then seeks its likeness in the world. When this likeness is not found, he must resort to the power of feelings and the weakness of language.

Shelley, for example, searches for an image that will transform an ordinary skylark into something more permanent, but he is forced to give the actual song of the bird precedence over any imaginative image. "What thou art we know not," he laments;

The Poetics of Epiphany

"What is most like thee?" The song of the bird may be "Like a Poet hidden," "Like a high-born maiden," "Like a glow-worm golden," and "Like a rose embowered." But the bird's "music doth surpass" all of these potential images. The song which is heard and produces an emotion cannot be successfully described. For Shelley, the power of the momentary feeling gives way to a sudden loss of vision and ends in a truth, not known or seen, but deeply felt beyond any specific representation. The epiphanies of Wordsworth and Coleridge transform sense perception into meaningful experience. Shelley's intellectualizing strain remains grounded in feelings that cannot always be verbalized. He does not often produce the epiphanic image that can radiate significance. Nevertheless, the moment that produces this feeling can be recorded as an epiphany.

Shelley often describes his search for that moment when "all things seem only one / In the universal Sun" ("To Jane. The Invitation"). A walk with Jane Williams and Mary gave rise to the two poems that most clearly achieve this powerful instant. The second of these poems includes an epiphany that is a prototype of Browning's infinite moment. Here the normal intellectualizing strain in Shelley gives way to a more objectified vision:

> How calm it was!—
>
> . . . .
>
>   The breath of peace we drew
> With its soft motion made not less
>   The calm that round us grew.—
> There seemed from the remotest seat
>   Of the white mountain-waste,
> To the soft flower beneath our feet
>   A magic circle traced,
> A spirit interfused around
>   A thrilling silent life,
> To momentary peace it bound
>   Our mortal nature's strife;—
> And still I felt the centre of
>   The magic circle there
> Was one fair form that filled with love
>   The lifeless atmosphere.
> ["To Jane. The Recollection," 33, 38–52]

Flashes of Internal Inspiration

Here epiphany transforms a noontide scene into a magic circle. The epiphany brings momentary peace and the sense of an interfused spirit. At the center of this magic circle is Jane, whose "fair form" inspires the otherwise lifeless scene. A negative equivalent of this epiphany occurs in "Stanzas Written in Dejection—December 1818, Near Naples," where perception is transformed into a "tone":

> I see the waves upon the shore
> Like light dissolved in star-showers, thrown;
> I sit upon the sands alone;
> The lightning of the noontide Ocean
> Is flashing round me, and a tone
> Arises from its measured motion,
> How sweet! did any heart now share in my emotion.
> [12–18]

The "tone" is rising toward the level of epiphany, but the epiphany is prevented by Shelley's solipsistic mood. The mood then turns, for this reason, from possible benediction into dejection.

"Lines Written among the Euganean Hills" is one of the few poems in which Shelley experiences an epiphany in and through the visible world. Like the lyrics to Jane, the poem records a perceptual experience that undergoes a powerful transformation in a sensitive mind. Shelley's description of the poem is reminiscent of Wordsworth's description of "Resolution and Independence." The poem records, Shelley says, "the sudden relief of a state of deep despondency by the radiant visions disclosed by the sudden burst of an Italian sunrise in autumn, on the highest peak of those delightful mountains." Wasserman quotes this comment and says that the poem establishes the existence of "isolated and self-enclosed moments of revelation and perfect existence that give worth to an otherwise worthless endurance: extraordinary spots of time 'bright, and clear, and still' (88), free from 'passion, pain, and guilt' (345), and constituted of unifying friendship and love." The noonday sunlight in the poem unifies the scene in the way that love unifies a life: "Metaphorically the poet's own day of illumination—which is also his poem—is one such 'silent isle' (329)."[25]

This island of calm is achieved in an epiphany that transforms the light of noon into an image of unity:

> Noon descends around me now:
> 'Tis the noon of autumn's glow,

The Poetics of Epiphany

> When a soft and purple mist
> Like a vaporous amethyst,
> Or an air-dissolved star
> Mingling light and fragrance, far
> From the curved horizon's bound
> To the point of heaven's profound,
> Fills the overflowing sky;
> And the plains that silent lie
> Underneath. . . .
> [285–95]

Shelley catalogues all of the objects that are unified by this powerful light of noon—leaves, vines, grass, tower, Alps, living things—and then admits that this unification occurs only in an epiphany in his mind:

> And my spirit which so long
> Darkened this swift stream of song,—
> Interpenetrated lie
> By the glory of the sky:
> Be it love, light, harmony,
> Odour, or the soul of all
> Which from heaven like dew doth fall,
> Or the mind which feeds this verse
> Peopling the lone universe.
> [311–19]

Shelley's skepticism does not allow him to describe absolutely the source of this revelatory elevation of consciousness. But the last lines clearly suggest that the epiphany is produced by a mind (the poet's) that peoples an otherwise empty universe.[26] These lines, not surprisingly, are reminiscent of the close of "Mont Blanc," where Shelley asks the mountain,

> And what were thou, and earth, and stars, and sea,
> If to the human mind's imaginings
> Silence and solitude were vacancy?
> [142–44]

The rhetorical question implies its answer; without the mind's imaginings, the mountain, earth, stars, and sea are "vacancy." The poem that precedes these lines also reveals the mood that can transform vacancy into meaning.

Flashes of Internal Inspiration

The source of all power in "Mont Blanc" is invisible, unseen in the ethereal altitudes of snow and mist. Power, when it appears, descends "in likeness" of the crashing Arve, a river that bursts "through these dark mountains like the flame / Of lightning through the tempest" (18–19). The image of startling natural light is once again used to suggest the moments of awareness. The resulting mental state is astonishingly similar to Coleridge's in "Frost at Midnight":

> Dizzy Ravine! and when I gaze on thee
> I seem as in a trance sublime and strange
> To muse on my own separate phantasy,
> My own, my human mind, which passively
> Now renders and receives fast influencings,
> Holding an unremitting interchange
> With the clear universe of things around.
> [34–40]

Shelley sees a waterfall crashing through a deep, jagged gash in the overwhelming mountain. This powerful perceptual image—"Dizzy Ravine! and when I gaze on thee"—gives way to a trance that is at once sublime and strange. Power shifts, as always in epiphany, from the visible world of things to the invisible world of mind.

The sensitive soul can possess a fantasy that is distinct from the objects revealed by sense. Like Wordsworth's mind, which half perceives and half creates, Shelley's mind renders *and* receives. The associative powers of mind, when confronted with a powerful perception, seek "among the shadows . . . some shade . . . Some phantom, some faint image." The shadows Shelley describes are the shadowy images of the mind. The terms "phantasy" and "phantom" suggest, as in Coleridge, that the mind can associate present perceptions with past experience, producing recognizable images in clouds, mist, or crashing river. Shelley describes his mind in this heightened state as a "legion of wild thoughts." It floats and wanders, seeking "Some phantom, some faint image" of the visible. Unlike Wordsworth, who uses this state of mind to focus more clearly on the objective world, Shelley lets his mind soar out from the visual perception that produces this heightened consciousness. In his epiphanies, Wordsworth intends to reveal the essence of a perceptual experience. Shelley's epiphanies, as "Mont Blanc" shows, become a way of moving beyond perceptions, for Shelley is more interested in revealing the source of his perception. As Bloom notes, Shelley calls poetry a "witch" in this passage because this kind of poetry is a form of magic.[27] It reveals a power that can affect the material world.

The epiphany in "Mont Blanc" emerges from the "sublime and strange" trance which envelops the poet as he confronts the ravine of Arve. This "Dizzy ravine" momentarily interrupts the normal flow of thought and reveals the "secret strength of things," the invisible world that can be seen by a mind capable of imagining the unseen in powerfully wrought images of visibility. The epiphany moves us from the visible ravine to an invisible, mental manifestation:

> In the calm darkness of the moonless nights,
> In the lone glare of day, the snows descend
> Upon that Mountain; none beholds them there,
> Nor when the flakes burn in the sinking sun,
> Or the star-beams dart through them:—Winds contend
> Silently there, and heap the snow with breath
> Rapid and strong, but silently!
> [130–36]

As in "Resolution and Independence" and "Frost at Midnight," a mental image achieves a mysterious power. None behold the snowflakes burned by the sun and illumined by the moon, yet the poet can imagine them in order to reveal the invisible source of the visible. The poem records Shelley's movement from a powerful experience of the visible toward his insight that the source of power is invisible. Just as the imagined snow is the invisible source of the visible river, so an invisible aspect of the mind is the source of the sublime trance that overwhelms the poet when he is confronted with this scene. "Silence and solitude" are never a vacancy to an active human mind which fuses disparate thoughts and images. In the process, such a mind peoples solitary scenes with its own creations and creates audible verbal images of visibility amid otherwise invisible silences. Poems become a way of producing images out of the imageless deep described by Demogorgon.

In "A Defence of Poetry," Shelley formalizes the relationship between certain momentary perceptions and poetic creation, revealing how the sensitive mind "peoples" solitude and silence. The moments recorded as literary epiphanies become, for Shelley, one of the major sources of poetic creation. Without feelings of momentary significance, which emerge from the ordinary events of the world, we are wrapped in a "film of familiarity" that "obscures from us the wonder of our being." When powerful moments occur they create "anew the universe after it has been annihilated in our minds by the recurrence of impressions blunted by reiteration." Joyce's epiphanies likewise emerge from a belief in the power of certain moments to focus consciousness into crystallizations of thought and feeling. The extent to which Joyce's idea of epiphany derives from Shelley can be clearly seen by comparing a number of passages:

SHELLEYAN "MOMENT"[28]	JOYCEAN "EPIPHANY"[29]
Sometimes associated with place or person, sometimes regarding our own mind alone, and always arising unforeseen and departing unbidden.	A sudden spiritual manifestation, whether in the vulgarity of speech or of gesture or in a memorable phase of the mind itself.
A word, a trait in the representation of a scene or a passion, will touch the enchanted chord.	That mysterious instant . . . very like to that cardiac condition which . . . Luigi Galvani . . . called the enchantment of the heart.
We are aware of evanescent visitations of thought and feeling. . . . they can colour all that they combine with the evanescent hues of this etherial world.	The most delicate and evanescent of moments.
Subdues to union under its light yoke all irreconcilable things.	(Occurs) when the relation of the parts is exquisite, when the parts are adjusted to the special point.
Arrests the vanishing apparitions (and reveals) the beauty of the internal nature (that is otherwise) concealed by its accidental vesture.	(The object's) soul, its whatness, leaps to us from the vestment of its appearance.
Transmutes all that it touches, and every form	The instant wherein that supreme quality of beauty,

The Poetics of Epiphany

moving within the radiance of its presence is changed by wondrous sympathy to an incarnation of the spirit which it breathes.	the clear radiance of the esthetic image is apprehended luminously by the mind.
Experienced principally by those of the most delicate sensibility and the most enlarged imagination.	He received an impression keen enough to afflict his sensitiveness very severely.
(Reveries) precede or accompany or follow an unusually intense and vivid apprehension of life.	He who utters it is more conscious of an instant of emotion than of himself as feeling emotion.
It compels us to feel that which we perceive.	The lyrical form is in fact the simplest verbal vesture of an instant of emotion.
Even in the desire and the regret they (these "moments") leave, there cannot be but pleasure.	The luminous silent stasis of esthetic pleasure, a spiritual state.
Makes familiar objects be as if they were not familiar.	The soul of the commonest object, the structure of which is so adjusted, seems to us radiant. The object achieves its epiphany.

Enchanted, evanescent, radiant, sensitivity, instant: the similarities in diction suggest that Joyce imported Shelley's ideas directly into his own theory of epiphany. Although we should not assume that the notions are identical, Shelley's "evanescent visitations" are remarkably similar to Joyce's "most . . . evanescent of moments."

Both of these columns, however, derive ultimately from Wordsworth. We could, in fact, add a third column that would suggest both Joyce's and Shelley's debt to the preface to *Lyrical Ballads*, where Wordsworth describes how the poet, one endowed with more "lively sensibility" than most and affected by "absent things as if they were present," is able to "throw" over "incidents and situations from common life" a "colouring of imagination, whereby ordinary things should be presented to the mind in an unusual aspect." Wordsworth grounds his verse in the quotidian by saying that poetry "sheds no tears 'such as Angels weep,' but natural and human tears." This kind of poetry can "boast of no celestial ichor" but only of "human blood." Yet, this poetry also has a magical power to perceive "similitude in dissimilitude," the principle that is "the great spring of the activity of our minds, and their chief feeder."[30] When the mind perceives such "similitude in dissimilitude," when it "subdues to union . . . all irreconcilable things" (Shelley) or adjusts parts to the "special point" (Joyce), the result is "radiance," "the light that never was, on sea or land"—epiphany.

The epiphanies I have been discussing derive from poetic applications of this relationship between experience and imagination. Shelley senses the associative aspect of the process when he says that these moments "colour all that they combine" with evanescent hues. For Shelley, poetry can be described as "the record of the best and happiest moments of the happiest and best minds"—minds that have the greatest capacity for these moments that ascribe a unity and coherence to otherwise random, insignificant events. For just this reason, Shelley tries to give the mute, inscrutable face of Mont Blanc a meaning. Wordsworth and Coleridge are more often successful with epiphany precisely because they are not seeking an absolute meaning for their perceptual experience. They are more willing to allow the poetic epiphany to radiate its significance *and* its mystery.

In all three poets, however, the literary epiphany becomes an increasingly important way of restoring to the world the value that had been removed by the mechanizing effects of skeptical empiricism. A mental state produces a sudden feeling of significance out of an ordinary experience. The result is "enchantment," "radiance," a "manifestation." Both Shelley and Joyce see the imagination as the source of these transformations:

SHELLEY	JOYCE
Imagination is as the immortal God which should assume flesh for the redemption of mortal passion.	In the virgin womb of the imagination the word was made flesh.

Imagination is an act of incarnation which formulates ideas as literary objects, experiences as poems. It is by no means coincidental that Joyce in his own "history of literature" gives the "highest palms" to Shelley and Wordsworth after Shakespeare. These two Romantic poets, who stand so far from Joyce in so many ways, are among the originators of a literary technique that plays a major role in the work of the greatest modern poets and novelists.

4

Browning's Modernism

The Infinite Moment as Epiphany

> It was a tree; there was the river; it was afternoon; here we were; I in my serge suit; she in green. There was no past, no future; merely the moment in its ring of light.
> —Virginia Woolf, *The Waves*

BROWNING'S MODERNISM has most often been seen as originating in his use of the dramatic monologue. Blending traditional poetic genres and emphasizing powerfully realized psychological states, the monologues have been described as a source of literary technique in authors as diverse as James, Conrad, Pound, Eliot, and Joyce. Such influences suggest that Browning's sense of character is his primary strength and that it combines with his dramatic ability to place a fictional consciousness in accurately circumscribed historical time. These arguments leave one essential question unanswered: to what extent is Browning sympathizing with his characters and to what extent is he passing judgment on them from some objective viewpoint outside the poem? This question has become an increasingly important focus of critical discussion in recent years. The notion of sympathy is affirmed by defenders of Browning's moral relativism, while the idea of a moral standard is advanced by those who defend his ability to identify dramatically with characters with whom he actually disagrees.[1]

Browning's poetry does indeed possess an essential modernism, one that originates not in the dramatic monologues themselves but in the imaginative impulse that underlies the monologues. This impulse, the "epiphanic imagination," underlies the moment of crisis and character revelation which his most successful poems so often exemplify. Such an imagination brings a powerful emotional intensity to bear on certain moments of experience. A similar intensity was described by Wordsworth in his spots of time and later by Joyce in the epiphanies of *Stephen Hero*. While critics have noted Browning's emphasis on the moment, no one has suggested just how the epiphanic consciousness develops nor why it proves so important to subsequent literature. William O. Raymond argues that Browning's poetry is characterized by imagery that "flashes forth at the peak of an emotional mood" and that the dramatic monologues represent a "distillation of a crucial moment of human experience . . . the revelation of the significance of the precipitous moment."[2] More recently, Carol Christ has claimed that many of the experiences described in Browning's poetry anticipate the epiphanies of Joyce.[3] Christ's analysis develops important connections between the Victorian dramatic monologue and modern poetic uses of the mask and persona. This link includes a changing Victorian sense of time that leads to an emphasis on fleeting experiences of transition in which a focused moment in an individual's life reveals character. Such experiences, which are central to many of Browning's greatest poems, become a defining characteristic of modern literature.

The dramatic monologue, as Browning employs the form, involves a sudden concentration of intense significance in the details of an otherwise ordinary experience. Character emerges not over time but as the product of a series of instantaneous recognitions. Fra Lippo Lippi, for example, emerges suddenly from the darkness into the torchlight surrounding the guard's faces. Lippi characteristically sees the world as if it were just created. He has achieved an Adamic awareness of immediate experience ("I always see the garden and God there / A-making man's wife"). Lippi sees the truth of his nature ("I'm a beast, I know") but achieves a final recognition in the sight of himself as the image of "Ecce Homo," emerging from his own brush:

> up shall come
> Out of a corner when you least expect,
> As one by a dark stair into a great light,
> Music and talking, who but Lippo! I!—
> Mazed, motionless and moonstruck—I'm the man!
> [360–64][4]

In the image of the self transformed in a painting, Lippi reveals one of the characteristics of Browning's epiphanies; they emerge from a character's autobiographical recollections and make their way into works of art. The ordinary once again reveals the extraordinary in such intensely focused moments of transformed consciousness.

Even in the grotesque nightmare world of "Childe Roland to the Dark Tower Came," Roland's final realization is rendered with the fleeting intensity of one moment of clear vision. "This was the place," Roland says, as though aware for the first time that his quest has a goal. The spot at first seems invisible, then suddenly is seen in clearly illuminated terms:

> Not see? because of night perhaps?—why, day
> Came back again for that! before it left,
> The dying sunset kindled through a cleft.
> [187–89]

Though still unclear in its meaning, the power of the experience cannot be doubted. It focuses years into an instant ("one moment knelled the woe of years"). We do not know why Roland is here, nor do we understand the significance of these events, but Roland clearly feels the importance of this culmination of his journey. Even if the ultimate meaning of his search remains unknown, the sense of final revelation is obvious. The apocalyptic close offers knowledge in the midst of uncertainty: "in a sheet of flame / I saw them and I knew them all." The identity of "them" remains unclear, as does the ultimate meaning of this quest. But the power of the feeling that envelops Roland cannot be doubted.

The image of a sunset, breaking through a cleft in the mountains, ushers in Childe Roland's "one moment." Browning may have drawn this image from a letter to Elizabeth Barrett, in which he compared his own poetic impulses to the flashes of light that emerged periodically from the narrow chink in a Mediterranean lighthouse. These insights are like this beam, which "only after a weary interval leaps out, for a moment, from the one narrow chink, and then goes on with the blind wall between it and you."[5] Such imaginative moments characteristically come suddenly, and when they end, the "blind wall" returns. The memory of the experience may last, but the intensity of the feeling fades. Discussing a similar phenomenon in a letter to Julia Wedgwood, Browning described "the rare flashes of momentary conviction that come and go in the habitual dusk and doubt of one's life."[6] In many cases, Browning's poetry vacillates between just such flashes of conviction and doubt.

Browning's epiphanies, like those of the Romantics, thus distinguish the object of value—the epiphanic moment—from any necessary interpretation of its meaning. The poetics of epiphany can be related to modern theories of art that suggest the primacy of the aesthetic experience. In such cases, interpretation—the poem's meaning—is not rendered less important but rather is dependent on the prior reception of an aesthetic perception. Hans Robert Jauss, for example, notes the "distinction between understanding and cognition, primary experience and the act of reflection in which consciousness returns to the meaning and constitution of its experience." Epiphany, like Jauss's "aesthetic experience," "occurs before there is cognition and interpretation of a work,"—or a perceptual event—"and certainly before all reconstruction of an author's intent."[7] Jauss is speaking of criticism, but his distinction also applies to the act of literary creation. Just as Wordsworth worried from 1799 to 1850 about what he could validly claim on the basis of certain childhood experiences, so Tennyson spent more than a decade trying to turn the powerful experiences of grief for Hallam into meaningful art. In Tennyson's case, even more than in Browning's, we find a continuing tension between the aesthetic power of the epiphany and its subsequent interpretation. Browning's fascination with the actual creation of art—"Fra Lippo Lippi," "Andrea del Sarto," "Abt Vogler," "Pictor Ignotus," "A Toccata of Galuppi's"—reflects a related concern with the process that transforms experiences into meaningful verbal signs.

We note Browning's personal belief in flashes of insight in a number of poems where central experiences in individual lives are presented as epiphanies. Cristina's would-be lover, trying to explain her glance at him, says,

3
Oh, we're sunk enough here, God knows!
    But not quite so sunk that moments,
Sure tho' seldom, are denied us,
    When the spirit's true endowments
Stand out plainly from its false ones,
. . . .

4
There are flashes struck from midnights,
    There are fire-flames noondays kindle. . . .

Bishop Blougram, while trying to describe his periods of unbelief, is forced to admit certain short-lived experiences and the intense emotions that accompany them:

> Just when we are safest, there's a sunset touch,
> A fancy from a flower-bell, some one's death,
> A chorus-ending from Euripides,—
> And that's enough for fifty hopes and fears
> . . . .
> The grand Perhaps! We look on helplessly.
> [182–85, 190]

The agnosticism of these passages—"the habitual dusk and doubt of one's life," "The grand Perhaps!"—contrasts with the emotional intensity of such momentary flashes of feeling. As Jerome Buckley has pointed out, this contrast is the essence of Wordsworth's spots of time, when the mind perceives "a unity greater by far than the sum of its separate impressions."[8] Such experiences are characterized by a feeling, not by a sustained ratiocination that can be discursively articulated. Their intensity, which derives from the ability of the epiphanic moment to transcend chronological time, makes them stand out from ordinary consciousness.

The majority of Browning's epiphanies derive from his idea that the power of human love can exalt a self and confirm an identity. When related to the love between two individuals, these moments often suggest a passage from the temporal to the eternal, as in "Cristina":

> 5
> Doubt you if, in some such moment,
> As she fixed me, she felt clearly,
> Ages past the soul existed,
> Here an age 't is resting merely,
> And hence fleets again for ages,
> . . . .
> 8
> . . . .
> And then, come the next life quickly!

This kind of moment provides a sense of personal immortality, at least for the soul capable of love. Two souls, by virtue of having once loved, will love forever. "Porphyria's Lover" perverts this view by trying to preserve the epiphany in an inverted sense. As a result, the epiphany becomes ironic:

The Poetics of Epiphany

>   she
> Too weak, for all her heart's endeavor,
> To set its struggling passion free
> . . . .
>   And give herself to me for ever.
> . . . .
>   at last I knew
> Porphyria worshipped me; surprise
>   Made my heart swell, and still it grew
>   While I debated what to do.
> That moment she was mine, mine, fair,
>   Perfectly pure and good: I found
> A thing to do. . . .

In the warped mentality of the lover, the moment of epiphany leads to murder. He kills Porphyria because he wants her forever as he saw her for an instant, as his, a body that would be beside him always. In a similar way, "My Last Duchess" describes a woman preserved forever in a painting. The smiles that would not stop are stopped by the duke, frozen on canvas to be used as he chooses. In this sense, the duke seeks to stop time.

The epiphany is always threatened by failure because of its fleeting nature. The perceptual details that bring on the epiphany change; the mind moves on. For Browning, this tendency to emphasize change is true no less of poetic inspiration than it is of the love between two individuals. For an instant, described by reference to illumination, the lovers in "Meeting at Night" find the perfect consummation of "two hearts beating each to each!" The sexual images relating to light only confirm the radiant quality of the experience. The waves "leap / In fiery ringlets"; the "blue spurt of a lighted match" reveals the faces of the lovers to each other. But like the light Browning had seen through the chink in the lighthouse, the sudden gleam gives way to a nonepiphanic state characterized by chronological duration. The lovers part at morning, not because they no longer love one another, but because fulfillment is part of a cycle that emerges from its opposite—in the lover's words, because "straight was a path of gold for him, / And the need of a world of men for me."

"Love among the Ruins" derives from this tension between the agelessness of the past and the powerful intensity of a present moment. The love that exists between the two unnamed individuals transcends centuries of warlike history. Behind the poem is the realization that these lovers will not physically outlast the ruins that surround them. Nevertheless, Browning suggests that the power of the emotion embodied in their temporal existence achieves, through its intensity, a status that is denied to the centuries. The lover in "Two in the Campagna," who longs for a feeling of permanence, loses his emotion as soon as he achieves it. The "good minute" arrives only to be snatched from him by the flow of his own rational thoughts:

> 10
> . . . .
>   I pluck the rose
> And love it more than tongue can speak—
> Then the good minute goes.

In an effort to understand the feeling, he loses it. Although the epiphany is short lived, Browning often suggests that there may be more to a moment than temporal chronology allows. This idea is not new to Browning—we have already noted its role in the Romantic poems—though the form he gives it is uniquely Victorian. Roma King describes this balance between ordinary and extraordinary in Browning, saying of Browning's poetry that its "art fixes firmly on this world, inscribing man's activities, indeed, but at the same time imbuing his efforts with a boundless significance."[9] The epiphanic imagination in Browning is revealed at those moments when an otherwise ordinary experience takes on the feeling of immense—Browning often says "infinite"—significance.

These "infinite moments" emerge from the ordinary and are described as infinite, not because they do last forever, but because they break down the normal flow of time, bestowing on certain instants a profound sense of kairotic timelessness, a feeling more important for itself than for any particular attempt to interpret its significance. The lover in "Two in the Campagna" loses the epiphany because he is preoccupied with the search for a specific rational thought that will solve his dilemma, a search that cannot pause to allow perceptual experience to dominate. The "good minute," when he catches the warmth of his lover's soul in his love for the rose, fades as he tries to interpret its meaning. In the end the speaker gains only a sense of his finite limitations and the infinite nature of his longings. For the epiphany to last, it must issue from

The Poetics of Epiphany

a powerful perception of the present and the mingled associations of the past, which can both exist in the intensely realized instant.

As DeVane has pointed out, "Two in the Campagna" represents the failure of the perfect understanding described in "By the Fireside."[10] In neither poem does Browning claim that the intense emotion that accompanies the epiphany lasts indefinitely. Rather, in "By the Fireside," he suggests how the epiphanic imagination renews and strengthens itself over time, giving rise to the conviction later stated in "One Word More" that "the minute makes immortal." It is not surprising that the most carefully articulated description of epiphany in Browning is also one of his most autobiographical poems. The literary use of epiphany, whether in Wordsworth's spots of time or Joyce's "most evanescent of moments," always derives from a conviction that the author has experienced such moments and that they can have far-reaching effects, both personal and artistic.

In "By the Fireside," Browning's poetic tribute to Elizabeth Barrett, the poet suggests how to achieve and preserve the intensity of a moment. The poem owes a debt to Shelley's epiphany of the "magic circle" in "To Jane: The Recollection," in which a "momentary peace" is found in a "thrilling, silent life" felt by the lovers. Browning's poem describes a journey taken by two lovers to a ruined chapel near Bagni di Lucca. After crossing a small bridge that leads to the chapel, they gaze through a grate in a window, then turn and cross the bridge in the opposite direction. They are suddenly halted by a powerful perception that gives way, as always in epiphany, to an intense emotion:

37

Oh moment, one and infinite!
    The water slips o'er stock and stone;
The West is tender, hardly bright:
    How grey at once is the evening grown—
One star, its chrysolite!

38

We two stood there with never a third,
    But each by each, as each knew well:
The sights we saw and the sounds we heard,
    The lights and the shades made up a spell
Till the trouble grew and stirred.

The one moment is identified with the one star. Just as the shining star cuts through the "hardly bright" evening, so this moment cuts through the ordinary moments that precede and follow it. The walk to the chapel begins with the poet's "heart, convulsed to really speak, . . . choking in its pride." This inability to articulate his true feelings is overcome by a powerful epiphany that makes speech unnecessary. Through the image of the one star, the poet resolves his crisis; the experience is transformed as it renders up meaning. "Rabbi Ben Ezra" employs the identical image of illumination:

> when evening shuts,
> A certain moment cuts
> The deed off, calls the glory from the grey.
> [91–93]

The shining star casts a spell over the lovers on the footbridge, evoking a dreamlike state: dreamlike not in the sense of distanced from reality but rather in the sense of possessing a feeling of heightened reality. The trouble that grows and stirs in the wake of this feeling consists of thoughts that follow the intense consciousness of the present. These thoughts then work to interpret the meaning of the epiphany.

Browning elaborates his notion of the way two lovers can achieve a spiritual unification through such moments. The important element is not the object or the events of the epiphanic moment but rather the feeling of unity and timelessness possessed by those who have such an experience. Even "a moment after," the initial power of the feeling fades, but it leaves something of its value behind:

> 48
> The forests had done it; there they stood;
>   We caught for a moment the powers at play:
> They had mingled us so, for once and good,
>   Their work was done—we might go or stay,
> They relapsed to their ancient mood.
>
> 49
> How the world is made for each of us!
>   How all we perceive and know in it
> Tends to some moment's product thus,
>   When a soul declares itself—to wit,
> By its fruit, the thing it does!

The forests have "done it" merely as the scene in which the epiphany takes place. The "soul" is the actual creator of the experience because it recognizes its ability to feel in this way. The fruit of the soul is its ability to identify itself with the object of experience, whether human beloved or shining star. Wordsworth, in *The Prelude*, claims that certain experiences retain a similar "fructifying" virtue in the mind. Such spots of time lead to the creation of a soul aware of its place in the universe. Browning, in the preface to *Sordello*, wrote, "My stress lay on the incidents in the development of a soul: little else is worth study." The incidents in which the soul develops are those that bear fruit by retaining a renovating virtue.

Browning's epiphanies are thus similar to Wordsworth's, although they almost always emerge from the intensity of the love relationship, rather than from a transformed vision of the natural world. From "all we perceive and know," the welter of our mental associations, moments occasionally emerge that can powerfully unify these associations. Any moment that leads to a soul's recognizing its connection with the object of its experience is likewise important. The feeling of unity reflects a harmony between the mind's associations and immediate experience. A single perception has unexpectedly and overwhelmingly brought a mass of mental material into focus.

For Browning, as for Joyce, the feeling of wholeness and harmony is primary, which is one of the reasons the state can be described as "infinite." The feeling of unity tends to collapse the distinction between past, present, and future. Walter Pater remarked on a similar relationship between time and such intensely felt moments. Pater's emphasis on the epiphanic moment, in fact, plays a central role in the development of the modernist aesthetic:

> Now it is part of the ideality of the highest sort of dramatic poetry, that it presents us with a kind of profoundly significant and animated instants, a mere gesture, a look, a smile, perhaps—some brief and wholly concrete moment—into which, however, all the motives, all the interests and effects of a long history, have condensed themselves, and which seem to absorb past and future in an intense consciousness of the present . . . exquisite pauses in time, in which, arrested thus, we seem to be spectators of all the fulness of existence, and which are like some consummate extract or quintessence of life.[11]

A "long history" is condensed in the vivid apprehension of a single impression. A predisposition is fulfilled by moments that help to produce, out of our own experience, a world "made for each of us." The intense consciousness of the present that allows this coalescence seems to block out past and future, giving the instant a durationless quality, a sense of the eternal.

In this regard, Browning's poetic impulse is primarily dramatic rather than lyrical. The epiphanic imagination demands the dramatic progression from a period of normal perception through the heightened perception that leads to the unexpected culmination of epiphany to the less emotional, more intellectual, attempt to interpret the significance of the powerful feeling. Browning's monologues successfully combine narrative and dramatic elements with the emotional intensity of the lyric. The result is a uniquely modern poem which, while breaking down the barriers of traditional poetic genres, also prefigures the narrative techniques that become central to the short stories and novels of the twentieth century. Epiphany begins as a way of ordering experience and becomes a way of organizing narrative structures.

Browning clearly suggests that an operation of mind is the cause of the epiphany. Once the "work is done" the lovers can "go or stay." The important aspect is not the scene itself but the powers that have been at work, producing an overwhelming sense of the importance of one gray evening sharply focused by a single flash from a greenish-yellow star. The product of the moment is that the "soul declares itself." The specific nature of these "powers" is never made clear. We do know, however, that a process of self-definition results: "I am named and known by that moment's feat." The moment elevates the perceiver and leads to a new awareness of the self's place in the world.

Even so elegiac a poet as Matthew Arnold, whose poems most often testify to the difficulties of self-elevation and connectedness with the world, holds out the possibility of such momentary fulfillment. "The Buried Life" describes the search for epiphanic flashes of insight, which, as in Browning, are related to a paradoxically selfless, but self-fulfilling, love:

> Only—but this is rare—
> When a beloved hand is laid in ours,
> When, jaded with the rush and glare
> Of the interminable hours,
> Our eyes can in another's eyes read clear,
> . . . .
> A bolt is shot back somewhere in our breast,
> And a lost pulse of feeling stirs again.

The Poetics of Epiphany

> The eye sinks inward, and the heart lies plain,
> And what we mean, we say, and what we would, we know.
> A man becomes aware of his life's flow. . . .
> [77–81,84–88]¹²

All of the terms of Browning's "good moment" are here: the sense of unity, the breakdown of the normal time sense, the powerful feeling that overwhelms any particular interpretation of the moment's meaning. There is a powerful sense that "unwonted calm" descends, that the instant is revelatory. In a Wordsworthian close, Arnold suggests that such epiphanic moments convey a vague but nonetheless powerful message to the recipient, a sense of the "hills where his life rose, / And the sea where it goes." In "Mortality," Arnold speaks of rare "hours of insight" which are surrounded on both sides by "hours of gloom." Only in these "hours of light" do we discern "all we have built," that is, all we have made of ourselves. During them we do not know "the gauge of time."

Arnold's epiphanies are most often connected with a sense of loss. For Arnold the powerful moment is more often a nostalgic hint, rather than a form of continuing confirmation. "To a Gipsy Child by the Sea-Shore" begins with an image of "sails that gleam a moment and are gone." The epiphany of the poem is negative; it reveals only the "majesty of grief" in this child's evocative face. In "The Strayed Reveller," the whirling energy of "eddying forms" that sweeps through the mind of the youth is broken by a moment when desire sees its object:

> And sometimes, for a moment,
> Passing through the dark stems
> Flowing-robed, the beloved,
> The desired, the divine,
> Beloved Iacchus.
> [277–81]

Arnold's poem "A Dream" evokes the timelessness of the epiphanic moment as well as its fleeting quality. In the poem—after asking, "Was it a dream?"—the poet and his companion, Martin, sail in a small boat down a swift-flowing Alpine stream. On a balcony of a cottage they see the forms of two women, Olivia and Marguerite. The women see the men in the boat, and suddenly a "more than mortal impulse fill'd their eyes." Then the epiphany occurs:

> Their lips moved; their white arms, waved eagerly,
> Flash'd once, like falling streams; we rose, we gazed.

> One moment, on the rapid's top, our boat
> Hung poised—and then the darting river of Life
> (Such now, methought, it was), the river of Life,
> Loud thundering, bore us by; swift, swift it foamed,
> Black under cliffs it raced, round headlands shone.
> Soon the planked cottage by the sun-warmed pines
> Faded—the moss—the rocks; us burning plains,
> Bristled with cities, us the sea received.

Arnold is struck by the sense of the racing, temporal river of life that tears the two men away from the objects of their desire. But he captures effectively the Browningesque sense that the moment of recognition is powerful: "Flash'd once . . . One moment . . . our boat / Hung poised." Once again we see the mind trying to solidify the passing scene into timelessness.

Epiphany typically strives to possess this timeless quality. Even in the historically placed monologues of Browning, the revelation of character in a sharply focused instant suggests that these moments are the truest representations of meaningful experience. This elevation of the ordinary becomes a defining characteristic of modern literature. Browning not only adopts Pater's emphasis on moments that merge past and future into an intense consciousness of the present but also anticipates Carol Christ's suggestion that, "when men no longer have a sure sense of the progress of time from creation to apocalypse, they relocate the 'end-feeling' in the moment." Christ notes that the idea of eternity under these circumstances becomes personal and psychological. Having lost confidence "that time is progressing toward an end point that will justify and reveal time's meaning and open out onto eternity, they attempt to conceive such an end as potentially present in every moment."[13] The desire for finality and completeness is transferred from the future into an intensely realized sense of the present. This attitude perhaps describes the Victorian state of mind, one that sought its clearest insights in a here and now that Carlyle would call the "divine moment," when the soul accepts the world as it is; "Here, in this poor, miserable, hampered, despicable Actual, wherein thou even now standest, here or nowhere is thy Ideal."[14]

In Browning's case, fulfillment is not potentially present in every moment but only in those rare moments which focus thought, feeling, and sense into a unity:

> Out of your whole life give but a moment!
> All of your life that has gone before,

> All to come after it,—so you ignore
> So you make perfect the present,—condense,
> In a rapture of rage, for perfection's endowment,
> Thought and feeling and soul and sense—
> Merged in a moment.
> ["Now," 1–7]

These moments are also centrally related to artistic creation. Abt Vogler finds a godlike power in "a flash" that occurs when three notes produce a chord that is "not a fourth sound, but a star." Browning's fascination with artistic creation is always exemplified in his poems about music. Music's effect, more emotional than intellectual, is like the effect of epiphany. Music takes Vogler out of time into timelessness. Fra Lippo Lippi paints "soul" not by painting the ineffable but by painting the physical body perfectly. By doing so he claims to add "life's flash" to the mundane. Art reveals the spiritual through an intense concentration on the visible. As always in the modern epiphany, the visible material world reveals the invisible psychic life. Browning likewise senses the autobiographical element that separates all art since the Renaissance from its traditional counterpart. Andrea del Sarto, the ultimate representation of the developing modern artist, declares, "I saw alike my work and self / And all that I was born to be and do" (47–48).

Thus Browning anticipates again the assertion made by Joyce that art emerges from an intense valuation of the ordinary. The role of the artist, according to Joyce, is "slowly and humbly and constantly to express, to press out again, from the gross earth or what it brings forth, from sound and shape and colour which are the prison gates of our soul, an image of the beauty we have come to understand."[15] This image of beauty need not be beauty as traditionally conceived. Often in Joyce, epiphany springs from the sordid, the base, and the trivial. Likewise Browning's love of the grotesque, his celebration of the ordinary, and his sense of the moment's ability to render up eternity all stem from this intuition that the poet, as Joyce said, creates by "transmuting the daily bread of experience into the radiant body of everliving life."

Characters in Browning's dramatic monologues are left to speak for themselves. They are neither introduced nor discussed after they have their say. As readers we are like the recipient of these intense moments; we reserve our judgment until the moment has passed. At the outset we simply share an experience. In the process we achieve a sense of an order and unity that can emerge from the randomness of experience. Browning's epiphanic imagination provides a sharpened focus for the details of ordinary life. Buckley sees a similar phenomenon operating in Wordsworth's spots of time. Such an instant, he says, gives "something of the assurance of value otherwise denied a secular age; it offers, at least for a moment the 'silent stasis,' the possibility of a fixed and ultimate pattern."[16] The world as described by the empiricists stops long enough for the poet to record an unwavering conviction. This conviction emerges not as an absolute meaning but as the record of a powerful feeling, unspecific in its value, but no less real. Such a moment defeats the dread of passing time not just by redeeming past memories, as in Wordsworth's proleptic epiphanies, but by possessing in itself—as Browning suggests—an adelonic feeling of the infinite and of the interconnectedness of things.

Browning's claims in this regard represent a pervasive modernist concern. Joyce is only one of those novelists and poets who testify to the importance of such moments. The short stories of Chekhov as well as the narratives of Henry James, Virginia Woolf, Joseph Conrad, and D. H. Lawrence all display a sense of such keenly focused moments in which significance is emotionally felt but not known with definitive certainty. A similar development occurs in poetry from Yeats to Seamus Heaney. A poem like Yeats's "Vacillation" begins in an ordinary coffee shop and ends in a blaze of secular benediction:

> While on the shop and street I gazed
> My body of a sudden blazed;
> And twenty minutes more or less
> It seemed, so great my happiness,
> That I was blessed and could bless.

As with Browning's "good minute," the experience is known by its feeling, not by its ultimate interpretation. The source of the epiphany is sudden and unspecified. Its results are powerfully felt but not discursively articulated. It lasts only twenty minutes and gives way to a return of ordinary consciousness. Eliot likewise testifies to

> the sudden illumination—
> We had the experience but missed the meaning,

> And approach to the meaning restores the experience
> In different form.
>
> ["The Dry Salvages," 2]

Any attempt to interpret the meaning will result in a change in the experience itself, which is described as pure and unmediated. As the experience of illumination is associated in the mind, it takes on meaning. But any particular meaning is not intrinsic to epiphany. It emerges only later, as a result of the processes of thought. Modern theories of meaning derive from a similar belief that meaning arises internally, as a function of thought, not externally as a function of the nature of reality.

The literary epiphany and its use by an imagination like Browning's clearly represents the modern poetic tendency toward open-endedness. While poems had traditionally sought to provide completeness of form and vision, the nineteenth century produced an increasing emphasis on the suggestive rather than the definitive aspect of experience. Christopher Clausen has observed that the Victorian period is characterized by a profound change in poetic scale. After 1860, he notes, "the truths of poetry that seemed to wear best were no longer the 'great truths' of which Wordsworth had spoken in *The Prelude,* but rather flashes of insight into experience, highly focused clarifications of life . . . amalgams of thought and feeling expressed in lyric form."[17] As early as 1799, however, such flashes of insight were being described in the earliest draft of the poem that would become *The Prelude.* The literary epiphany begins in Wordsworth's spots of time and goes on to become increasingly important as a means of representing this highly focused, nondefinitive aspect of experience. Browning's infinite moment suggests that epiphany can crystallize an instant of the present into a moment of overwhelming emotion, the meaning of which unfolds after the experience in countless mental associations. It is clear in this sense that literature comes to be not only written epiphanically but also read in the same way, in light of the almost limitless associations surrounding immediate experience.

THE POET AS MAGUS: *The Ring and the Book*

> Now let me try . . . to fix the moment in one effort of supreme endeavor. This shall endure. From discord, from hatred . . . my shattered mind is pieced together by some sudden perception.
>
> —Virginia Woolf, *The Waves*

Browning's *Ring and the Book* is the most modern of the Victorian long poems. Its modernity has usually been described in terms of Browning's use of the dramatic monologue to express varying, and often conflicting, points of view. The emphasis on narrative determined by character is a technique that becomes a mainstay of modernist fiction. Equally important to the modernity of *The Ring and the Book*, however, is the role of the author as expressed in the poem and the emphasis Browning places on certain momentary mental states, expressed in a complex and variable timeframe. Browning's poetics evolved gradually toward the poem he considered his masterpiece, resulting in an elaborate theory of the relationship between the reality a poet undertakes to describe and the truth that is contained in poetic creation. This theory develops out of Browning's tendency to employ an epiphanic imagination. Viewed from the perspective of these innovative aspects, the narrative poem Browning published in 1868–69, much more than the work of Dickens, George Eliot, or Thackeray, is the ancestor of the modern novel. The fictions of Virginia Woolf, Joyce, Lawrence, Faulkner, and others owe a debt to Browning that has not been fully explored. At the same time, the poetic credo Browning advances in *The Ring and the Book* becomes a source of subject and style from Yeats to present-day poets.

In 1860, Browning felt a pressing need to tell the story of the Franceschini murders in its entirety. As soon as he had discovered the long-forgotten Old Yellow Book and been riveted by its sordid tale, he noted his willingness to add whatever fiction might be necessary to the historical "facts" so that they might yield up their underlying truth. This poetry was to be imaginative, but with a purpose that lay partly in asserting the relationship between facts and the creative fictions that might bring dead facts to life. Describing the composition of *The Ring and the Book*, Browning compares the poet to three creators: God, a magus, and Elisha. He expresses the godlike aspect of the poet in characteristically Victorian fashion. The poet does not create ex nihilo, says Browning, but rather is a resuscitator who "Repeats God's process in man's due degree / Attaining man's proportionate result." This poet is not Shelley's, who, like the God in Tasso's dictum, *merita nome di Creatore.* Rather, Browning suggests that man's products are, like man, inferior to the source of his creation. More important is Browning's comparison of the poet to a "mage," a magus, or magician. Like magi, poets cannot create the raw materials of creation. They can, however, return seemingly dead facts to life by a process similar to the rekindling of a dying fire. They can fan Shelley's coal into a flame.

For Browning, poetry originates in the individuals who are able to create, in themselves, an "impulse." This self-originating energy "Makes new beginning, starts the dead alive, / Completes the incomplete and saves the thing" (1.733–34). This process of completing the incomplete parallels the leap which allows an ordinary object or event to take on a new significance in the mind. Like the wicks of lamps, the faded aspects of experience can be "breathed on" by a creative spirit and reilluminated. In the process, artists can "mimic creation," to provide what Browning calls "galvanism for life." This reference to the galvanic process reminds us of Browning's "ring," the image that describes the creation of his book-length poem. To fashion a ring, gold ore is mixed with an alloy for strength and bathed in acid to preserve its shine. This process affects the gold's external characteristics but not its essence. The term "galvanism" refers to the electrical bonding of zinc to steel in order to increase the steel's strength and prevent tarnishing. It also refers to any administration of an electrical shock. The term derives from Luigi Galvani, the Italian physiologist whose electrical experiments on nerve tissue helped inspire Mary Shelley's *Frankenstein*.[18] Galvani was later quoted by Joyce in his description of the "enchantment of the heart" which characterized the emotions associated with the literary epiphany. Browning's reference to galvanism and to the illuminated lampwicks of experience suggest how the epiphanic imagination evident in Browning's lyrics becomes central to the monologues that compose *The Ring and the Book*.

For Browning, the poet is like a magus because he or she does not "make man" but rather—as Coleridge had suggested—raises phantoms, or ghosts. Such ghosts are neither illusory nor unreal; they are the legitimate products of an active mind that works on the raw materials of experience. The raw materials, as Browning's language clearly suggests, are not conceived of as a single, unified whole but rather as fragments that imply a whole. The mind must construct a unity out of these materials, which are the objects of consciousness. Then the incomplete can be perceived as complete, and a unity can be derived from the fragments. When intuition finally does occur, it is always, according to Browning, a product of self-projection:

> I can detach from me, commission forth
> Half of my soul; which in its pilgrimage
> O'er old unwandered waste ways of the world,
> May chance upon some fragment of a whole,
> Rag of flesh, scrap of bone in dim disuse,
> Smoking flax that fed fire once: prompt therein
> I enter, spark-like.
> [1.749–55]

This passage critiques the impulse behind the literary epiphany that begins in Wordsworth and is finally named by Joyce. The poet, an essentially active agent, finds scraps of flesh and bone—Yeats will appropriate Browning's image directly in "The Circus Animals' Desertion"—which are then fired with an electrifying spark from within consciousness. The origin of inspiration could not be more clearly described as internal. A part of consciousness ("half my soul") goes into the mundane, waste ways of the world, where it chances upon isolated fragments that can be sparked to life. Facts are combined with the "smoking flax" of emotion and sparked by the imagination. Thus animated by the imagination, these objects can be transformed into artistic creation. The ring, in Browning's metaphor, must be rendered malleable and then shaped. Just such a process occurs in the accumulation of details that make up *The Ring and the Book*.

The result is surprisingly indefinite, more like the individual brushstrokes of an impressionist canvas than the detailed wholes of a realistic painting. The need thus exists for differing points of view, or varying versions of the same event, from which a generalized truth can be extrapolated. Such an imaginative creation, says Browning, emerges surrounded by a kind of fog:

> led forth last
> (By a moonrise through a ruin of a crypt)
> What shall be mistily seen, murmuringly heard,
> Mistakenly felt.
> [1.756–59]

The new literary product is a fact from the past that is reanimated by a sensitive mind. Brought forth from the crypt of the past, the fact is illuminated by powers of consciousness that can give it a new life. The result is "mistily seen, murmuringly heard, / Mistakenly felt," not because it is intrinsically vague, but because the meaning of such a creation cannot be clearly articulated. Like the epiphanies recorded in Browning's lyrics, the facts that come to light in this way cannot be unequivocally articulated. Meaning in such cases does not depend on a simple correspondence between experience and a truth to which the experience corresponds. Rather, the reilluminated fact depends on countless associations: rags, scraps, and smoking flax, which combine to produce a sharpened, radiant image. Browning therefore tells the story of the Roman murder through the mouths of numerous historical speakers. The monologues resonate with a richness of personality and character placed there by the poet but nonetheless true to the facts as understood by Browning. The effect of such illuminations of character is more felt than immediately understood. On these terms Browning sees the truth emerging from his poem, not preceding it. Such truth is an ore to be mined and alloyed, not simply a treasure waiting to be uncovered.

Browning also likens the poet to Elisha, the biblical prophet who used physical means to reanimate the corpse of a dead child:

> and he went up
> And lay upon the corpse, dead on the couch,
> And put his mouth upon its mouth, his eyes
> Upon its eyes, his hands upon its hands,
> And stretched him on the flesh; the flesh waxed warm:
> And he returned, walked to and fro the house,
> And went up, stretched him on the flesh again,
> And the eyes opened.
> [1.764–71]

This is Browning's defense of poetic realism. Poets do not create the facts; they breathe life into them. The biblical account and Browning's version both suggest that the miraculous aspect of Elisha's resuscitation is secondary to his physical contact with the child. When his staff placed on the body fails to effect a cure, he employs his own breath and bodily warmth. By comparing Elisha's act to poetic creation, Browning radically distinguishes his view of inspiration from Milton's nightly muse or the blinding states of extrasensory rapture described by the metaphysical poets. On Browning's account, poets must engage the world in an immediate, powerfully sensuous way. They must fuse their "live soul and that inert stuff." The objects of consciousness and consciousness itself can then cohere in an alliance of parts that allows the seemingly dead world to "warm" and "come to life." In the revelatory flashes of insight that testify to this process, poets find another source of artistic creation. The poem itself becomes the visible sign that such a coherence has occurred. Epiphanies in *The Ring and the Book* record those moments when characters—Pompilia, Caponsacchi, the Pope—experience such a coherence and convert coincidental coherence into meaning.

The poem not only contains numerous epiphanic passages, it also sets forth a theory of epiphany. Browning consistently uses images of brilliant sparkling, flashing, and flaring to describe the mental effects of certain events. He also explains how a sensitive mind turns the historical record of these events into poetry. Browning elaborates his poetics in the first section of the poem, which is itself entitled "The Ring and the Book." The significance of the epiphanies Browning describes, like the significance of the historical events that produced them, is not closed. Both radiate their significance outward: one in the minds of readers of this Victorian poem, the other in the mind of the poet who revitalizes history. In the case of a long poem like *The Ring and the Book,* the meaning emerges "note by note." Like a musical score, the poem achieves its total meaning as a product of a combination of parts. In a similar way, the Romantic self achieves an identity by combining empirical impressions into a composite of significantly related parts. Such a meaning, however, built up note by note, is significant because it can reach beyond the particulars and therefore can "mean beyond the facts." In such a case, each concrete image becomes a touchstone. These touchstones—many of them epiphanic—then can anchor meaning without enclosing it.

For a poet, according to Browning, the truth of art always emerges from a valuation of the ordinary. What objects does the poet choose as subjects? What events possess the significance that warrants their transformation into poems?—those which exist with a certain vividness in the mind, those that mix with the materials already in the mind to produce a revitalized object. Not only is "fiction which makes fact alive, fact too." Poetic fictions are actually a means of selecting from the welter of "facts" those details which bear most directly on the underlying truth of a given situation. The truths of poetry, Browning suggests, can only be told "obliquely." This obliqueness, however, reveals the closest approximation to an absolute truth. The truth emerges from within the poet and is mixed with external facts in order to quicken a material world that seems otherwise dead and subject to the strictures of passing time.

One clearly focused image, however, is never enough for Browning. In this regard he remains firmly entrenched in the Victorian sensibility, regardless of the extent to which he anticipates modern literary developments. What separates the highly wrought epiphanies of the nineteenth century from their twentieth-century counterparts is the poet's desire for these epiphanies not to exist in isolation. The quality of aesthetic isolation, which determines a poem's value for the Symbolists and the Imagists, is the one most dreaded by Tennyson and Browning. For these two poets, the image produced by the epiphany, no matter how powerful in itself, must exist in relation to a transcendent reality. Its associations can thus extend infinitely. Likewise, Wordsworth never wants his images to stand on their own. Instead, they must combine with other similarly focused moments and point toward a unitary truth suggested by each individual representation. Coleridge and Keats, on the other hand, begin the tradition that allows epiphanies to exist in aesthetic isolation. Coleridge's "phantoms" and Keats's "isolated fine verisimilitudes" are eventually transformed into the "symbols" of Yeats and the "images" of Pound.

Not coincidentally, Browning chooses images from Coleridge and Keats to suggest the danger of recording mere "panel" images of experience. Thus, says Browning, the Coleridgean epiphany of "frost at goblin-time" which "startled the moon" should not stand by itself in a "House of Fame" (1.1353–54). This image suggests the fear of aesthetic isolation recounted in Tennyson's "Palace of Art." Without a direct connection to life, the images of art are sterile and cold. For this reason, Browning continues, Keats's epiphany of autumn, "August's hair afloat in filmy fire" which "swooned there and so singed out the strength of things" (1.1355–57), is unable to exist in a void. For Browning, epiphanies themselves, like the associations from which they derive, must be combined and focused into a unity. Browning's choice of these two epiphanies suggests that he clearly understands the increased importance of such moments in nineteenth-century poems. In *The Ring and the Book*, Browning suggests a synthesis, not only of clusters of associations that produce epiphanies, but of the epiphanies themselves, into a unity that can be identified with truth, a unity all the more powerful because of the multeity that characterizes it. "Learn and love," he says, not only each individual, and powerful experience, but

> Each facet-flash of the revolving year!—
> Red, green and blue that whirl into a white,

> The variance now, the eventual unity,
> Which make the miracle.
> [1.1361–64]

Experience is momentary and fragmentary. This strain in Browning is modernist. But beyond the fragments, the traditionalist Browning still seeks a "miracle," a whole that can reflect and focus all of these facet-flashes into a unity identified with God.

The poet, says Browning, is like "a glass ball with a spark a-top." Once again Browning employs an image drawn from an early electrical apparatus to suggest the power that originates in the creative intellect. The "magic fire that lurks inside" is capable of igniting the scraps of the world, of providing a radiant quality by sparking the smoldering flax of experience into flame. The mind must always seek to overcome its linearity. The imagination ordinarily can show only "one tint at a time." When these tints are combined, however, the result is a single color that possesses all of the shades while revealing none of them individually. Likewise, the modern epiphany does not need to reveal any of the specific associations that gave rise to its initial significance. Contained in such highly focused moments are all of the ideas, thoughts, feelings, and sensations that contribute to the epiphany's subsequent power. Just as one temporal instant can suggest infinity because of its seemingly limitless associations—Browning's infinite moment—so one fragment of experience can imply a whole, of which it is only a particularly suggestive part.

In this way the variable truths of the monologues of *The Ring and the Book* contribute to a truth greater than the sum of their parts. As the Pope suggests, the human mind is the place where this unification ultimately occurs. Our knowledge of the unity of things is a function not of the nature of the world but of our own human capabilities:

> Man's mind, what is it but a convex glass
> Wherein are gathered all the scattered points
> Picked out of the immensity of sky,
> To re-unite there, be our heaven for earth,
> Our known unknown, our God revealed to man?
> [10.1311–15]

This passage points toward a particularly modern view of human psychology. The mind makes a model of reality on its own terms; it focuses the diversity of events into a coherent whole. Shelley had earlier described life as a "dome of many coloured glass" which stained "the white radiance of eternity." For Shelley, the disparate fragments of sensation present in the mind indicate the curse of a fallen state. For Browning, the same image is reversed to become a description of man's mind, a place where the scattered points unite to produce a symbol of the eternal. The mind can thereby produce a "heaven," knowledge amid uncertainty, and a God revealed in the mind. The reuniting of these "scattered points" produces a constrained vision,—"heaven for earth," heaven in human terms. The problem that remains is the one that so often confronts Browning: how does this finite vision provide an index for the absolute? In the terms of epiphany, how can disparate associations unite to form a significant whole?

Browning's poetic technique partially solves this problem. The modernist who accepts Browning's epistemology but denies his theology requires a different solution. For Browning, the solution lies in telling the truth obliquely, in the same way one sees the world. The result shall "breed the thought," not only in the poet, but in all of the poet's readers. Except for those startling flashes recorded as epiphanies, a poet can achieve little more. *The Ring and the Book* develops this aspect of Browning's earlier monologues and reverses one of the dominant traditional ideas about narrative. Instead of offering a unitary theme developed through specific details, Browning presents the details of life as a function of variable human character. Narrative details can thus be conflicting and complementary by turns. Themes emerge, not as a product of Browning's mind, but as a product of the mind of each reader who accommodates and interprets the multifarious details of the story.

The role of the reader in this process is clearly described when Browning says, "Here be facts, charactery; what they spell / Determine, and thence pick what sense you may!" (3.837–38). As with individual epiphanies, the role of interpretation is a function not of the poet but of the reader. Instead of containing one possible interpretation, the text suggests numerous directions of developing significance. Browning's appeal to the reader is not an appeal to find a hidden truth, cloaked in the narrative details, but a truth which

>nowhere, lies yet everywhere in these—
>Not absolutely in a portion, yet
>Evolvible from the whole.
>[10.229–31]

Browning's poetic theory suggests that truth is not a given but something that develops through effort and choice. This same kind of internal effort characterizes the epiphanic form of imaginative inspiration.

Browning's Pope, in book 10 of *The Ring and the Book*, describes his eyes in just these terms. This fictional Innocent III grounds the truth available to humans not in a divine dispensation of special sight to special souls but in the perceptual details of physical sight intensified by the sensitive mind:

> eyes grow sharp by use,
> I find the truth, dispart the shine from shade,
> As a mere man may, with no special touch
> O' the lynx-gift in each ordinary orb.
> [10.1242–45]

Browning claims that there is "no special touch" of external inspiration involved in this process. The eye is ordinary; it has no supernatural powers that enable it to see, catlike, in the dark. What improves with use is not our capacity to receive divine inspiration but rather our ability to derive from nature a sense of unity behind the passing flux of fragmentary sensations. We grasp this sense by allowing consciousness to become almost hypersensitive to the details of ordinary experience.

This notion is not the conventional Victorian view of truth, but it is not unique to Browning. As Walter Houghton has noted of Victorianism, "The scientific view that all things, material and human, were in constant flux, changing under the inevitable influences of many and complex factors, could make all truths seem relative only to a particular moment." The moment becomes important not only as a temporal mode of perception—in a rapid, variegated sequence—but also because it becomes the form in which evidence is marshaled and truth is presented. William Buckler goes as far as to define "modern man" in terms of epiphany: "dignified, worthy of his humanness, but not romantically climactic . . . he may have epiphanic moments as his mythic reassurances occasionally inflate, but as those moments are clustering, they are scattering too."[19] Bergson's phenomenological emphasis on direct experience as a succession of mental states represents one important outcome of this focus on moments. His notion of *durée réelle*, or "real time," suggests that the flow of all mental states is dynamic rather than static.[20] Dynamism of this kind is also an aspect of all evolutionary models of history, biological or social.

Browning's epiphanies derive from his emphasis on the paradoxically momentary and dynamic nature of immediate experience and his conviction that the poet is a "mage," or magician, who can "raise a ghost." Ghosts are raised—Browning once again reminds us of Coleridge—when the poet "by a special gift, an art of arts," uses "more insight and more outsight" (1.737, 739, 740) to produce images or symbols that can order experience. The result is a truth determined by an act of mind rather than by a state of affairs in the external world. "In Browning's poetry," as Betty Flowers has noted, "it is these inner moments which are explored, not the moments in which outer actions occur."[21] These moments of sudden shifts in emphasis, when what was previously unimportant becomes significant or powerfully symbolic, are analogous to the idea that underlies Victorian evolutionary thinking. As Stephen Toulmin and June Goodfield suggest:

> The most profound lesson of Darwin's work is that new creations of great functional significance often come into existence as by-products of processes, all of whose manifest goals lie in quite other directions; and the merits of these novelties depend, not on their conformity to any long-term historical tendency, but on their immediate appropriateness to the particular situation at hand. This is equally true for both organizations and institutions. If there is a key to the understanding of all history, it consists in recognizing not its single-directedness, but rather its multiple opportunism.[22]

Toulmin and Goodfield do not note that this profound lesson also applies to individual consciousness, where powerful moments change the expected direction of thought and produce long-lasting results. Epiphanies emerge from just such mutations of mind and replace a static, teleological view of meaning with a dynamic, developmental model. William James argues that Darwin revealed "the power of chance happenings to bring forth 'fit' results if only they have time to add themselves together."[23] Epiphany reveals a similar power in poetry; chance happenings and coincidences bring forth beneficial results when associated with mental contents that "add themselves together" to elevate consciousness.

Hans Myerhoff has connected such dynamic associationism with nineteenth-century historicism, which discovers a universal law, structure, or continuity beneath the flux of history or consciousness. Myerhoff cites the evolutionary laws of Darwin, Huxley, and Spencer; the cyclical laws of Vico, Nietzsche, and Spengler; and the dialectical laws of Hegel, Marx, and Comte.[24] These theories of progress all derive from a dynamic association that can fuse "elements ordinarily divided according to objective time." In the nineteenth century, Myerhoff notes, the sudden connection of previously unrelated ideas is described as "most vivid in sleep, dreams, and fantasies."[25] This view results in a new emphasis on states of mind which can transcend ordinary temporality and produce an eternity interpreted not as infinite durational time but as timelessness. The countless unrelated details of history can then be organized around mental models—suggestive symbols which convey an ordered sense of significance. In a similar way, Browning's *Ring and the Book* builds up details in the minds of Guido, Pompilia, Caponsacchi, the Pope, the lawyers, and the townspeople to reveal a cumulative truth which must account for all of the details. David Newsome has recently suggested that there are

> moments—"spots of time," perhaps—when the concrete image gives us greater assurance, when the abstraction is for a moment solidified, and we can be certain that what might have seemed a mere acknowledgement was in truth a living passion. . . . At such moments as these, what a person thought becomes truly what a person felt, and a lifeless abstraction has become a living idea.[26]

Epiphany for Browning serves this role of transforming mental abstractions into "living ideas."

Browning's monologues suggest how moments of crisis can reveal the ultimate truths of character. Character, for Browning, is ultimately defined through choice, particularly the choices that occur after moments of epiphanic intensity. The involuntary epiphany in Browning always leads to conviction. Those who choose rightly—Pompilia, Caponsacchi, the Pope—achieve completeness. Those who choose wrongly—Guido and the Comparini—can find completeness only in death, if at all. "You never know what life means until you die," Guido claims at the end of his final monologue, still failing to realize that Pompilia and Caponsacchi can know the meaning of life most intensely in their moments of moral choice. For all of the characters in the Franceschini murder case, the crucial choices will always follow on the heels of highly wrought

The Poetics of Epiphany

moments of epiphany which allow a self to transform raw experience into meaning: Pompilia decides how to respond to her imprisoned life; Caponsacchi chooses to rescue a married woman; the Pope chooses to condemn Guido to death. The question always centers on a self responding to such moments and their potential for meaning. From this interaction between self and circumstance, significance emerges.

Pompilia makes her fate meaningful by longing to "grasp the lightning" that will save her from her nightmare life with Guido. She identifies this lightning with Caponsacchi in a moment of epiphany. Pompilia's fate is in her own hands, achieved through choice, not destiny. Caponsacchi likewise suggests the internal origins of this form of inspirational self-definition:

> Pompilia spoke, and I at once received,
> Accepted my own fact, my miracle
> Self-authorized and self-explained.
> [6.918–20]

To claim that a miracle is authorized and explained by the self is to make inspiration a matter of psychological receptivity, not external impulse. The result of this self-originating miracle is a natural phenomenon that reveals the truth of Caponsacchi's situation:

> Afterward,—oh! I gave a passing glance
> To a certain ugly cloud-shape, goblin-shred
> Of hell-smoke hurrying past the splendid moon
> Out now to tolerate no darkness more,
> And saw right through the thing that tried to pass
> For truth and solid, not an empty lie.
> [6.922–27]

Caponsacchi's heightened sensitivity transforms a dark cloud scudding across the moon into an image of Guido, the lying forger who tries to blot out the light of Pompilia's goodness. But more than simple self-awareness determines the possibility of elevating the power of experience in this new way. The mind must act to value not only those experiences indicative of external power but those which produce a more immediate and personal meaning. With this emphasis, significance can suddenly be derived from unexpected sources. "The true, / The good, the eternal," says Caponsacchi, are to be found

>   not alone
> In the main current of the general life,
> But small experiences of every day,
> Concerns of the particular hearth and home:
> To learn not only by a comet's rush
> But a rose's birth.
>   [6.2090–95]

This passage is central to an understanding of Browning's epiphanies. They derive not from the general current of life, not from the universal, but from the particular circumstances of individual experience. Just so, Caponsacchi says, he will live and learn "out of the low obscure and petty world." The ordinary rose's birth, perceived by a single consciousness, is as powerful as the comet's rush because of its potential to mean something to an individual. An individual telling his or her truth, however, does so only in terms of fragmentary flashes of personal, private revelation. To the court, Caponsacchi can only say,

> After all, I shall give no glare—at best
> Only display you certain scattered lights
> Lamping the rush and roll of the abyss:
> Nothing but here and there a fire-point pricks
> Wavelet from wavelet: well!
>   [6.1171–75]

While the dark abyss continues to roll around each individual consciousness, the mind is nonetheless able to throw out scattered, fragmentary lights, the tips of illuminated waves—like the flashes from Browning's lighthouse—which always end quickly, returning the mind to its normal trough between the wave crests of light.

In *The Ring and the Book,* Browning reverses Milton's dictum and attempts to justify man's ways to God, that is, to suggest how man can, within his limitations, approximate a complete, unlimited understanding. Browning intends his poem to demonstrate from the horrible outward details of the tale a sense of the redemptive quality of certain moments. This broad solution is largely a product of Browning's own theology. Unlike the initially fearful epiphanies of Wordsworth, for Browning epiphany almost always serves to exalt experience by bringing immense significance to bear on moments of transformed consciousness. In an epiphanic imagination like Browning's, characterization is not a matter of uncovering a hidden

The Poetics of Epiphany

essence or soul but of showing the evolution of a soul through moments of crisis and personal revelation. Two of the most exemplary epiphanies in the poem are the meeting of Pompilia and Caponsacchi and the Pope's condemnation of Guido.

The meeting between Pompilia and Caponsacchi combines epiphanic language and structure into a characteristically Browningesque epiphany of the power of human love to rise above the mundane circumstances of life and avow an awareness of changelessness. Pompilia agrees to be rescued, not to save herself, but to save the baby she knows she is carrying. Her pregnancy, rather than her desire to escape, precipitates her decision. Once Pompilia has agreed to the rescue, she awaits Caponsacchi's arrival with intense expectation. She compares him, in her mind, to a legendary flaming stone that was changed into a sword to save a Christian virgin pursued by heathens. She describes him as the lightning that will save her. The epiphanic moment is prefigured by her description of this legendary miracle; the miracle "fixed the flash" of the fiery stone in order to save the girl. The phrase clearly suggests a power of mind that is capable of solidifying an instant in time.

When Pompilia sees that Caponsacchi has come to rescue her, the image of his face becomes just such a means of solidifying the chaos around her. Countless past associations are focused in one instant of clear sight. The uncertainty of her situation and her own doubts about the wisdom of this course of action are fused into a changeless moment of vision—"no change / Here, though all else changed in the changing world!" Richard Altick and James Loucks have seen this moment, "the moment of their meeting," as "the great spiritual epiphany of the poem," the point at which "hesitation ceases, and ignorance gives way to steady vision."[27] The careful use of verb tenses allows Pompilia's phrase to radiate in two directions. The world goes on changing while the power of this single perception stops all alteration in Pompilia's mind. The vision of Caponsacchi's face is also permanent and timeless, though it subsequently changes all of the other relationships in Pompilia's life. The two meanings are equally balanced in Browning's carefully described epiphany:

> And still, as the day wore, the trouble grew
> Whereby I guessed there would be born a star,
> Until at an intense throe of the dusk,
> I started up, was pushed, I dare to say,

> Out on the terrace, leaned and looked at last
> Where the deliverer waited me: the same
> Silent and solemn face, I first descried
> At the spectacle, confronted mine once more.
> So was that minute twice vouchsafed me, so
> The manhood, wasted then, was still at watch
> To save me yet a second time: no change
> Here, though all else changed in the changing world!
> [7.1404–15]

Pompilia then speaks, and Caponsacchi answers:

> He replied—
> The first word I heard ever from his lips,
> All himself in it,—an eternity
> Of speech, to match the immeasurable depth
> O' the soul that then broke silence—"I am yours."
> [7.1442–46]

The simple words "I am yours" echo in Pompilia's ears with immeasurable profundity. The epiphany transforms his "silent and solemn face" into an image of eternal changelessness, his simple words into the echo of an infinite soul.

This occasion, as Pompilia notes, is the second time she has seen Caponsacchi's face, for earlier in the year their eyes met at a spring carnival play. In this instance as well, the narrative is organized as an epiphany. Pompilia has just heard two lovers on stage declare their love for one another when she sees a single, unknown face in the crowd. At the same moment, a bunch of tied candies falls in her lap. The actual thrower of this "foolish twist of comfits" is Canon Conti, Guido Franceschini's cousin. But their startling effect combines with the predisposition created by the stage lovers' declaration to focus Pompilia's attention intently on the face she has just seen in the crowd, the face of Giuseppe Caponsacchi, "silent, grave, / Solemn almost" (7.989–90).

The frozen image reminds Pompilia of a psalm she has often heard:

> There is a psalm Don Celestine recites,
> "Had I a dove's wings, how I fain would flee!"
> The psalm runs not "I hope, I pray for wings,"
> Not "If wings fall from heaven, I fix them fast,"—

Simply "How good it were to fly and rest,
Have hope now and one day expect content!"
[7.991–96]

Pompilia's association of Caponsacchi's face with this psalm reveals clearly the nature of the epiphany. The vision is not a theophanic product of divine intervention; no wings have fallen from heaven, no prayers have been answered from above. Instead it is "simply" the association of a single, silent face in a crowd with Pompilia's heartfelt desire to escape her nightmarish life and save her child. In the same way that her mind associates the candies in her lap with Caponsacchi—even though they were thrown by someone else— so Caponsacchi's face is associated with Pompilia's desperate desire to escape. Whether such an association is accidental or not is irrelevant; it is powerfully moving, whatever its cause. The association finds significance in the actual texture of experience, which is why epiphanies become so important in the twentieth century. Even without the unifying framework of a commonly accepted theology, the power of such experiences cannot be doubted. Some epiphanies do have religious significance, as in the poetry of Gerard Manley Hopkins and the late poems of T. S. Eliot. Epiphany itself, however, is neither religious nor secular; it is a form of meaning that derives from the way the mind associates and transforms the details of its awareness into clusters of significance.

Caponsacchi's feelings as Pompilia gazes on him for the first time echo her later ascription of an eternal aspect to such a gaze. Of the initial meeting of their eyes he says:

That night and next day did the gaze endure,
Burnt to my brain, as sunbeam thro' shut eyes,
And not once changed the beautiful sad strange smile.
[6.434–36]

The Mona Lisa–like changelessness of this paradoxically sad smile cuts through the transitory nature of the surrounding moments and impresses Caponsacchi's mind with a supersensuous intensity. The open-ended image of Pompilia's sad smile invites analysis and illustrates the fertile ground that critics have found in Browning's poetry. Interpretation becomes a matter of paying extremely close attention to subtle shifts in tone, nuance, and suggestion. Often the meaning of a specific phrase or image will suggest two equally likely—and sometimes conflicting—interpretations. As in epiphany itself, this kind of ambiguity is likely to result from a keen attention to the actual texture and details of experience. This vagueness and open-endedness is not a weakness; it suggests the potential richness of a single smile, a nod of the head, or a meeting of eyes.

The term "epiphany" appropriately describes the early glances between Pompilia and Caponsacchi, as confirmed by her comparison of her "star"—Caponsacchi— to the star that heralded an earlier theophanic epiphany:

> So did the star rise, soon to lead my step,
> Lead on, nor pause before it should stand still
> Above the House o' the Babe,—my babe to be. . . .
>   [7.1448–50]

In this revealing passage, Pompilia compares her own child to Christ and Caponsacchi to the star that led the magi to the stable. As already suggested, the Christian epiphany is more specifically a theophany. And as Pompilia has claimed earlier, Caponsacchi's arrival displays, not divinity, not "wings fallen from heaven," but a simpler—though no less deeply felt—earthly revelation: "How good it were to fly and rest, / Have hope now, and one day expect content." The wings we fly by, for Browning, are wings of our own making. They may carry us upward, but like the wings of Icarus, they are bound by the limitations of their materials. In the case of epiphany, the limitation is the human mind. The wings we make for ourselves Abt Vogler calls the "broken arcs of earth," which can nevertheless suggest the "perfect round of heaven." These arcs are fragments that point toward a whole. In the same way, the fragmentary sensations of a single mind struggle toward the unified consciousness of an identity. Epiphany, in Browning, suggests the extent to which a single consciousness can achieve a godlike state.

In describing the meeting between Pompilia and Caponsacchi, Browning seems removed from the autobiographical materials which are so often the source of the literary epiphany. Browning is closer than first seems apparent, however, if we compare the meeting of Pompilia and Caponsacchi with the epiphany of the lovers— Browning and Elizabeth—in "By the Fireside." In both cases the image of the star is central. In "By the Fireside," the "moment, one and infinite" is identified with the single evening star. Pompilia likewise imagines her salvation in these terms: "as the day wore, the trouble grew." In the dusk that envelops the lovers in "By the

Fireside," the identical anxiety is felt—"the trouble grew and stirred." In the same poem, Browning defines the result of the epiphany as

> some moment's produce thus,
> When a soul declares itself—to wit,
> By its fruit, the thing it does!
> [243–45]

This goal is perfectly realized in the circumstances that surround Pompilia and Caponsacchi. Their souls declare themselves as a result of the first sight that passes between them: Pompilia, by requesting that she be rescued; Caponsacchi, by finally agreeing to spirit away another man's wife for noble reasons.

The "moment, one and infinite" of "By the Fireside" is also echoed in Pompilia's momentary glimpse of Caponsacchi's face, as well as in the first words he speaks—"I am yours." Pompilia claims that these words are spoken in a moment of kairos, in an epiphanic instant that resonates eternity. Pompilia hears three simple words—"I am yours"—which can contain a lifetime of meaning for her situation, and identifies this meaning with the image of a rising star. As I have already noted, Caponsacchi as rising star has his counterpart in the "one star, its chrysolite!" that catalyzes the infinite moment of the lovers in "By the Fireside." The story of Pompilia and Caponsacchi is autobiography at one remove. Like much else in *The Ring and the Book*, their epiphanic meeting is a fusion of Browning's own emotional life with the details of the seventeenth-century Roman murder story. Elizabeth Barrett Browning's inability to understand Browning's fascination with the story and her criticism of his attempts to transform such a sordid tale into poetry testify to the profoundly personal level of Browning's involvement in the complex emotions described in the poem.

Browning's epiphanies do not always center on a powerful relationship between two individuals, nor do they derive necessarily from autobiographical sources. The second great epiphany in *The Ring and the Book* occurs at the close of the Pope's monologue, where Browning's persona offers an epiphany as his reason for sentencing Guido to die at the gallows:

> For the main criminal I have no hope
> Except in such a suddenness of fate.
> I stood at Naples once, a night so dark

> I could have scarce conjectured there was earth
> Anywhere, sky or sea or world at all:
> But the night's black was burst through by a blaze—
> Thunder struck blow on blow, earth groaned and bore,
> Through her whole length of mountain visible:
> There lay the city thick and plain with spires,
> And, like a ghost disshrouded, white the sea.
> So may the truth be flashed out by one blow,
> And Guido see, one instant, and be saved.
> [10.2117–28]

The Pope compares the possibility of Guido's conversion on the gallows to a totally natural occurrence, an epiphany of the lightning that suddenly illuminated the city of Naples on a night so dark the earth seemed to have disappeared. Just as the Pope's vision was transformed when the invisible earth was suddenly revealed, "white the sea," like a "ghost disshrouded," so Guido may see the truth of his sinful character at the moment of death. In the powerful epiphany of Naples, the Pope's mind turns the darkened earth into a laboring mother who groans and bears up a city "thick and plain with spires." A perceptual illusion—that the city no longer exists—reveals a psychological truth when the lightning flashes. The truth can always be "flashed out by one blow" in "one instant," in a blaze of recognition. Whatever the orthodoxy of Browning's theology, he relies on a completely naturalistic epiphany to describe the change in the Pope's state of mind.

Browning's emphasis on highly focused flashes of imaginative revelation and his use of the dramatic monologue to convey such moments lead in two directions—one poetic, the other prosaic. The poetics of epiphany develops through the sensual moments of the Decadents into the symbols of Yeats, leading ultimately to the imagistic fragments of Pound and the dramatic monologues of Pound and Eliot. As a narrative technique, epiphany provides a way of moving from one intense perception to the next and thereby presenting independent truths of character rather than universal truths of nature. This application of epiphany reaches from Joyce and Woolf through Faulkner to Pynchon. When DeVane claims that "the evolution of the dramatic monologue through Browning leads directly to the stream of consciousness of Joyce,"[28] he is commenting on the increased importance of internal psychological states to fiction. The literary epiphany becomes one of the prime vehicles of this movement, suggesting not a specific interpretation of the meaning of mental events but rather one way that consciousness moves from one ascription of significance to the next. Childe Roland's epiphany of sunset in "Childe Roland to the Dark Tower Came"—a sheet of flame that reveals all his predecessors—is perhaps not surprisingly the direct ancestor of Tyrone Slothrop's epiphany of rockets in Pynchon's *Gravity's Rainbow*:

> 6:43:16 BDST—*in the sky right now* here is the same unfolding, just about to break through, his face deepening with its light, everything about to rush away and he to lose himself, just as his countryside has ever proclaimed . . . slender church steeples poised up and down all these autumn hillsides, white rockets about to fire, only seconds of countdown away, rose windows taking in Sunday light, elevating and washing the faces above the pulpits defining grace, swearing *this is how it does happen—yes the great bright hand reaching out of the cloud*.[29]

As the hand of God had once been said to reach out of the clouds, Pynchon says, so the rockets are now reaching out of the sky at this moment, a moment named—6:43:16 BDST—and frozen in a revelation, a modern version of apocalypse.

In the closing section of *The Ring and the Book*, Browning leaves the monologues for a final summation. In a strikingly modern conceit, he admits the arbitrariness of narrative endings: "Here were the end, had anything an end." He suggests that even a book-length poem is finally able to convey its message in one instant of blazing meaning:

> Thus, lit and launched, up and up roared and soared
> A rocket, till the key o' the vault was reached,
> And wide heaven held, a breathless minute-space,
> In brilliant usurpature: thus caught spark. . . .
>
> [12.2–5]

Just such an image becomes the controlling metaphor of *Gravity's Rainbow:* the rocket pauses for an instant at the apogee of its flight, just long enough for silence to descend with a meaning that awaits the destructive explosion for its end. The story of Guido Franceschini is likewise delivered up to the reader—"you have seen his act . . . over and ended, falls and fades." For Browning, "Art remains the one way possible / Of speaking truth" (12.843–44). The poem tells a truth obliquely and in the process is able to "mean beyond the facts." This continuing meaning involves the reader in a creative act. The separation of the poet's power and the reader's power is central to the epiphanic imagination. It assumes that the poet's role is that of presenter, not interpreter, of experience. The role of interpretation is left to the reader, who, in Browning's words, "judges" and so creates a new significance out of new associations. The epiphanic imagination produces poems that do not *tell* their significance but rather *are* significant, insofar as they can be accommodated into patterns of meaning by any consciousness. In modern literature, the reader plays just such a determining role in the meaning of literary texts. Interpretation becomes a new form of creation.

In Browning, the autobiographical epiphanies of Wordsworth become a means of characterization. By locating the epiphany in the consciousness of a literary character, Browning prepares the way for the novelists of the next century. The epiphanies of Browning record an intensified experience in which feeling overwhelms interpretation, giving rise to interpretation only after the fact. During such moments time seems to stop or to dissolve into a nontime that is identified with eternity. During these same moments a pattern is suggested or a focus is achieved which concentrates varied mental phenomena into a single overpowering image. This image possesses, by virtue of its associations, a mysterious, powerful, and personally enriching quality. The effect is always one of manifestation, not only of the essence of the objects involved, but also of the processes of mind by which this feeling of integration is achieved. The epiphanic imagination reveals at once the world and the mind's ability to make sense of the world.

5

Victorian Versions of Epiphany

Tennyson's Secular Mysticism: The Epiphanic Trance Poem

> A sonnet is a moment's monument,—
> Memorial from the Soul's eternity
> To one dead deathless hour.
> —Rossetti

NORTHROP FRYE'S comment that the word "mystic" has brought nothing but confusion to the study of Blake applies equally well to the study of Tennyson. Since the earliest biographies, critics have tended to accept without question the suggestion that Tennyson was a mystic, or at least that he had experiences of a kind that can only be called mystical. Sir Charles Tennyson claimed that his grandfather "was at heart a mystic with a capacity for true mystical experience." Harold Nicolson uses the term to describe Tennyson's greatness: "The mystical genius of Tennyson comes upon one in a flash, and there can be no question of the reality of his emotion and his impulse." Nicolson's comment that "there can be no question" as to the validity of Tennyson's impulse suggests, however, that there may well be such a question and reveals one problem with all mystical experience—it rests ultimately on the judgment of the individual in question. Basil Willey sees Tennyson as "not unacquainted with flashes of mystical insight," while Carlisle Moore bases his analysis of the poet's faith on "the mystical quality of his own vision and experience." Even Alan Sinfield, in his discussion of the modernity of *In Memoriam*, describes Tennyson's "dependence upon mystical experience," although Sinfield connects this tendency in Tennyson with the exclusively mental reality of the symbolists.[1]

The meaning of "mystical" in each of these cases remains regrettably unclear. Willey offers perhaps the most straightforward definition: he claims that experiences like those of Tennyson represent "this oneness with the real," a "contact with 'that which is.'"[2] Even this terminology is overly vague, however, when used to define a word that most often has an explicitly theological reference. None of the critics cited suggests how the "reality" perceived by Tennyson in his exceptional states differs from the reality I perceive before me on my table, or how Tennyson's contact with "that which is" differs from Keats's aesthetic identification with the sparrow in the gravel outside his window. Without further explanation, such uses of the word "mystical" and its cognates are vague and do not help us to understand Tennyson's poetry.

The term "mystic," particularly when applied to a poet rather than to an avowed religious mystic, has a confusingly wide range of meanings. The *Oxford English Dictionary* defines the term variously as "pertaining to the mysteries of the faith," "union with or absorption into the Deity," "union with the Divine nature by means of ecstatic contemplation," and "spiritual apprehension of truths that are inaccessible to the understanding." References to Tennyson's poetry have relied on one or more of these definitions. The O.E.D. also offers one purely secular use of the term, the so-called recent use which is defined as "inspiring an awed sense of mystery," as in—the O.E.D. quotes Tennyson's "Morte D'Arthur"— "an arm / Clothed in white samite, mystic, wonderful." Such a definition, which has its origins in the Victorian era, comes closest to any valid general use of the term in reference to the poet of *In Memoriam*. More important for my argument, however, is the sense in which the term "mystic" fails to describe the impulse behind Tennyson's so-called mystical poems.

Confusion about this issue originates, in large part, in Tennyson's own interest in what he called "trances," states of altered consciousness that occurred throughout his life and were often associated with poetic composition. In the most well-known description of these experiences, the aging poet reported,

> A kind of waking trance I have frequently had, quite up from boyhood, when I have been all alone. This has generally come

upon me thro' repeating my own name two or three times to myself silently, 'till all at once, as it were out of the intensity of the consciousness of individuality, the individuality itself seemed to dissolve and fade away into boundless being, and this not a confused state, but the clearest of the clearest, the surest of the surest, the wierdest of the wierdest, utterly beyond words, where death was an almost laughable impossibility, the loss of personality (if so it was) seeming no extinction but the only true life.[3]

Most critics have understood this account to describe the experience that leads to mystical vision in a number of Tennyson's poems. Others have been more skeptical. Robert Preyer thinks that Tennyson's concentration on his own name makes this case one of simple self-hypnosis.[4] A. Dwight Culler has commented on the incantatory quality of this repetition and its relation to Eastern forms of transcendental meditation.[5] In the most recent biography of the poet, Robert B. Martin cites Tennyson's own comments, made late in his life, about these alterations of normal consciousness. After 1848, Martin writes, the poet "began referring openly, for the first time, to his own trances, which he ascribed either to gout or to his passing voluntarily into an extra-sensory state through a form of self-hypnotism or meditation."[6] Martin discusses Tennyson's recurrent fears of epilepsy and their relationship to gout, a disease from which the poet clearly suffered. The imaginative stimulation that often signals the onset of a gout attack, Martin notes, is very similar to the visionary aura that can precede an epileptic seizure. Visual imaginations are particularly well developed in individuals who suffer from both complaints. R. C. Zaehner, in his *Mysticism, Sacred and Profane,* takes this skeptical reading to the extreme and advocates a complete denial of any mysticism in Tennyson. Zaehner defines mysticism broadly as "a direct apperception of the Deity; the mystic *knows* that God is in him and with him." He then quotes Tennyson's description of his trance state in full and notes: "It is surely significant that it never occurred to Tennyson to connect this experience with God. . . . the experience, praeternatural though it undoubtedly was, did not suggest the presence of God at all."[7]

Zaehner's denial of mystical status to this trance state is borne out by Tennyson's own comment that the loss of personality involved in his trances always admitted an element of doubt (note his parenthetical "if so it was")—and his assertion that the state emerged from "the intensity of the consciousness of individuality" (Tennyson's own individuality) rather than from a consciousness of divine otherness. At the same time, Tennyson does in certain instances suggest that such an experience *may* involve contact with a divine force. The confusion in Tennyson's case is compounded by his Victorian willingness to define human mental qualities in spiritual terms. "'Personality,'" he said, "as far as our intelligence goes, is the widest definition and includes 'Mind,' 'Self-consciousness,' 'Will,' 'Love' and other attributes of the Real, the Supreme, 'the High and Lofty One that inhabiteth Eternity Whose name is Holy.'"[8] This kind of general definition only confuses the issue further. Mysticism in all of its definitions demands a certainty about the nature of experience that is always lacking in Tennyson. Eliot's comment about the power of Tennyson's doubt suggests how unwilling the poet was to place a final interpretation on even his most powerfully felt experiences. This tendency to allow the power of experience to supercede any particular interpretation connects Tennyson's revelations with the modern epiphany.

Jerome Buckley comes perhaps closest to the truth about Tennyson when he says that the "I" of *In Memoriam* "finds in his mystical insight the surest warrant for spiritual recovery." This diction leaves the ascription of mysticism up to the poet, not the critic. It is one thing for a poet to claim to have had a mystical insight, and entirely another for a critic to agree that such an ascription is valid. Emphasizing this distinction, Buckley argues that Tennyson "had been familiar with such 'spots of time' from his childhood, and there was, of course, ample literary precedent for his use of 'mystical' materials." The phrase "use of 'mystical' materials" suggests that mysticism in Tennyson's case is a way of describing experience rather than making an epistemological claim about the nature of experience. On Buckley's terms, the verbal or literary representation, more than the experience, can be called mystical. The event takes on suprasensible qualities because the author says it does and because there is no other way of describing a particularly powerful event in language. Buckley's use of the term "spots of time" to describe Tennyson's deeply felt conjunctions between the mind and external nature points to the parallels I have been suggesting between autobiographical events and their transformation into poetry throughout the century. It is revealing that Buckley concludes by citing Kierkegaard, who, while denying the possibility of any actual mystical union, demanded a "moment of passion" in which the possibility of significance was more important than the specific contents of the experience of meaning, in which the emotional assertion of a belief becomes more significant than any claims about the specific contents of the belief.[9]

I do not argue that Tennyson never had an experience that could be described as mystical. Such an issue rests almost solely on the definition of the term. Rather, I suggest that a careful examination of Tennyson's poems that have most often been called mystical reveals them to be more closely allied with the form of meaning found in Wordsworth's spots of time and Browning's infinite moment, a form of meaning that can be discussed critically by reference to the term "epiphany." Not only the most well known of these poems—section 95 of *In Memoriam*—but a number of Tennyson's lyrics describe a revelatory experience grounded in this world, a revelation that originates not in an external source but in the mind of the poet. Important from the point of view of modern poetry—in which epiphany becomes a commonplace—are those poems in which Tennyson testifies to a vaguely understood, but powerfully felt, apprehension of the essence of an object or event. Often in Tennyson's "trance" poems we see the sudden mental focusing of disparate details that characterizes epiphany. The meaning of the experience is evolved internally, not imposed from outside. The revelation is sudden and unexpected, yet it completes a powerful psychic predisposition, fulfilling an anticipation unexpectedly by combining diverse mental contents into a single powerful image that radiates significance. Tennyson's characteristic skepticism, uncertainties, and ambivalences testify to the fleeting nature of his moments of conviction. He was, like Wordsworth, subject to revelatory "gleams," "flashes," and "shocks" that were intensely vivid at the time of their cognition, emerging unexpectedly out of ordinary events, and were then turned over and reworked in the mind, becoming the subject matter for some of his greatest poems.

In Tennyson, the manifestation of power in experience is almost always directly related to the process of poetic composition. The concept of epiphany can thus be extremely useful in resolving the characteristic uncertainties of such a poet, for it can reveal these uncertainties and mysteries as strengths rather than weaknesses. Tennyson's own description of his trance state expresses an interplay between individual and universal, a sense of an objective essence beyond immediate sensation. The tension between the objective aspect of an event and its imaginative transformation in the mind produces a new poetic image that radiates power. Events otherwise trivial or accidental take on a new significance. The event's meaning cannot be fully explained or articulated, and yet, although "beyond words," the experience leads to continuing efforts at poetic description.

Tennyson described his trance state in these terms throughout his life. As late as 1885, in "The Ancient Sage," a poem he described as "very personal," Tennyson noted that

> more than once when I
> Sat all alone, revolving in myself
> The word that is the symbol of myself,
> The mortal limit of the Self was loosed,
> And past into the Nameless.
> [229–33][10]

The sage goes on to tell how such a "loss of Self" leads to "such large life as matched with ours / Were Sun to spark," invoking the language of radiance. The poem includes no trance but rather a description of the trance state; there is no epiphany, but only talk about epiphany. The poem takes place a "thousand summers ere the time of Christ" and laments our "thin" human minds, which constantly seek to force the "Eternal Now" into temporal categories. The sense of boundlessness, the accompanying loss of self, and the description of an eternity contained in the present connect Tennyson's trances with Browning's infinite moment of atemporal awareness.

"The Ancient Sage" also provides an important clue to the actual details of Tennyson's revelatory experiences by suggesting that a secular, indeed skeptical, turn of mind characterizes even the most powerful of his visions. The sage argues powerfully that it is impossible to establish the central issue of all religious thinking—immortality: "Thou canst not prove thou art immortal, no / Nor yet that thou art mortal." In fact,

> nothing worthy proving can be proven,
> Nor yet disproven: wherefore thou be wise,
> Cleave ever to the sunnier side of doubt,
> And cling to Faith beyond the forms of Faith!
> [66–69]

"Faith beyond the forms of Faith" characterizes an entire school of twentieth-century theology. Tennyson suggests, in terms that would not be unfamiliar to Kierkegaard or Tillich, that an individual believes, not on the basis of an indubitable insight into the nature of reality, but on the basis of a search for consistent "form" amid the seemingly unordered vagaries of life.[11]

The relationship between momentary insight and objectively verifiable truth worried Tennyson from his earliest days as a poet. "Armageddon," the composition he wrote as a teenager and later revised into the prize-winning "Timbuctoo," echoes Wordsworth's "light that goes out" but with a fading sense that reveals an "invisible world":

> Each failing sense,
> As with a momentary flash of light,
> Grew thrillingly distinct and keen.
> [2.27–29]

This state leads not to a vision of God but to a view of the wonder and expansiveness of the human soul:

> I wondered with deep wonder at myself:
> My mind seemed winged with knowledge and the strength
> Of holy musings and immense Ideas,
> Even to Infinitude. All sense of Time
> And Being and Place was swallowed up and lost
> Within a victory of boundless thought.
> [2.40–45]

Such a state unites the poet with the "Unchangeable" but leads to a strictly personal, humanized form of devotion—"Yea! In that hour I could have fallen down / Before my own strong soul and worshipped it." This passage is a clear echo of Wordsworth's "To my soul I say, I recognize thy glory."

Not surprisingly, Tennyson's view of apocalyptic Armageddon ends with a characteristically Wordsworthian epiphany:

> The clear stars
> Shone out with keen but fixed intensity,
> All-silence, looking steadfast consciousness
> Upon the dark and windy waste of Earth.
> There was a beating in the atmosphere,
> An indefinable pulsation

> Inaudible to outward sense, but felt
> Through the deep heart of every living thing,
> As if the great soul of the Universe
> Heaved with tumultuous throbbings on the vast
> Suspense of some grand issue.
> [4.24–34]

This pulse sounds remarkably like the beating of the poet's own heart; the epiphany can originate in a physical sensation. It is described as powerfully felt, and yet its ultimate significance remains elusive. The diction of the passage indicates clearly that Tennyson is operating within the confines of the new form of poetic meaning first developed in Wordsworth's spots of time. Certain experiences, because of their powerful interconnections in Tennyson's mind, achieve an importance in the memory that allows them to assume a value far beyond their initial significance. Such experiences reveal a mind keenly aware of its ability simultaneously to perceive and alter the contents of experience.

One of Tennyson's strikingly modern epiphanies appears at the close of "Audley Court," a poem often considered trivial by critics because of its seemingly obvious conclusion—that certain moments in a life are happier than others. But the poem's simplicity is deceptive. "Audley Court" is in fact an almost direct precursor of Wallace Stevens's "The Idea of Order at Key West." In Tennyson's poem, the poet and his friend, Francis, are walking home late after a singing match and picnic. They want to prolong the day but

> ere the night we rose
> And sauntered home beneath a moon, that, just
> In crescent, dimly rained about the leaf
> Twilights of airy silver, till we reached
> The limit of the hills; and as we sank
> From rock to rock upon the glooming quay,
> The town was hushed beneath us: lower down
> The bay was oily calm; the harbor-buoy,
> Sole star of phosphorescence in the calm,
> With one green sparkle ever and anon
> Dipt by itself, and we were glad at heart.
> [78–88]

The genesis of the poem is the sight of a harbor buoy that appeared and disappeared in the sea. The first time Tennyson saw this buoy he was unable to tell what it was. The image reminds us of the flickering lighthouse beacon that Browning compared to his own moments of revelation. This buoy's role in the composition of Tennyson's poem, in addition to suggesting a sudden revelatory illumination, is hinted at in the poem's earlier song, a lyric with rhythmic echoes of a lover's departure and return: "I go tonight: I come tomorrow morn. / I go, but I return." The theme of the poem centers around the cycle of departure and return made manifest in a buoy that flickers off and on.

"Audley Court" is more significant than most responses to the poem would indicate. James Kincaid's comments are typical, as he claims that it possesses only a "gentle" irony and a "simple affirmation of the value of. . . that moment of happiness."[12] The poem, on the contrary, suggests that such moments of certainty are few and far between and that they represent a rare state of fulfillment. In the Francis of "Audley Court" we see a version of Arthur Hallam, five years dead when the poem was composed in 1838. Hallam had died after a sea crossing to Europe; Francis's song claims that "The sea wastes all." Francis details the futility of most human endeavor and then makes a simple request—"let me live my life." The poem responds to this request with a simple folk song of love to Ellen Aubrey that concludes, "I go, but I return." The shining buoy of "Audley Court," with its "green sparkle," reminds us of the chrysolite star that catalyzes Browning's epiphany in "By the Fireside." For Tennyson, the sparkling buoy becomes the symbol of reappearance demanded by the lover who longs to know that things which vanish can return. This theme becomes particularly evident when the simple yet profound moment of happiness is seen in the context of lessening stability in the later years of the narrator's life. The poem goes on to note that, amid "the fallow leisure" of life, the narrator became a "rolling stone of here and everywhere." Such instability is countered, however, in the focused moment of fulfillment represented by the epiphany of the flashing buoy. The exact significance of the moment, beyond the gladness felt by Francis Hale and the narrator, remains as elusive and fleeting as the phosphorescent point of light at sea that becomes the focus of their emotion. But as I have already suggested, the epiphany always stands to gain in power by not being fully explained, by sustaining a sense of power and mystery.

Arthur Hallam's relationship to the Francis Hale of "Audley Court" is confirmed in section 89 of *In Memoriam*, where a strikingly similar event is recorded. "Audley Court" was composed in 1838; section 89 in 1835 or 1836. In section 89, Tennyson describes a visit to Somersby, when he and Arthur listened to songs on the lawn and were able to "break the livelong summer day / With banquet in the distant woods." Not only the energetic singing and picnicking but the tone and diction of specific lines echo the details of "Audley Court":

> We talked: the stream beneath us ran
> The wine-flask lying couched in moss,
>
> Or cooled within the glooming wave;
> And last, returning from afar,
> Before the crimson-circled star
> Had fallen into her father's grave,
>
> And brushing ankle-deep in flowers,
> We heard behind the woodbine veil
> The milk that bubbled in the pail,
> And buzzings of the honied hours.
> [43–52]

Images often associated with epiphany—"the glooming wave," the "crimson-circled star"—and the sensuous Keatsian evocation of the "honied hours" all suggest the intensity of transformed vision found in "Audley Court." In both cases, the vivid details of a carefully described perceptual scene give rise to a mental state that is seen as beatific and beneficent. Wallace Stevens achieves a remarkably similar epiphany in "The Idea of Order at Key West," when the "Blessed rage for order" sought by the narrator is achieved in the bobbing lights of the fishing boats that master the night and portion out the sea: "Fixing emblazoned zones and fiery poles, / Arranging, deepening, enchanting night." In both Tennyson's poem and Stevens's there is a clear movement from perception of phenomena to an apprehension of spirituality.

For Tennyson, such elevations of the ordinary through a powerful act of mind are not restricted to natural scenes. His suggestion that the mere repetition of his name could bring on a sort of waking trance indicates that words themselves had an incantatory power over him, a power similar to that reserved in Wordsworth for natural scenes, in Coleridge for heightened intellectual or altered states of consciousness, and in Browning for events associated with a human loved-one. The enchanting power of words over Tennyson is detailed in "Far-Far-Away," a poem the poet described by saying, "The words 'far, far away' had always a strange charm for me." Wordsworth's "Stepping Westward" records a similar verbal effect when the simple words "What, you are stepping westward?" uttered by a stranger seem "a sound / Of something without place or bound" that give the poet "spiritual right / To travel through that region bright." In Tennyson's case, this charmed effect results in a poem that has been called "mystical" by many but that actually suggests a heightened psychological state rather than a revealed transcendental reality. The first draft of the poem employed an autobiographical "I" which was later changed to a more distanced third person "he." The poem suggests that words alone can induce an altered state of consciousness:

> What vague world-whisper, mystic pain or joy,
> Through those three words would haunt him when a boy,
>   Far-far-away?
>
> A whisper from his dawn of life? a breath
> From some fair dawn beyond the doors of death
>   Far-far-away?

The association of "mystic" with vagueness and the paradoxical fusion of pain and joy suggests the epiphanic open-endedness I have been ascribing to Tennyson's revelatory moments. In this lyric, language transcends immediate sense experience, provoking thoughts of worlds beyond this world and leading to a mood in which the normal categories of emotional response are broken down in a single, all-encompassing mystery. The evocative term "world-whisper" reoccurs in the poem "New Year's Eve," where it is once again associated with a paradoxical and exclusive opposition of emotions. Here the world-whisper is described as a "haunting notice, neither grief, nor joy."

The poem "De Profundis: The Two Greetings" is often considered one of Tennyson's most mystical utterances, which is particularly surprising when we consider the poem's claim that the "main miracle" of the universe is neither the divine creation of the material world nor "finite/infinite" space and time. The only miracle stated in the poem is Tennyson's utterly human cry to the "darling boy," an assertion from the poet to his son that "thou art thou, / With power on thine own act and on the world." Implicit here is the suggestion that man possesses the power, through consciousness, to create a world that is his own and yet can reflect the external world. In an earlier poem, Tennyson testifies to the role of man as the creator of all that can be known:

> There is no rest, no calm, no pause,
>   Nor good nor ill, nor light nor shade,
> Nor essence nor eternal laws:
>   For nothing is, but all is made.
> ["All thoughts, all creeds"]

All is made, that is, insofar as all is acted on by the human mind. Tennyson is finally willing to leave the unknown beyond the realm of human knowing. Two of Tennyson's greatest fears throughout his life were that the mind would prove to be a deceiver and that belief could not rest on experience but depended entirely on a faith that could always admit of doubt. These fears were encouraged by a historical age that increasingly demanded empirical, scientific evidence for any knowledge that might lay claim to certainty.

For the poet, the notion of mental creation rests on the power of words. In Tennyson's case, his own name repeated over and over or a phrase like "far-far-away" can evoke imaginative associations that reveal a coherence between seemingly disparate sense impressions, establishing a new significance for commonplace events. The repetition of his own name could produce a feeling of the boundlessness of the self's place in the universe. Likewise, the repetition of a phrase could reconcile thoughts of past and present into hints of preexistence and immortality. In much the same way, Wordsworth's drowned man, Coleridge's icicles, and Browning's evening star have the power to reconcile countless associations in the poet's mind. The result is a feeling of sudden elevation, a manifestation of a central process of the mind which, by working on the raw materials of sensation, turns them into an image of significance and permanence.

As Frye has noted, "To the poet the (single) word is a storm-center of meanings, sounds and associations, radiating out indefinitely like the ripples of a pool." Frye adds that this very indefiniteness leads the poet to write a poem, striving for a "unity of words in which these radiations have become the links of imaginative cohesion."[13] In Tennyson's case, we sense that the formal properties of a poem—its metrical subtleties, rhythms, and rhyme scheme—reach precision as a way of assuring a form of undeniable certainty in the face of continuing metaphysical doubts. His technical excellence

The Poetics of Epiphany

becomes one way of revolting against external chaos. Tennyson's own identity—in name or image—often becomes the only object on which he can rest this kind of certainty. On these terms, *In Memoriam* can be seen as an elegy for Tennyson's own earlier self as well as for the lost self of Hallam. More generally, Tennyson's intense consciousness of his own individuality often subverts the stated aims of his poetry.

These issues appear most clearly in section 95 of *In Memoriam*, the "trance" most often cited as proof of Tennyson's "mystical" tendencies. Once again, however, a close look at the background of this lyric and of Tennyson's subsequent claims about his experience reveals the evening at Somersby to be firmly grounded in this world rather than in any transcendent spiritual apprehension. Tennyson begins on the lawn of the rectory, left alone reading the letters of the dead Hallam. Suddenly he feels a "living soul" flashed on his own being. This soul was described by Tennyson at different times as the soul of Hallam or of God or both, the confusion resulting primarily from the poet's having changed the pronoun "his" (referring to the soul) to a more distanced "this" in later versions of the text. According to Tennyson, this significant change resulted from his desire not to confuse readers about the nature of the experience. Instead, the alteration seems to have led to confusion not only in Tennyson's mind but also in the minds of many interpreters of the poem.

Almost all critics have accepted a mystical, or at least extrasensory, source for this experience. Moore calls it "a record of genuine mystical experience, a clear sign from a beloved spirit in the next world which, because it effected, or seemed to effect, the dispelling of all religious doubts, had all the earmarks of a conversion comparable in its way with St. Paul's."[14] Just how this experience might be seen as a conversion is nowhere made clear. Religious conversion always begins in a belief that is doubted and then finds a confirmation in experience; it never originates in an experience out of which new meaning evolves. E. D. H. Johnson cites "the mystical revelation of the ninety-fifth," while John Jump calls the section a record of "a mystical experience of a sort Tennyson knew at intervals throughout his life."[15] Willey calls the event "quasi-mystical" but nowhere explains how this term differs from "mystical."[16] I do not minimize completely the value of such judgments but suggest only that the term "mystical" used in such contexts sheds almost no light on the nature of Tennyson's experience or its relationship to this central section of his elegy to Hallam.

Philip Collins, more recently and by contrast, cites section 95 as a moment when the poet was—quoting Tennyson— "carried away out of sense and body, and rapt into mere existence" and argues that a "secularity may, finally, be observed in Tennyson's account of his experience 'out of time.'" Collins concludes by saying that the poet "escaped beyond the usual 'bounds of human thought' by means more human than divine."[17] In all of the poems examined so far in this book, we have seen how just such an escape is possible without an appeal to an identified otherness beyond the poet. Tennyson, as we shall see, has valid poetic reasons for describing a "soul" that flashed on his. It does not follow that such an epiphany cannot be interpreted theophanically; in Hopkins and the later Eliot, this theophanic aspect becomes the defining characteristic. But the new epiphany, a strictly human escape from the ordinary bounds of thought, derives its usefulness as a critical term from its psychological origins and its formal literary properties. Seen in this light, section 95 of *In Memoriam* reveals a more complex aspect of Tennyson's own revelatory states than is ordinarily observed. To argue that the poem records a modern literary epiphany and not a traditional mystical vision is not to reduce its power and meaning but rather to give it a wider range of applicability and significance.

Crucial to any understanding of the flashing soul of section 95 is a careful analysis of the language used in the sections of the poem that precede this climactic scene. Sections 90 through 94 each record a version of the expectation that will be fulfilled in the epiphany of section 95. In the first two of these sections, the poet calls out to the spirit of Hallam—"come thou back to me," "Come, beauteous in thine after form." Almost immediately, however, Tennyson doubts the validity of any physical vision suggesting instead the likelihood of a series of weaker "spiritual presentiments." There will be no "visual shade," but perhaps the nonphysical "Spirit himself, may come." We ask here: what could this spirit be if not a powerfully realized image in the mind? At each stage of preparation for the climactic section 95, Tennyson reduces the force of his claims and undermines his own certainty by modifying his versions of the sort of awareness that may be vouchsafed a human being. By the end of section 93 he has moved from a longing for an actual vision of his dead friend to a request that, even in the midst of his human "blindness," he may at least be allowed to "feel" that Hallam's "ghost" is near. In section 94 Tennyson finally states his actual conditions for "union" with the dead and reveals that the spiritual can be linked with the living through a purely human agency—imagination. Spirits, like the dead Hallam's,

>haunt the silence of the breast,
>Imaginations calm and fair,
>The memory like a cloudless air,
>The conscience as a sea at rest.
>[9–12]

Such spirits haunt the breast of the living as "Imaginations," a function of both memory and conscience. The locale of these dead spirits is here described in completely human terms that involve not transcendence but imagination, not mysticism but epiphany.

The revelation comes to Tennyson with the force and form of a literary epiphany. Tennyson's poem, remarkably Wordsworthian in structure, recounts an experience that is as much aesthetic as it is spiritual. As Joyce suggests and as Wordsworth demonstrates, the terms "aesthetic" and "spiritual" need not be mutually exclusive. The group on the lawn at Somersby has been engaged in an energetic activity all evening, singing "old songs." Gradually they leave Tennyson alone with his thoughts in one of the last places in which he saw Hallam alive. His powerful predisposition is described when he says, "A hunger seized my heart." As he reads the letters of his dead friend, a physical sensation he describes on three separate occasions as "strange" sweeps over him. The words on the page move his sensibility until he is engulfed by a feeling of unity and aionic timelessness:

>So word by word, and line by line,
>   The dead man touched me from the past,
>   And all at once it seemed at last
>The living soul was flashed on mine,
>
>And mine in this was wound, and whirled
>   About empyreal heights of thought,
>   And came on that which is, and caught
>The deep pulsations of the world,
>
>Æonian music measuring out
>   The steps of Time—the shocks of Chance—

> The blows of Death. At length my trance
> Was cancelled, stricken through with doubt.
>
> [33–44]

This passage has always been seen as the climax of this section of the poem. For many critics it represents the turning point of *In Memoriam*. At this moment there is an achievement of kairos (the crucial moment turned to useful account) and also of aiōn (the temporal instant rendered suddenly eternal). But for all of its intensity, this climax is not the final achievement of section 95 or of the entire poem. Tennyson's diction is explicit, and its precision casts continuing doubt on the status of this flashing soul. The living soul seemed to be flashed on Tennyson's, and even this "seeming" is described in terms not ordinarily associated with the mystical. The empyreal heights are "of thought," strangely intellectual for an experience supposedly of pure spirit. The pulsations the poet feels are said to be of "the world." Tennyson perhaps is simply becoming aware of the beating of his own excited heart in the quiet of the darkened lawn. We recall lines from "The Lotus-Eaters": "And deep-asleep he seemed, yet all awake, / And music in his ears his beating heart did make" (35–36). Traditional inspiration, mystical or otherwise, always involves a pervasive awareness of the divine or of another world. It is revealing in this regard that Tennyson's "Æonian music" measures out not only the "steps of Time" and "blows of Death" but also the "shocks of Chance." Such shocks describe the accidents that bring together various mental contents into a focused image or mood. In the subsequent stanza Tennyson reveals that the poem records a change not in the world but in his own state of mind. Words cannot describe, he says, nor intellect reach "that which I became."

Tennyson's uncertainties about this experience are confirmed as the trance, for all its power, is almost immediately "cancelled, stricken through with doubt." The epiphanic moment usually ends with doubt, but the effect remains. Even Moore, in defending Tennyson's mysticism, acknowledges that it is "the nature, not the actual occurrence of the experience that the poet doubts."[18] This doubt suggests not the realm of transcendence but simply the poet's own awareness of his distinct identity. Tennyson's doubts emerged most clearly when he altered the original "His living soul was flashed on mine / And mine in his was wound" to its present impersonal form, "The living soul was flashed on mine / And mine in this was wound," thus distancing himself from any distinct sense other than self-awareness. "The first reading, 'his living soul,'" Tennyson commented, "troubled me, as perhaps giving the wrong impression." Later he added, "I have often had the feeling of being whirled up and rapt into the Great Soul."[19] Tennyson clearly saw the Somersby Rectory experience as involving his own identity, however much he may have altered the event for artistic purposes. It was another of those experiences he had known since childhood when the consciousness of his individuality expanded until it seemed to "dissolve and fade away into boundless being," that is, until the self came to be identified with the universe.

In a note to the trance of section 95, Tennyson provides an important clue to the effect of the epiphany of Somersby Rectory. "The trance came to an end in a moment of critical doubt," he wrote, "but the doubt was dispelled by the glory of the dawn of the 'boundless day.'" The trance was important to Tennyson's subsequent life as the true epiphany of the poem because its effect persists, manifesting the mind's power to bestow immense significance on the ordinary experience of a sunrise. Section 95 ends with a creative breeze that rises to become an image of reconciliation and fulfillment:

> And sucked from out the distant gloom
>   A breeze began to tremble o'er
>   The large leaves of the sycamore,
> And fluctuate all the still perfume,
>
> And gathering freshlier overhead,
>   Rocked the full-foliaged elms, and swung
>   The heavy-folded rose, and flung
> The lilies to and fro, and said
>
> "The dawn, the dawn" and died away;
>   And East and West, without a breath,
>   Mixt their dim lights, like life and death,
> To broaden into boundless day.

This vividly realized sunrise, with its imagined voice, represents the outcome of the epiphany. Certainty (a manifestation of unity) comes not in the flashing soul that leads to doubt but in the powerful realization that follows: the light of dawn transformed into a voice in the breeze, a mixing of natural lights which connects night and day, reaffirming the epiphanic union between dead and living.

This event is not a mystical union of supernatural spirits but a realization of a psychological unity behind the diversity of the senses that can imaginatively connect the living and the dead in a sensitive mind. It is dawn itself, the mixing of two dim lights into sudden boundless brightness, that is both objectively real and poetically imagined in Tennyson's mind. The poet may be able to doubt the contents of his "trance" (as Keats does at the close of "Ode to a Nightingale": "Was it a vision, or a waking dream? / Fled is that music—do I wake or sleep?"), but he cannot doubt the powerful feeling of significance that comes to be associated with an otherwise normal experience. The accidental fact that night has passed during Tennyson's reverie takes on a profound significance, enabling the dawn suddenly to stand for the lasting truth Tennyson has been seeking throughout the poem.

A later poem, often overlooked by Tennyson scholars, describes the experience of section 95 in completely human terms. In 1861 Tennyson traveled to the Pyrenees, returning to a spot he had visited with Hallam in 1830. The journey was filled with memories of his friend and led to the composition of a poem entitled "In the Valley of Cauteretz," of which he later said, "Altogether I like the little piece as well as anything I have written."[20] In the poem, Tennyson is walking beside a "stream that flashest white." The sound of this stream grows strangely louder as night begins to fall. As the noise of the waters increases, the three decades since his visit to the spot with Hallam seem to roll away like mist. Finally, Tennyson addresses the stream:

> all along the valley, down thy rocky bed,
> Thy living voice to me was as the voice of the dead,
> And all along the valley, by rock and cave and tree,
> The voice of the dead was a living voice to me.

The voice of the dead here is nothing more complex than memory joining the present sound of a cascading river to a powerful recollection of the past. The image is not epiphanic because it suggests neither the manifestation of a new mental construct nor a literal transformation. But the scene does indicate that the voice of Hallam can be brought back "from the dead" by as simple a phenomenon as walking beside a rocky stream where the two once walked together. Section 100 of *In Memoriam* asserts, "I find no place that does not breathe / Some gracious memory of my friend." Returning to section 95, we may ask: where would such a situation be more likely to occur than on the lawn of Somersby Rectory, where Tennyson was alone with Hallam's letters in an emotional state described as "a hunger"? The letters, we now realize, are treated in that scene as something physically sensed. Spirituality in section 95 emerges from the epiphanic transformation of the contents of the letters into a powerful sense of soul.

Tennyson's continuing doubts about the validity of his experience of Hallam's (or the divine) soul are articulated even more clearly in section 122 of *In Memoriam,* in which imagination is described as the source of any such elevation of the self:

> Oh, wast thou with me, dearest, then,
>   While I rose up against my doom,
>   And yearned to burst the folded gloom,
> To bare the eternal Heavens again,
>
> To feel once more, in placid awe,
>   The strong imagination roll
>   A sphere of stars about my soul,
> In all her motion one with law;
>
> If thou wert with me, and the grave
>   Divide us not, be with me now. . . .

Tennyson's uncertainty about the status of this experience and his suggestion that the activity of "strong imagination" was its source remove the Somersby Rectory trance from the class of mystical visions which conform to a preexisting belief. The passage states unequivocally that it was Tennyson ("I") who "rose up" in a yearning, not that any external fulfillment was actually achieved in the trance. Tennyson, like Wordsworth in *The Prelude,* continually seeks the significance of those elevations of consciousness that occur when,

>   As in the former flash of joy,
> I slip the thoughts of life and death;
>
>   And all the breeze of Fancy blows,
>   And every dew-drop paints a bow,
>   The wizard lightnings deeply glow,
>   And every thought breaks out a rose.

This description of epiphany employs the same image that Wordsworth describes as "the gleam, / The light that never was, on sea or land." The breeze is of "fancy"; the "lightnings" are those of a poetic magician, a wizard. The imagery of Tennyson's passage recalls the breaking of dawn on the boundless day after the night on the rectory lawn. The predisposition of desire, Tennyson's yearning, gives rise to a strong "roll" of imagination that transforms an image of natural illumination into an epiphany that unifies thoughts of life and death.

T. S. Eliot's claim that Tennyson was "capable of illumination which he was incapable of understanding" fails to acknowledge Tennyson's remarkable ability to express the vague and often contradictory nature of his most powerful experiences.[21] Eliot, as we shall see, explores very similar illuminations in *Four Quartets*. The concept of an open-ended epiphany allows us to see how such ambiguity can become a strength, indeed, how it guarantees Tennyson's stature as a major poet. Tennyson's honesty about his doubts has led to some unfair criticism. Paull F. Baum, for example, remarking on the change of language in 1878, claims that Tennyson's gloss of the "flashing soul" as "the Deity, maybe" betrays a "weakness inherent in Tennyson's character. . . . we have a right to expect some sort of clear statement: either it *was* the Deity—for the purposes of the poem, of course—or it was not."[22] Not only is this unwillingness to make a final statement not a weakness of character; it represents that which is most modern in Tennyson's poetry, that is, his willingness to suspend judgment in the face of experience, allowing significance to emerge from events rather than imposing significance upon them. When interpretation follows a powerful experience in Tennyson, the result often involves a range of conflicting, or at least ambiguous, meanings.

The modern literary epiphany differs from previous forms of inspiration in its sense of the qualitative value of experience as experience, without any appeal to a specific evaluation of its contents. For this reason Tennyson's interpretive glosses tend to weaken the effect of the epiphany. This relationship between epiphany and a heightened imagination is stated clearly in "Merlin and the Gleam," written late in Tennyson's life and perhaps his most autobiographical poem. The gleam, the "Magic" that Merlin/Tennyson has followed throughout life, is a symbol of the epiphanic imagination. Such an illumination, said Tennyson of "Merlin and the Gleam," "signifies in my poem the higher poetic imagination." The poet first senses this gleam during his own experiences of childhood and later in the poetic images derived from Wordsworth:

> Innocent maidens,
> Garrulous children,
> Homestead and harvest,
> Reaper and gleaner.
> [55–58]

The gleam fades, not unexpectedly, with the death of Hallam, restored only when it draws "to the valley / Named of the shadow," suggesting the vale of Cauteretz rather than Somersby Rectory. The gleam henceforth is wed to the "melody," the music of poetry. Though Merlin/Tennyson is growing older, he sees the gleam whenever it passes "the dead man's garden." Toward the close of his life Merlin finally sees the gleam of poetic imagination as the highest achievement available to man: "All but in Heaven / Hovers the Gleam." Then, echoing "Ulysses," he calls on all young mariners to recognize the gleam for what it is: not sunlight, moonlight, or starlight, but the light of the human mind. Tennyson beseeches these poetic mariners to follow this gleam, in fact to chase it before it vanishes; that is, before its possessor, the magician, dies. "Merlin and the Gleam" is an autobiography of the epiphanic impulse—the desire to create literary epiphanies—in the life of one of its foremost practitioners.

Only once does Tennyson actually describe the mind's psychological power to elevate the trivial or commonplace by an action that connects powerful mental states with simple images:

> Strange, that the mind, when fraught
> With a passion so intense
> One would think that it well
> Might drown all life in the eye,—
> That it should, by being so overwrought,
> Suddenly strike on a sharper sense
> For a shell, or a flower, little things
> Which else would have been past by!
> ["Maud," 2.2.8]

The mind fastens onto little things when already in the grip of a predisposition, a heightened emotional sensitivity. We recall Wordsworth's encounter with the leech-gatherer of "Resolution and Independence," Coleridge's attention to the flickering light on the grate in "Frost at Midnight," and Browning's sight of the evening star in "By the Fireside." Once the mind strikes "on a sharper sense," it can move beyond the bounds of sense perception and complete an image by an act of creative imagination. The revelation emerges from experience and finds its completion in a poem. Consciousness finds itself reified in language. The literary epiphany becomes a way of bestowing significance on events that would have been otherwise "past by." In discussing Tennyson's revelations, we should not forget that he said of *In Memoriam*: "It's too hopeful, this poem, more than I am myself," and added, "I think of adding another to it, a speculative one, bringing out the thoughts of 'The Higher Pantheism,' and showing that all the arguments are about as good on one side as the other, and thus throw man back more on the primitive impulses and feelings."[23] When most himself, Tennyson was always drawn to these primitive feelings as well as to the "little things" that could reveal such impulses in experience. The result is often a dialogue between the experience of self and the experience of the world that produces immense poetic energy.

The epiphanic imagination does not seek to replace one set of historically valid circumstances and meanings with another but to find a common ground for all experiences of significance. This focus limits the definitiveness of the claims made in epiphanic poems but widens the range of their possible meanings. The epiphany—words which manifest power—becomes a rich source of meaning, a mine to be quarried, a mysterious wilderness of potential and continuing significance. The experience is described in a way that conveys a clear sense of the objective validity of the object or event it reveals and combines that sense with an awareness of the mind's power as imaginative creator. The mind itself, as Joyce's verbal insight suggests, can shed light (phainein) upon (epi) the powerfully felt objects of experience. For this reason Joyce suggests that the term "epiphany" can be applied both to the experience of significance and to the literary form it assumes in a sensitive, creative mind.[24] In addition, of course, the poet can produce epiphanies that have no immediate connection with actual experience. Unlike those traditional inspirations and conversions that arise from preexisting convictions and beliefs, the modern epiphany unites the arbitrary with the meaningful, turning the ordinary into something profound. As De Quincey realized, "The fleeting accidents of a man's life, and its external shows, may indeed be irrelate and incongruous; but the organising principles which fuse into harmony, and gather about fixed predetermined centres, whatever heterogeneous elements life may have accumulated from without, will not permit the grandeur of human unity greatly to be violated."[25] A poet like Tennyson is finally unwilling to ascribe his vision completely to a literary or psychological source and often retains theological language, which he nowhere fully espouses. But careful attention to the way he expresses the details of his own revelations allows us to place them closer to the epiphanies of Wordsworth and Browning than to any traditional form of mysticism.

Hopkins and the Return to Theophanic Epiphany

> "There is nothing insignificant—nothing."
> —Coleridge

Writing to Alexander Baillie in September 1864, Gerard Manley Hopkins sought to minimize the importance he attached to the word "inspiration." "The word inspiration need cause no difficulty," Hopkins wrote; "I mean by it a mood of great, abnormal in fact, mental acuteness, either energetic or receptive, according as the thoughts which arise in it seem generated by a stress and action of the brain, or to strike into it unasked."[26] Fifteen years later, this same Hopkins declared, "I find myself both as man and as myself something most determined and distinctive, at pitch, more distinctive and higher pitched than anything else I see. . . . Nothing else in nature comes near this unspeakable stress of pitch, distinctiveness, and selving, this selfbeing of my own."[27] For the poet who saw his deepest fulfillment in the orthodox vows he took in 1877 to become a member of the Society of Jesus, such sentiments may seem inconsistent. Viewed in light of epiphany, however, these assertions about the mental source of inspiration can be connected with his almost unbearable sense of personal identity to yield important clues about the sources of power in Hopkins's poetry. Both ideas also point toward epiphany as a new way of describing certain powerful experiences, a way of recording this high "pitch" of self.

When Seamus Heaney, in a 1974 lecture before the British Academy, compared Hopkins's poetry to the fire that is at once *in* a piece of flint (as potential) and also struck *from* the flint (as a spark), he was emphasizing the complexity of a literary technique that continues to be explored by numerous contemporary poets: "The poem is apparently dismissed as something let go or let fall almost accidentally; there is an understated tone to the phrase; an understatement artists are prone to when speaking about a finished work in order to protect the work's mystery and their own."[28] Heaney suggests that the result of such a process is a poem which, like "the fire i' the flint / Shows not till it be struck." The flint of the world does not reveal its fire until struck by the mind of the poet. Hopkins expressed an identical sentiment in a fragment (no. 91) written in 1864:

> The rainbow shines, but only in the thought
> Of him that looks. Yet not in that alone,
> For who makes rainbows by invention?
> . . . .
> The sun on falling waters writes the text
> Which yet is in the eye or in the thought.[29]

Throughout his poetic career Hopkins worried, as Wallace Stevens would, about the transformations that the mind wrought on the objects of sense. He experienced countless instances in which the essence of an object or event was revealed for a moment in the mind. He also sensed clearly that the "text" written by the "sun" was actually "in the eye or in the thought."

Hopkins employs epiphany as a way of describing experience and as a poetic form. The important role played by this form of meaning will become clear through an examination of a number of his poems and his comments about their origins and significance. Hopkins displays a powerful poetic tension between intense consciousness of self and an equally vivid awareness of the external world, a tension that finds a resolution in the modern literary epiphany. Significance, in these cases, arises in the mind out of experiences which produce radiant images in place of complete understanding. This tension ultimately finds a theological resolution in many of Hopkins's poems, as it does in the later poems of T. S. Eliot. But the conflict between perception and invention also underlies the movement in Hopkins from the confident assertions of his early work to the despair and anguish of his later poems. The shift suggests, not a fundamental change in the poet's religious outlook, but rather an increasing honesty about the sources of his own inspiration and the kind of meaning he could justifiably attach to his own most powerful feelings.

Language, in many of Hopkins's poems, emerges from the

The Poetics of Epiphany

powerful perceptual experience that yields a small, but significant, insight. Every object in the world becomes, like an Emersonian fact, a potential source of spiritual illumination in the mind: "All things therefore are charged with love, are charged with God and *if we know how to touch them* give off sparks and take fire, yield drops and flow, ring and tell of him."[30] I have added emphasis here to emphasize Hopkins's continuing belief in the human power that allows these manifestations to occur. Hopkins believes in "essences" like those that Stephen Daedalus finds revealed in moments when his spiritual eye achieves focus. The only difference is that Hopkins defines these essences literally and theologically, while Joyce defines them in figurative, aesthetic terms. These essences have been identified with Thomistic *quidditas* and Scotian *haecceitas*, concepts with which Hopkins and Joyce were both familiar. For Hopkins, the scholastic notion of this kind of essence can always be seen as an object's identity in the mortal realm (no. 57):

> Each mortal thing does one thing and the same:
> Deals out that being indoors each one dwells,
> Selves—goes itself; *myself* it speaks and spells,
> Crying *What I do is me: for that I came.*

Hopkins's value as a poet, particularly for those who do not share his dogma, has been enhanced by the emphasis he places on this identity and on the poet's ability to "touch" objects in a way that will allow them to "give off sparks and take fire." We recall that Browning used just such language to describe poetic inspiration in *The Ring and the Book.* This process produces suggestive images rather than discursive reasoning because, as James Scully says, speaking of Hopkins, "at any given moment, human reality harbors more crystallizations and confusions than are admitted by the processes of reason."[31]

Revelation in Hopkins always flows from an experience of the world to an interpretation of its significance, placing him directly in the line of descent I have been tracing. His theology emerges not before but after his sensuous apprehension of the world, an apprehension so intense that it demanded new words and new metrical forms to embody its power in language. Repeatedly, however, Hopkins testifies to the self-originating source of immediate revelation, the active agency of the mind in the conversion of ordinary events into meaningful experience. Describing the worn timber-framed arches of an ancient barn, for example, he is struck by the active role of the observer, as well as by the consequences of passivity: "I thought how sadly beauty of inscape was unknown and buried away from simple people and yet how near at hand it was if they had eyes to see it."[32] The object's essence as inscape is revealed by an eye that has the power to perceive its instress. Even Hopkins's coinages "inscape" and "instress" anticipate Joyce's contention that the mind has the power to realize a privileged sense of the identity of an object in an otherwise ordinary perceptual act. Inscape, which Hopkins defines as the essence of any object or image, is clearly related to quidditas, which Stephen Daedalus connects with epiphany. In a similar way, Hopkins's instress, like Stephen's claritas, suggests the power that reveals these essences in the mind of the observer. Hopkins derived his theology from his experience of the world. He therefore came to see many of his epiphanies as theophanies, or manifestations of a revealed divinity. Such poems include modern literary epiphanies, however, because they originate in a powerful physical perception and demonstrate how particular objects in the world can become sources of meaning (i.e., can be made manifest) in the mind.

Hopkins's kingfishers thus "catch fire" in the human mind. His dragonflies "draw flame" only insofar as a sensitive consciousness is able to perceive their inscape via their instress. Otherwise, their essences are "unknown and buried away." The individual, not the world, has the power—as Hopkins says—to "make each morn an Easter Day." Like Emerson, Hopkins believes that every fact can become an "Epiphany of God." This power derives directly from the soul's ability to "Gather gladness from the skies" and "Take a lesson from the ground." Hopkins nowhere suggests that we come to the truth apart from our experience of the world. Instead he seeks, as he says in "The Blessed Virgin compared to the Air we Breathe," a plurality of experiences that will awaken "New Nazareths in us . . . New Bethlems." Such experiences can, in turn, testify to the unity behind the distinctiveness that separates the world into, as John Pick says, "an endless catalogue of sharply individuated selves."[33] Using the epiphanic language of illumination, Hopkins describes this discovery of meaning as "a flash," "a beacon," "shivelights," "firedint," a "spark," and "wildfire." But such illuminations are always to be found through the objects of this world (no. 77):

> Then may I upwards gaze and see
> The deepening intensity
> Of the air-blended diadem,

The Poetics of Epiphany

> All a sevenfold-single gem,
> Each hue so rarely wrought that where
> It melts, new lights arise as fair,
> Sapphire, jacinth, chrysolite,
> The rim with ruby fringes dight,
> Ending in sweet uncertainty
> 'Twixt real hue and phantasy.
> [113–22]

This early poem, "Il Mystico," hints that the revelation may not always lead to a theological confirmation but can point instead to an uncertainty about where the world ("real hue") leaves off and imagination ("phantasy") begins. Browning's "One star, its chrysolite!" emerges at just such a moment of heightened perceptual intensity and ends, not in a confirmation of traditional inspiration, but in "uncertainty," like the lights of "Il Mystico." As Browning states, "The lights and shades made up a spell / Till the trouble grew and stirred." "Trouble" and "uncertainty" follow the focused epiphanic moment as the mind seeks to understand the significance that is at first only felt.

In Hopkins, epiphany becomes theophany only later, when the moment of power is interpreted by the mind. When the experience stands on its own, it always possesses that radiant quality which characterizes Wordsworth's spots of time and Browning's infinite moment. "The Starlight Night," for example, begins with a purely descriptive, nonevaluative praise of the power of the stars to blaze their distant lights into this world. The perceptual detail and the emotional response achieve the characteristic elevation of epiphany:

> Look at the stars! look, look up at the skies!
>   O look at all the fire-folk sitting in the air!
>   The bright boroughs, the circle-citadels there!
> Down in dim woods the diamond delves! the elves'-eyes!
> The grey lawns cold where gold, where quickgold lies!
>   Wind-beat whitebeam! airy abeles set on a flare!
>   Flake-doves sent floating forth at a farmyard scare!

The passage is reminiscent of one of Wittgenstein's comments about the category mistake of solipsism: "Look at the blue of the sky and say to yourself 'How blue the sky is!'—When you do so spontaneously—without philosophical intentions—the idea never crosses your mind that this impression of colour belongs only to *you.*"[34] In Hopkins, this mood fades as soon as the mind goes to work on powerfully perceived objects of experience. Once emotion (indicated by Hopkins's exclamation points) gives way to interpretation, the richness and immediacy of the perception diminish:

> Ah well! it is all a purchase, all is a prize.
> Buy then! bid then!—What?—Prayer, patience, alms, vows.
> . . . .
> These are indeed the barn; withindoors house
> The shocks. This piece-bright paling shuts the spouse
>   Christ home, Christ and his mother and all his hallows.

Images of unlimited light give way to images of enclosure as the stars are replaced by a determinate Christ and Mary that hallow by enclosing all.

In a number of poems, Hopkins separates the perception that causes revelation from its interpretation and considers the psychological source of inspiration. This distinction is not possible in traditional religious inspiration, where the experience is a manifestation of preexisting meaning rather than a trigger to a new manifestation in the mind. "The Candle Indoors," for example, describes a flashing perceptual sensation that seeks an order in the mind of the perceiver:

> Some candle clear burns somewhere I come by.
> I muse at how its being puts blissful back
> With yellowy moisture mild night's blear-all black
> Or to-fro tender trambeams truckle at the eye.

The eye, as perceiver, is the source of the pause that leads the mind to wonder. The candle's essence, its "being," has the simple but profound ability to return bliss to the world by the simple process of uplifting the observer. The poet's eyelashes, as Hopkins noted, are the proximate cause of the split "trambeams" of light that direct the mind's questioning. Pure description of the image drops away, however, as soon as the interpretive powers of mind go to work on the scene (no. 46):

> By that window what task what fingers ply,
> I plod wondering, a-wanting, just for lack
> Of answer the eagerer a-wanting Jessy or Jack
> There / God to aggrándise, God to glorify.

The eagerness of Jessy or Jack to aggrandize and glorify God will lead them quickly to an answer. Meanwhile, the "wondering, a-wanting" Hopkins—the "I" of the poem—is less willing to let the pure experience of bliss give way to explanation. The last two stanzas of the poem reproach this attitude, articulating a fear that too much emphasis on pure experience may leave the poet "blind" and a "liar."

Such a tension between the moment of illumination and the mind's desire to understand the source of its insights is also the theme of "The Lantern out of Doors," a poem Hopkins called a companion to "The Candle Indoors." Hopkins's lantern is another version of Browning's fleeting lighthouse beam and Tennyson's flickering buoy, appearing and disappearing behind the rolling waves. All three images are sources of wonder, passing inspiration, and ultimately sources of poetry (no. 40):

> Sometimes a lantern moves along the night.
>   That interests our eyes. And who goes there?
>   I think; where from and bound, I wonder, where,
> With, all down darkness wide, his wading light?
>
> Men go by me whom either beauty bright
>   In mould or mind or what not else makes rare:
>   They rain against our much-thick and marsh air
> Rich beams, till death or distance buys them quite.
>
> Death or distance soon consumes them: wind
>   What most I may eye after, be in at the end
>   I cannot, and out of sight is out of mind.

In these lines Hopkins demonstrates an awareness of the accidental aspect of experience. Of the notion that the eyes "wind," he says, "I mean that the eye winds / only in the sense that its focus or point of sight winds and that coincides with a point of the object and winds with that."[35] This bringing together of eye and object can yield significance only after the mind seeks to understand this "co-incidence" between itself and the specific object—"I think; where from and bound, I wonder."

Up to this point, the poem recapitulates a characteristic Victorian fear that was expressed by Matthew Arnold in "Rugby Chapel," where "the life / Of mortal men on earth" is seen as a fearfully transient rise and fall. For Arnold, men live

> Striving blindly, achieving
> Nothing; and then they die—

> Perish;—and no one asks
> Who or what they have been,
> More than he asks what waves,
> In the moonlit solitude mild
> Of the midmost Ocean, have swelled,
> Foamed for a moment, and gone.

For Hopkins, partly for this reason, the epiphanic lantern light will not suffice. The mental manifestation, in Hopkins's case, always needs a theophanic buttress, lest it become only the flickering instability feared by Arnold and embraced by Hopkins's Oxford tutor, Walter Pater. Pater's longing to "give nothing but the highest quality to your moments as they pass, and simply for those moments' sake" is the state dreaded by Hopkins, a state in which the privileged moment stands only for itself, without reflecting any wider significance.

Hopkins agrees with Pater in his emphasis on certain formal aspects of experience but disagrees completely with Pater's concentration on form alone. While Pater's epiphanies celebrate the unconnectedness of fleeting, intense perceptions, Hopkins seeks always to fit his epiphanies into a wider system of meaning, an accepted orthodoxy. Pater found all such orthodoxies untrue to the details of his experience:

> To burn always with this hard, gem-like flame, to maintain this ecstasy, is success in life. In a sense it might even be said that our failure is to form habits: for, after all, habit is relative to a stereotyped world, and meantime it is only the roughness of the eye that makes any two persons, things, situations, seem alike. While all melts under our feet, we may well grasp at any exquisite passion, or any contribution to knowledge that seems by a lifted horizon to set the spirit free for a moment, or any stirring of the senses, strange dyes, strange colours, and curious odours, or work of the artist's hands, or the face of one's friend. . . . With this sense of the splendour of our experience and of its awful brevity, gathering all we are into one desperate effort to see and touch, we shall hardly have time to make theories about the things we see and touch. What we have to do is to be for ever curiously testing new opinions and courting new impressions, never acquiescing in a facile orthodoxy.[36]

The Poetics of Epiphany

Pater's theory of epiphany derives from Keats's sense of the "isolated fine verisimilitude," that moment that redeems itself from the flux of passing sensations, and from Coleridge's sense of the strangeness of the elevations of the ordinary produced by the sensitive mind. Pater's view also rests on Coleridge's claim in the *Westminster Review* of January 1866: "To the modern spirit nothing is or can be rightly known except relatively and under conditions." In a similar way, Wordsworth's spots of time record the poet's ability to revitalize past experiences of momentary elevation. For Hopkins, all such transformations of experience have value only if they can be subordinated to a larger system of theological meaning. Wordsworth often moved from epiphany to claims about a transcendent realm. But Hopkins is the first of the poets of epiphany to demand that these powerful and personal elevations of consciousness be interpreted as confirmations of theological dogma.

Pater's unwillingness to commit himself to any system or theory that demands abandoning the purity of experience lies behind the rise of the secular epiphany in the twentieth century. For Hopkins, by contrast, this fear of orthodoxy represents the danger that must be countered by the notion of a revealed, immanent divinity. "The Lantern out of Doors" cannot end in the uncertainty of "all down darkness wide" nor in the "wading light" that leaves consciousness in a questioning state of wonder. Hopkins's epiphanies become theophanies when the image produced by the mind is transformed further into a trope of a dogma that demands assent. Such an assent ends not in mystery but in a final, self-validating assertion of understanding:

> Christ minds: Christ's interest, what to avow or amend
>   There, éyes them, heart wánts, care haúnts, foot fóllows kínd,
> Their ránsom, théir rescue, ánd first, fást, last friénd.

The image of Christ restricts the meaning of the epiphanic opening of "The Lantern out of Doors" to a specifically orthodox interpretation.

Hopkins's epiphanies do not emphasize the structure of the moment to the same extent as Tennyson's, Browning's, or Wordsworth's, partly because Hopkins desires to see each fleeting moment as part of the continuum of Christian time. The notion of kairos, and more specifically aiōn, is antithetical to the Christian notion of a chronological time that moves inexorably from a distant, mysterious creation to the ultimate revelation of apocalypse. Hopkins's imagination is most powerful in the excruciating intensity of the present moment realized by the perceiving self. But Hopkins is held back from a full embrace of the moment, even the perfectly realized moment of epiphany, by his faithful desire to "wait till morn eternal breaks." Until that moment he feels himself capable only of intimations of immortality.

Hopkins's vision of every object as a manifestation of divinity derives not only from the scholastic doctrine of immanence but also from a sense of each "dull despised fact" that has the power to become "an Epiphany of God." Hopkins in "The Windhover," begins with a powerful perception ("I caught this morning morning's minion, kingdom of daylight's dauphin, dapple-dawn-drawn Falcon, in his riding") moves toward a Romantic identification with the source of power ("My heart in hiding / Stirred for a bird,—the achieve of, the mastery of the thing") and ends by subtitling the poem with an orthodox ascription of final meaning ("To Christ our Lord"). From Hopkins's point of view we are no longer left to wonder about the meaning of this bird. God now is not manifested in experience itself, as was always the case in traditional revelation. Instead, theophany in Hopkins is achieved only as a result of a particular interpretation which follows the experience. The experience itself, the "dearest freshness deep down things," whether bird, stars, or poplars, retains the open-ended quality of the modern epiphany.

Hopkins's devotional lyrics find meaning *through* the world but *in* the mind. All religious poems, whether by Hopkins, Donne, Herbert, or Crashaw, are finally intellectual achievements; the mind attains a beauty "past change" only by consciously connecting itself with a closed system of meaning. In Hopkins's case, the poet returns the concept of epiphany to a theological framework by claiming a specifically divine origin, not only for the created world, but also for the means by which the poet perceives the world. It is revealing, as a result, how little the subtitle enters into the actual texture of a poem like "The Windhover." If we remove "To Christ our Lord," the poem is a pure epiphany. And yet, for Hopkins, to remove the orthodox subtitle would render the poem meaningless. In such poems, Hopkins demonstrates, both before and after his ecclesiastical vows, that the power of unmediated experience can overcome all his attempts at interpretation.

Hopkins's poem "Winter with the Gulf Stream," for example, is a remarkably modern poem, written while he was at school and first published in 1863. The surprising aspect of this poem is Hopkins's refusal to move beyond a straightforward description of the scene, thus leaving the implicit significance of the experience unstated. Instead, he allows the image of illumination to radiate its intensity without demanding an analysis of its meaning. This experience is as Paterian a moment as we will find in Hopkins. The poem begins with a powerful, almost Hardyesque evocation of winter which prepares the way for the epiphany:

> The boughs, the boughs are bare enough
> But earth has never felt the snow.
> Frost-furred our ivies are and rough
>
> With bills of rime the brambles shew.
> The hoarse leaves crawl on hissing ground
> Because the sighing wind is low.
>
> But if the rain-blasts be unbound
> And from dank feathers wring the drops
> The clogged brook runs with choking sound
>
> Kneading the moulded mire that stops
> His channel under clammy coats
> Of foliage fallen in the copse.
>
> A simple passage of weak notes
> Is all the winter bird dare try.

Hopkins beautifully invokes both the calm and the decay that characterize the coming of winter. The poem sounds like Hardy's "Darkling Thrush" ("The tangled bine-stems scored the sky / Like strings of broken lyres") approaching the end of an exhausted century. The lines also echo Shelley's "Sensitive Plant" and Browning's "Childe Roland to the Dark Tower Came." Grotesque images alternate with stillness, as though the hissing ground, the clogged brook, and the weak-noted bird are all waiting for something to happen. What eventually does happen—as always in epiphany—is ordinary: the sun sets. The description of the scene possesses all the characteristics of the modern epiphany:

> The bugle moon by daylight floats
>
> So glassy white about the sky,
> So like a berg of hyaline,
> And pencilled blue so daintily,

Victorian Versions of Epiphany

I never saw her so divine.
But through black branches, rarely drest
In scarves of silky shot and shine,

The webbed and the watery west
Where yonder crimson fireball sets
Looks laid for feasting and for rest.

I see long reefs of violets
In beryl-covered fens so dim,
A gold-water Pactolus frets

Its brindled wharves and yellow brim,
The waxen colours weep and run,
And slendering to his burning rim

Into the flat blue mist the sun
Drops out and all our day is done.

The floating moon triggers a series of associations that include the patterned light in the west, the reefs of purple flowers cut by the river, and the narrowing edge of the sun that vanishes suddenly in the shining mist. The bugle moon "announces" this sharply realized image. But the actual epiphany is achieved in the stunning finality of the sun, which fulfills its role not by flaming brightly before setting but by dropping into undifferentiated mist and dramatically ending the day. The burning rim gives way to night, bringing forth a sudden awareness that finality may be one form of fulfillment. The end of day becomes, via this epiphany, the most honest way of resolving the fears associated with winter in the poem's opening. Hopkins ends the poem, not by promising spring, but by suggesting that the watery west into which the sun dies may possess a warmth of its own, a "Gulf Stream" that is not a warmth of continuation but an ending ("our day is done") that becomes a paradoxically resonant fulfillment. The image of sun dropped into the "flat blue mist" evokes the emotional power of the scene. It radiates significance without positing a final meaning. The poem manifests the mind's awareness but does not restrict that awareness; it leaves open the question of exactly what it means. The poem is not theophanic but rather a pure example of the modern epiphany.

Toward the end of Hopkins's career we find him refusing to allow experience to speak for itself in this powerful way. The poet of "Carrion Comfort," "No worst, there is none," "To seem the stranger lies my lot," and "I wake and feel the fell of dark," all written in 1885, has retreated from the world of perceptual awareness into an intellectual realm. Nevertheless, he still recognizes his fears (no. 132):

> In the staring darkness
> I can hear the harshness
> Of the cold wind blowing.
> I am warmly clad,
> And I'm very glad
> That I've got a home.

The home of Hopkins's faith is, as Hillis Miller has noted, contingent upon "a violence done to the self great enough to transform it completely." Miller also describes the fearful consequences of the failure of this vision: "The central religious experience of his last years is the prolonged anguish of spiritual paralysis, dryness of soul, an absence of God and the failure of grace. . . . It seems as if God has withdrawn from the self and from the world."[37]

As a poet, Hopkins withdraws from the world just when he realizes his own role in the inspirations he had described as "a mood of great . . . abnormal mental acuteness." Even in the depths of a mood that has "crush'd my heart, and made me dumb," a mood that ends poetry by demanding inarticulateness ("Cry Pardon, and then be dumb") the poet can still recognize himself as the source of his condition. He can still recognize this "selving, this selfbeing of my own," a sense of personal identity more "determined and distinctive and higher pitched than anything else I see" (no. 127):

> Trees by their yield
> Are known; but I—
> My sap is sealed,
> My root is dry.
> If life within
> I none can shew
> (Except for sin),
> Nor fruit above,—
> It must be so—
> I do not love.
>
> Will no one show
> I argued ill?
> Because, although

> Self-sentenced, still
> I keep my trust.

"Self-sentenced" like so many earlier sinners—particularly Puritan sinners—Hopkins longs for death as a justification, a proof of the faith he has kept in life. Such a dark night of the soul is central, not only to Catholic and Puritan traditions, but also to the secular despair of the Victorians. In Hopkins's case, the source of despair is an absence. "My lament," he says, "Is cries countless, cries like dead letters sent / To dearest him that lives alas! away." Later he begs the absent "lord of life" to "send my roots rain." When the world is no longer enough, the poet cries out, "I want the one rapture of an inspiration."

The decline of Hopkins's poetic vision is related, at least in part, to his fear that his mind, and his mind alone, was the source of inspiration and creation. Paradoxically, this same power is most responsible for his value to modern poetry:

> Not of all my eyes see, wandering on the world,
> Is anything a milk to the mind so, so sighs deep
> Poetry tó it, as a tree whose boughs break in the sky.
> ["Ashboughs," sec. a., 1–3]

Wordsworth had cited an identical image of tree branches against the sky as the source of his own dedication to a poetry of new images. In the Fenwick note to "An Evening Walk," he quotes lines from the poem ("And fronting the bright west, yon oak entwines / Its darkening boughs and leaves in stronger lines") and says:

> This is feebly and imperfectly expressed, but I recollect distinctly the very spot where this first struck me. It was in the way between Hawkshead and Ambleside, and gave me extreme pleasure. The moment was important in my poetical history; for I date from it my consciousness of the infinite variety of natural appearances which had been unnoticed by the poets of any age or country . . . and I made a resolution to supply, in some degree, the deficiency.

Even more than Wordsworth, Hopkins seeks the natural appearance unnoticed by others, the dappled, fickle, freckled thing, the ordinary intensified. Hopkins is perhaps as great a master of naturalistic details as any of his Romantic predecessors.

Hopkins finally sees the eye as a wanderer, searching the world for perceptual details that can stimulate the mind. The tree "whose boughs break the sky" can become a "milk to the mind," a source of mental activity, emotion ("sighs"), and finally a source of "Poetry." In "Nondum," Hopkins claims that all our knowledge must come from this world; even when we raise a psalm, "No answering voice comes from the skies." The power of Hopkins's epiphanic imagination seeks continually to explain the "glories of the earth" while admitting that the "hand that wrought them all"—Isaiah's God in hiding—remains inscrutable. He suggests that each of us "in his own imagining" sets up "a shadow" in the seat of divinity. We are left, so far as experience is concerned, in a state that is finally mysterious and indeterminate (no. 23):

> And still th'abysses infinite
> Surround the peak from which we gaze.
> Deep calls to deep, and blackest night
> Giddies the soul with blinding daze
> That dares to cast its searching sight
> On being's dread and vacant maze.

We should not doubt Hopkins's orthodoxy at this point, even if being itself is "dread and vacant." We should see his vision as finally grounded in this world, however, a world which can, in its most vital moments, spur the imagination:

>   the strong
> Spur, live and lancing like the blowpipe flame,
> Breathes once and, quenched faster than it came,
> Leaves yet the mind a mother of immortal song.
>   ["To R.B."]

The mind fans the sparks of life into flame. Like Shelley's womb of the imagination, the mind is the mother of poetry. Those poems in which Hopkins tries to interpret the meaning of his experience are theophanic when they seek to establish a theological ground for meaning. But they do not explain experience in theological terms. The immediate source of Hopkins's theophanies is always the modern epiphany, in which a subjective point of view, "the peak from which we gaze," unites with the infinite "deep" of the mind to "giddy" the soul into a momentary elevation of consciousness.

6

Epiphany in Twentieth-Century Poetry

YEATS: THE ARTIFICER OF THE "GREAT MOMENT"

>   That mirror
> Whose magic penetrates like a dart,
>   Who lifts that mirror
> And throws our mind back on us, and our heart,
>   Until we start?
>   —Thomas Hardy, "Moments of Vision"

WE CAN CONCLUDE a study of epiphany in the nineteenth century by suggesting the continuing importance of this new form of meaning in twentieth-century poetry. The concept of epiphany clearly provides a means of connecting those poems that focus on a powerfully realized moment of transformed consciousness. Although a complete analysis of these developments in the twentieth century is beyond the scope of this book, a look at poems by Yeats, Eliot, Wallace Stevens, and Seamus Heaney suggests the contemporary importance of the literary form first explored in Wordsworth's spots of time.

The majority of poets who use epiphany in the twentieth century employ the term in Joyce's secular sense. An exception is Eliot, who, like Hopkins, returns epiphany to a theological framework. All uses of epiphany in the twentieth century can be related to Arthur Symons's *The Symbolist Movement in Literature,* a book described by Eliot as "an introduction to wholly new feelings . . . a revelation."[1] Symons's book on nineteenth-century French Symbolists played an often-noted role in the early poetics of Yeats and Eliot, as well as in Joyce's literary theory. It emphasized the perceptual immediacy of experience and momentary states of mind and gave British writers a new justification for what Verlaine called "sincerity and the impression of the moment followed to the letter," a movement already underway in England among the Aesthetes and the Decadents. Rimbaud and Mallarmé, for example, both sought to return literature to the realm of the spiritual, not by means of religious orthodoxy, but by establishing a direct connection between immediate experience and meaning. The symbol came to be seen as the mind's way of participating in a timeless, nonphysical reality.

In 1899, Symons employed terms remarkably similar to those that Joyce would appropriate five years later in his definition of "epiphany." Symons wrote:

> Here, then, in this revolt against exteriority, against rhetoric, against a materialistic tradition; in this endeavour to disengage the ultimate essence, the soul, of whatever exists and can be realized by the consciousness; in this dutiful waiting upon every symbol by which the soul of things can be made visible; literature, bowed down by so many burdens, may at last attain liberty, and its authentic speech.

This revolutionary tone of liberation led writers to see *The Symbolist Movement in Literature* as a manifesto; symbols could transform experience. "As we brush aside the accidents of daily life," Symons concluded, "in which men and women imagine that they are alone touching reality, we come closer to humanity."[2] But this brushing aside does not involve an ignorance of immediate sensation. In fact, it calls for a new emphasis on every nuance of perceptual detail, every impression. This perceptual attention can then be combined with an act of creative imagination in order to show forth the soul of "whatever exists and can be realized by consciousness." Our "real position," Symons adds, is made clear to us only in "moments" of "overpowering consciousness," which come like "blinding light or the thrust of a flaming sword."[3] Or as Joyce later suggests, "The soul of the commonest object, the structure of which is so adjusted, seems to us radiant. The object achieves its epiphany."[4]

Symons's ideas also underlie Ezra Pound's dictum, in "A Retrospect," that "Only Emotion Endures." Imagism can be compared with the general tenets of symbolism, particularly insofar as Pound defines an "Image" as "that which presents an intellectual and emotional complex in an instant of time." Equally important is Pound's claim that the literary "presentation of such a 'complex' instantaneously," like the focused associations in all literary epiphanies, provides "that sense of sudden liberation; that sense of freedom from time limits and space limits; that sense of sudden growth."[5] For Pound, the Chinese ideogram is important precisely because it provides "a vivid shorthand picture of the operations of nature." The imagist poem, by virtue of the very precision of its images, possesses this same power to convey in cryptic form the operation of a mind that finds its place not in nature but in complex interactions with nature.

Of course it would be a mistake to push these similarities too far. Epiphany, as is apparent in nineteenth-century poets already discussed, is merely one way of producing significance in poems. While similarities exist among all those twentieth-century poets who employ the technique, epiphany often serves widely divergent poetic ends. Thus for Pound, the vague suggestiveness achieved by many symbolist poems is a poetic weakness. He prefers the hard outlines provided by the pure image, outlines which present a complex of emotion and intellect in an instant. Pater's emphasis on the intensified, epiphanic moment of awareness is adopted for differing reasons by different groups: by the Decadents as a way of emphasizing sensations, by the Symbolists as a way of focusing fragments that can radiate meaning, and by the Imagists as a way of producing a clean, precise "shorthand" of experience.

Yeats, who later admired Pound's ability to associate numerous ideas into images that seem to "drift into the mind by chance," was deeply influenced by Symons's work. *The Symbolist Movement in Literature* was dedicated to Yeats, whom Symons called "the chief representative of the movement in our country." In his essay "The Symbolism of Poetry," Yeats demonstrates the appropriateness of this dedication by stressing the importance of an emotional response to experience on the basis of the data provided by the senses: "All sounds, all colours, all forms, either because of their preordained energies or because of long association, evoke indefinable and yet precise emotions . . . and when sound, and colour, and form are in a musical relation, a beautiful relation to one another, they become, as it were, one sound, one colour, one form." Once this unification of perceptual fragments has occurred, the result is an "emotion that is made out of their distinct evocations and yet is one emotion." The more perfect this fusion of parts, "the more powerful will be the emotion, the power, the god it calls among us."[6] An indefinable yet specific emotion emerges from an image that unifies perceptual fragments into a symbol. This symbol manifests an almost godlike power in consciousness. Such aesthetic manifestations constitute Yeats's definition of the literary epiphany.

This passage is not the first place in which Yeats allies the imagination with the process of evoking "the emotion, the power, the god." In his essay on Blake's imagination he notes that Blake learned from Boehme and others that "imagination was the first emanation of divinity, 'the body of God,' 'the Divine members.'" More important, says Yeats, is Blake's contention that "the imaginative arts were therefore the greatest of Divine revelations."[7] Yeats's view is related to Shelley's claim that imagination is the "immortal god" that should assume flesh (i.e., manifest itself in a poem) for the redemption of "mortal passion." Epiphany in both Shelley and Yeats involves the manifestation of a process of mind that reveals the essence of experience through language. Yeats, like Shelley, wants to identify these manifestations of power not with an orthodox divinity but with archetypal patterns. At the same time, he always anchors these revelations in the self.

In *Per Amica Silentia Lunae*, Yeats explains his moments of elevation by saying, "I begin to study the only self I can know, myself." He suggests certain moods of the mind that bring about revelation grounded in this world and based on a conjunction of mental images. Revelations, says Yeats, emerge in moments that are both timeless and "luminous." At "certain moments," emotional elevation is accompanied by powerful images which are drawn "from *Anima Mundi*," from the world soul, "embodied there and drunk with that sweetness." At such moments, the recipient of the inspiration feels as if the instant "would, like a country drunkard who has thrown a wisp into his own thatch, burn up time." The mood lasts not longer than an hour, and yet, while in the grip of its "happiness," Yeats is unable to hate and is "in the place where the Daimon is," on a bridge between the material and the spiritual realm.

Yeats then describes such a moment occurring while he is reading his own verse, "sitting in some crowded restaurant, the open book beside me, or closed, my excitement having overbrimmed the page."[8] The identical scene occurs in the revelatory elevation of consciousness in his poem "Vacillation," when the surroundings of a crowded London shop are suddenly transformed by a "blazing" sensation in Yeats's body, a benediction that reveals that he is "blessed and could bless." The self is transformed internally by a recognition of its own power as the source of experience. Yeats reaches the same conclusion in the final lines of "A Dialogue of Self and Soul." The spiritual soul cries, "Only the dead can be forgiven," and ends its part of the dialogue in silence—"But when I think of that [the forgiven dead] my tongue's a stone." The self, by contrast, sees the world for what it is and is thereby able to rise beyond the soul's silent benediction:

> We must laugh and we must sing,
> We are blest by everything,
> Everything we look upon is blest.[9]

This sentiment is not a platitudinous conclusion but the complex emotion that eventually finds resolution in Yeats's concept of tragic joy.

Earlier in *Per Amica Silentia Lunae,* Yeats connects the unifying powers of the mind with the ability to perceive, through moments of integrated consciousness, what Joyce calls "a sudden spiritual manifestation of the essence of an object or event." Yeats writes, "Only in rapid and subtle thought, or in faint accents heard in the quiet of the mind, can the thought of the spirit come down to us but little changed; for a mind that grasps objects simultaneously according to the degree of its liberation does not think the same thought with the mind that sees objects one after another."[10] Yeats concludes that to perceive truly we must focus on the mind's ability to hold numerous associations in a single image which can become a symbol. A Yeatsian symbol defeats the mechanistic model of mental activity which had held sway ever since Locke and Hume posited an unending series of rapid, successive thoughts. "Hammer your thoughts into unity," Yeats demands of those who would see the world through symbols.[11] He is even willing to connect this form of insight with the order that the mind bestows on the accidental randomness of experience. The "Daimon" of imagination "descends" into consciousness, Yeats says, not in a "straight line but zigzag, illuminating the passive and active properties . . . it is the sudden lightning, for all his acts of power are instantaneous. We perceive in a pulsation of the artery."[12] Yeats draws this image from Blake's *Milton*, where Blake identifies the instant with poetic inspiration:

> For in this Period the Poet's Work is Done: and all the Great Events of Time start forth & are conceived in such a Period, Within a Moment, a Pulsation of the Artery.
> [1.29.1–3]

Yeats's mythology places such revelatory perceptions in a spiritual realm which—like Joyce's use of the term "spiritual"—emphasizes the spirit of the percipient; that is, the imagination of the poet. In this sense, Yeats's identification of poetic inspiration with the symbol-making capacity bears comparison to Coleridge's phantom-producing imagination, Wordsworth's resonant spots of time, Shelley's imaginative coal fanned into flame by the breath of experience, and Browning's poet with the "spark a-top," a magus who brings the dead facts of the material world to life. Yeats seeks to explain the continuing mysteries of this process by reference to his complex theory—expounded in *A Vision*—of the phases of the self, of spirits and identities which are described as little more than hypostatized imaginative entities. Whatever Yeats's final relationship to the definitive statements of *A Vision*, he continually admits the relationship between meaningful mysteries and deep levels of the mind. Of his poem "The Cap and Bells," he says, "The poem has always meant a great deal to me, though, as is the way with symbolic poems, it has not always meant quite the same thing."[13] The possibility of defining poetic meaning this way begins in English with Wordsworth. The poem, like the experience from which it is derived, may not have a single meaning but may radiate significance in a number of directions.

Yeats's romantic legacy is clearly apparent when he identifies revelation with self-realization *and* self-abnegation, the very paradox that had so absorbed the Romantics: "I am awake and asleep, at my moments of revelation, self-possessed in self-surrender."[14] Not since Coleridge had poetic inspiration been so specifically defined as a mental state which achieves the not-self through the self. The imaginative poet, says Coleridge,

> by sacred sympathy might make
> The whole one Self! Self, that no alien knows!
> Self, far diffused as Fancy's wing can travel!

>   Self, spreading still! Oblivious of its own,
>   Yet all of all possessing!
>   ["Religious Musings," 153–57]

For Yeats, this paradoxical achievement of not-self in self becomes the defining characteristic of poetic inspiration. The result is a poem caught in time which can point beyond time, a poem that begins in the particularized distinctness of this world but reflects on the desired resolution of all distinctions into a unity. The symbol becomes important for Yeats largely because it assumes an independent life. "We artists," he wrote in "The Cutting of an Agate," "are the servants not of any cause but of mere naked life, and above all of that life in its nobler forms, where joy and sorrow are one, Artificers of the Great Moment."[15] It is important that Yeats distinguishes this moment from those moments emphasized by the Rhymers of the 1890s. In his essay "Modern Poetry," Yeats separates his own poetic practice from that of poets who wished, following Pater, "to express life at its intense moments, those moments that are brief because of their intensity, and at those moments alone."[16] Such an achievement is not sufficient for Yeats because it is restrictive rather than suggestive.

How is Yeats's "Great Moment" realized in the artifice of a poem, and how is it distinct from the Paterian moments from which Yeats disassociated himself? An examination of Yeats's poem entitled "A Memory of Youth," which appeared in 1914 in *Responsibilities*, demonstrates how Yeats's poetics operates to produce a characteristically modern epiphany. The achievement of the poem is not an elevation into another world but a clear vision of this world. I quote the poem in full because its narrative movement is partly responsible for the epiphanic effect achieved in the closing lines:

>   The moments passed as at a play;
>   I had the wisdom love brings forth;
>   I had my share of mother-wit,
>   And yet for all that I could say,
>   And though I had her praise for it,
>   A cloud blown from the cut-throat North
>   Suddenly hid Love's moon away.
>
>   Believing every word I said,
>   I praised her body and her mind

> Till pride had made her eyes grow bright,
> And pleasure made her cheeks grow red,
> And vanity her footfall light,
> Yet we, for all that praise, could find
> Nothing but darkness overhead.
>
> We sat as silent as a stone,
> We knew, though she'd not said a word,
> That even the best of love must die,
> And had been savagely undone
> Were it not that Love upon the cry
> Of a most ridiculous little bird
> Tore from the clouds his marvellous moon.

This poem succeeds not only because of its remarkable shifts of tone and powerful final lines but also because of its sudden, subtle reversals. The speaker, though moved by love, nonetheless observes these moments like a spectator. His mood is completely darkened when the clouds block the moon; he assumes that love does not last. The second stanza then recounts a series of human attempts to overcome the surrounding natural and emotional darkness. These efforts—the poet's praises of his lady—fail, and the lovers are left silent, almost stunned by the recognition that "even the best of love must die."

Having suggested that the lovers are about to be "savagely undone," Yeats focuses suddenly on a trivial cry from a bird. In the world of facts, this simple birdsong is accidentally conjoined with the sudden appearance of the moon from behind a cloud. In the world of the lovers, however, and in the words of the poet, this accidental conjunction of events is transformed into a radiant image of affirmation. The epiphany of the poem is completed in the adjectives "ridiculous" and "marvellous." The "ridiculous little bird" grounds the experience completely in the world of ordinary events, while love's "marvellous moon" displays the mind's ability to redeem the self from darkness in a revelatory illumination. The poem ends in a radiant vision of love in the mortal world, a love that is at once flawed and blessed. Man's "resinous heart" is the only fuel for this image, but the revelation is nevertheless able to flame "upon the night."

Yeats is concerned to record the instant of transformation, the moment when man's resinous heart consumes itself and yet sheds a momentary light in the process. "Everything that man esteems / Endures a moment or a day" ("Two Songs from a Play"), not because of the nature of the object, but because man's esteem is a fleeting emotion. "Among School Children" achieves an epiphany when the "brightening glance" suggests to the "sixty-year-old smiling public man" that dancer and dance are not to be distinguished. The final transformed image of dancer merged with dance is an epiphany because it records a "momentary wonder" like that seen in the children's eyes in the opening stanza of the poem.

Yeats's belief that the sensitive mind searches for such epiphanic revelations in experience is confirmed by "The Magi." In the "mind's eye" of the poet, the recipients of the Christian epiphany are transformed into eternal, cyclical seekers after revelation. "Unsatisfied" by the last epiphany they have seen, they look beyond "Calvary's turbulence," "hoping to find once more . . . the uncontrollable mystery on the bestial floor." In the poet's visionary imagination, these "pale unsatisfied ones / Appear and disappear." But their eyes are "fixed," focused like those eyes that gaze on the "Marbles of the dancing floor" in "Byzantium." Such eyes are receptive to the sight of "Flames that no faggot feeds, nor steel has lit, / Nor storm disturbs, flames begotten of flame." In the last two stanzas of "Byzantium," Yeats draws together the images that produce epiphanies in "Two Songs from a Play," "Among School Children," and "The Magi." The "bestial floor" becomes the marbled "dancing floor" that yields up "furies of complexity." The resinous heart that "flames upon the night" becomes the flame "that no faggot feeds," a flame of a mind that illuminates these "complexities of fury" and ends by

> Dying into a dance,
> An agony of trance,
> An agony of flame that cannot singe a sleeve.

The flame, like the trance, is a nonphysical function of mind. But it can yield up, via epiphany, a physical image of "that dolphin-torn, that gong-tormented sea."

Toward the end of his poetic career, Yeats sensed that poetic epiphanies originated not in a world of symbolic mental structures but in the simplest details of ordinary experience. The "masterful images . . . / Grew in pure mind, but out of what began?" he asks in "The Circus Animals' Desertion." They began in the most mundane details imaginable: "the sweepings of a street, / Old kettles, old bottles, and a broken can." Like Browning's junk heap of fragments which the poet sparks to life, Yeats's trivial details are elevated not in and of themselves but only in "the foul rag-and-bone shop of the heart." These elevations work through poems to achieve "Profane perfection of mankind," the goal Yeats sets forth in "Under Ben Bulben." Like the "profane joy" that signals Stephen Dedalus's epiphany of the bird-girl of Sandymount Strand, Yeats's "profane perfection of mankind" is the result of the "Poet and sculptor" who "do the work," reversing traditional inspiration in the process. Instead of bringing an external God into the realm of the human, the Yeatsian poet, like the Joycean artist, brings "the soul of man to God," that is, elevates the soul of man by a powerful attention to the details of ordinary life.

Eliot: History as a "Pattern of Timeless Moments"

> I lie along the deck against the engine-house, from which the smell of lukewarm grease exhales. Gigantic mists are marching under the French cliffs, enveloping the coast from headland to headland. The sea moves with the sound of many scales. . . . Beyond the misty walls, in the dark cathedral church of Our Lady, I hear the bright, even voices of boys singing before the altar there.
> —Joyce, *Epiphanies*

In the twentieth century, T. S. Eliot's later poems strive to continue Hopkins's return of the literary epiphany to a theological framework. Unlike Hopkins, however, Eliot in *Four Quartets* is able to find in the "privileged moment" not only a source of temporary theophanic revelation but a symbol of divinity itself. He achieves this goal by resolving all oppositions—water and fire, ends and beginnings, time past and time future—into a unity that can be identified with the source of salvation. Eliot places immense burdens on momentary experience in *Four Quartets*, which the moment can bear because it has been expanded into a timelessness—like Browning's infinite moment—of both kairos and aiōn: "What might have been and what has been / Point to one end, which is always present" ("Burnt Norton," 1).[17] Eliot sees this moment not only as one that hints at eternity, however, but as a new point of view, a vision sub specie aeternitatis. Eliot seeks to move beyond time, to find a "still point" described not as a "fixity" but as a point where "past and future are gathered" into a "dance." Like Wordsworth ("the soul— / Remembering how she felt, but what she felt / Remembering not"), Eliot can only say, "*there* we have been: but I cannot say where. / And I cannot say, how long, for that is to place it in time" ("Burnt Norton," 2).

Eliot's connection with the new literary epiphany is confirmed when he claims that "only through time time is conquered." We must focus on our moments—the rose garden, the rain-washed arbor, the "draughty church at smokefall"—in order that they may be involved, through memory, with "past and future." In clusters of associations that yield a powerful image, we can achieve what Eliot calls "the timeless moment." In such instants, we focus not solely on Pater's "intense moment / Isolated" but also on a "lifetime burning in every moment." This lifetime is not of "one man only / But of old stones that cannot be deciphered." No matter how complete our understanding, we still sense archetypes that hint rather than explain. Even in his most outwardly orthodox poems, Eliot is restrained by a sense of man's mortal limitations. As Denis Donoghue has pointed out, the words in Eliot's poems always come from, and point toward, "the other side of silence."[18]

Eliot's sense of the way moments of revelation arrive ties him most closely to the modern literary epiphany.

> Sudden in a shaft of sunlight
> Even while the dust moves
> There rises the hidden laughter
> Of children in the foliage
> Quick now, here, now, always—
> ["Burnt Norton," 5]

The revelatory moment comes suddenly in an image of illumination that unites "now, here, now" with eternity. Eliot's children remind us of the voice that Augustine heard from a neighboring house which triggered his conversion. Eliot wants to experience an Augustinian revelation, but he cannot achieve the description of God made manifest in experience that characterizes traditional religious inspiration. Instead, Eliot laments the extent to which our emotionally felt moments of insight precede, and remain distinct from, all attempts at interpretation:

> The moments of happiness—not the sense of well-being,
> Fruition, fulfilment, security or affection,

> Or even a very good dinner, but the sudden illumination—
> We had the experience but missed the meaning,
> And approach to the meaning restores the experience
> In a different form, beyond any meaning
> We can assign to happiness.
>   ["The Dry Salvages," 2]

This recognition of the possibility of a powerful experience that can exist apart from its "meaning" represents for Eliot a lament, but also an achievement.

Like the Wordsworthian renovation that occurs through an imaginative transformation of the contents of memory, experience for Eliot emerges in a different form once our conscious mind has bestowed significance. History is a "pattern / Of timeless moments," disparate and distinct, yet capable of finding a meaning in the mind's willingness to make a choice. Once the mind has made a choice identified with faith, Eliot, like Hopkins, can make a commitment to an absolute meaning. At this point the mind moves from epiphany to theophany, from a manifestation grounded in this world to a manifestation interpreted as divine. "The only hope or else despair," claims Eliot in the analysis of his own willed decision, "Lies in the choice of pyre or pyre— / To be redeemed from fire by fire." The choice is not actually a choice, once the distinction is collapsed in the unifying image of Christian incarnation. The pyre is destructive or redemptive, infernal or purgatorial; the difference is only one of interpretation and commitment.

"The Dry Salvages" is the central section of *Four Quartets* in this connection. It deserves a more literal reading, as Donoghue argues, than is suggested by Hugh Kenner or Donald Davie.[19] The misunderstanding surrounding this section of *Four Quartets* arises, in part, because Eliot is speaking not so much about himself as about prevailing currents of contemporary thought. If we disengage Eliot's own voice from the modulating voice of the narrator of "The Dry Salvages," we find a serious attempt to distinguish experience from any significance assigned to it. Like Hopkins, Eliot wants to "read" the world. The difficulty emerges when the "text" of the world overwhelms any attempt at understanding. Eliot is therefore thrown back, at one point, on a surprisingly Wordsworthian critique of the origins of understanding which he modifies with theories derived from Jung, Frazer, Weston, and Nietzsche:

> I have said before
> That the past experience revived in the meaning

> Is not the experience of one life only
> But of many generations—not forgetting
> Something that is probably quite ineffable:
> The backward look behind the assurance
> Of recorded history, the backward half-look
> Over the shoulder, towards the primitive terror.
>   ["The Dry Salvages," 2]

Whether Eliot is expressing his own view or parodying the view of others is unimportant to my argument. The passage, in either case, suggests those primitive impulses described by Tennyson when he said that he longed to write a companion piece to *In Memoriam* that would be less optimistic and more true to the ambivalences inherent in man's nature. Eliot points out that, as we revive momentary experience in the mind, we move from a sense of ourselves as individuals toward a realm of meaning that is somehow below consciousness and behind human history. We understand one isolated, fragmentary experience, Eliot suggests, by referring it to "the experience of . . . many generations."

As long as Eliot limits himself to describing the details of perceptual experience, he achieves the tone and diction of the literary epiphany. One such perceptual emphasis occurs in his description of the Dry Salvages themselves. Anchored amid the "ground swell" where the rolling buoy "Clangs / The bell," these sea-washed rocks become another avatar of the "strong brown god" who is invoked in the opening lines of *Four Quartets*. This "river" god is "sullen, untamed and intractable," reminiscent of the gods of pre-Christian epiphany who were seen in strictly anthropomorphic terms. The "god" present in this sea can be described imaginatively only by reference to the fragmented objects that become the voice of a powerful psychic force. The sea

>   tosses up our losses, the torn seine,
> The shattered lobsterpot, the broken oar
> And the gear of foreign dead men. The sea has many voices,
> Many gods and many voices.
>   ["The Dry Salvages," 1]

Like Tennyson's flickering buoy and Browning's flashing lighthouse, Eliot's clanging buoy measures out a "time not our time," one "older than the time of chronometers."

Searching for an image that will clarify the sense of a "sudden illumination," Eliot finds the sea-washed rocks of the Dry Salvages before him:

The Poetics of Epiphany

> the ragged rock in the restless waters,
> Waves wash over it, fogs conceal it;
> On a halcyon day it is merely a monument,
> In navigable weather it is always a seamark
> To lay a course by: but in the sombre season
> Or the sudden fury, is what it always was.
> ["The Dry Salvages," 2]

These lines actually critique an epiphany rather than present one. The manifestation of an object's essence ("what it always was") comes, says Eliot, during a "sombre season" or "sudden fury." The fury implies the energy of inspiration, describing one of the ways the vision can arrive. The sombre season suggests Wordsworth's "season of calm weather," during which the soul can suddenly transcend perceptual limits and travel to the source of its strength. Any object, like the rocks Eliot describes, can change its role in the human mind as a result of particular psychic circumstances. But behind these varying points of view lies the object's "essence," that aspect of its existence which remains always the same and which is, when perceived by humans, more felt than understood. When this essence is made manifest, the human mind clearly is the active agent in the revelation.

In "Little Gidding," Eliot describes a meeting with the personified ghost of English poetry, a figure who, in the first draft of the poem, is identified with Yeats. The encounter, perhaps not surprisingly, parallels Wordsworth's epiphanic encounter with the leech-gatherer in "Resolution and Independence." Eliot's version is almost a parody of Wordsworth's experience, in its emphasis on a self-consciously poetic tone. Yet Eliot's message in this section of the poem is to be taken seriously. In "Little Gidding," the dreamlike quality of the meeting with this ghost, the sense of benediction, and the strangely satisfying, yet ultimately unknowable, nature of the illumination all echo Wordsworth's poem. Eliot, describing himself as a poet worried about poetry, meets a spectral figure walking in the midst of war-scarred London and catches

> the sudden look of some dead master
> Whom I had known, forgotten, half recalled
> Both one and many; in the brown baked features
> The eyes of a familiar compound ghost
> Both intimate and unidentifiable.
> ["Little Gidding," 2]

The union of "intimate" and "unidentifiable" describes the paradoxical aspect of the literary epiphany—its enigmatic, yet revelatory, quality.

Eliot tells this ghost, "The wonder that I feel is easy, / Yet ease is cause of wonder." Wonder has arrived in a "sombre season," an "uncertain hour" that is described as an "intersection time / Of meeting nowhere, no before and after." While in the grip of this wonder, Eliot is willing to admit that his understanding may lie in abeyance—"Therefore speak: / I may not comprehend, may not remember." Eliot's meeting with the Yeatsian ghost of English poetry, like his description of the wave-washed Dry Salvages, achieves an epiphanic sense of the essence of experience, even though the event is outwardly described as a dream. The ghost, like the rocks, provides an epiphanic image that unifies *Four Quartets*—the image of a refining fire that consumes in order to restore:

> From wrong to wrong the exasperated spirit
> Proceeds, unless restored by that refining fire
> Where you must move in measure, like a dancer.
> ["Little Gidding," 2]

Earlier in *Four Quartets*, Eliot had described the "still point of the turning world" as a "dance." Yeats himself pointed out that we do not know the dancer from the dance at such a moment of unification between self and experience. This unity can, in fact, be defined as that moment when the self becomes the essence of its own activity. The ghost who has imparted knowledge of the refining fire to Eliot leaves not like an angel but like a leech-gatherer: "In the disfigured street / He left me, with a kind of valediction."

For Eliot, such a moment is not left to radiate its significance in "intimate" yet "unidentifiable" ways. His epiphanies in *Four Quartets* always move toward a theophanic identification of "fire and rose" with the image of Christian incarnation. Religious commitment never derives from epiphany for Eliot. Instead, epiphany confirms a preexisting faith. This confirmation occurs after the experience has been interpreted as having a theological significance. Like Hopkins, Eliot returns the literary epiphany to a theological framework by connecting such moments with a choice that derives religious commitment from intellectual paradox, disciplined faith from rational uncertainty:

> For most of us, there is only the unattended
> Moment, the moment in and out of time,

The Poetics of Epiphany

> The distraction fit, lost in a shaft of sunlight,
> The wild thyme unseen, or the winter lightning
> Or the waterfall, or music heard so deeply
> That it is not heard at all, but you are the music
> While the music lasts.
>
> ["The Dry Salvages," 5]

The experiences that give rise to epiphany are associated by Eliot with meaning that moves from partial insight toward a theophanic image of God made manifest on earth through Christ.

Eliot attests to a truth beyond this world that validates and anchors all the uncertainties of life. It is a truth identified with the life of faith that transcends death by way of the Christian cross. Experience provides

> only hints and guesses,
> Hints followed by guesses; and the rest
> Is prayer, observance, discipline, thought and action.
> The hint half guessed, the gift half understood, is
> Incarnation.
>
> ["The Dry Salvages," 5]

Eliot relies on the literary epiphany because his revelation does not come in a blinding flash of insight but as a hint, partly guessed and only partly understood. Wordsworth asks for just such a state of mind in "Ode to Duty" when he seeks the "confidence of reason" from a personified Duty. Like Eliot in *Four Quartets*, the later Wordsworth longs for "a repose that ever is the same." Such a stasis is achieved only for an instant in epiphany. In the image of incarnation, however, Eliot finds a lasting way of reconciling the Bradleian opposition between appearance and reality, another description of the gap that ordinarily separates the temporal from the eternal.

For Hopkins, by contrast, theophany is achieved not only in the image of Christ but also in every object that is able to flash forth its essence and thereby reveal the spark of its origins and its identity ("What I do is me: for that I came"). Hopkins connects identity and divinity in all of the objects of creation. Insofar as an object has an essence, that essence can be identified with God. For Eliot, however, the incarnation of God in Christ is the only image that ultimately reveals divinity to man. At the same time, Eliot never insists on a solution through dogma. Like Hopkins, he is willing to anchor his own certainty in experience. For both Hopkins and Eliot, the hints and guesses produced by experience can be turned, via prayer and discipline, into a single image that resolves all oppositions:

> Here the impossible union
> Of spheres of existence is actual,
> Here the past and future
> Are conquered, and reconciled.
> ["The Dry Salvages," 5]

While the literary epiphany seeks to make the ordinary extraordinary, the theophanized epiphanies of Hopkins and Eliot seek to make the impossible possible. They attempt not simply to establish significance but to transcend mortality. For neither poet, however, is this goal ever to be achieved in life. For Hopkins, this realization finally becomes a longing for physical death. Eliot likewise admits that such a goal is final; it will cost "not less than everything." But at the same time, Eliot expresses a willingness to continue as an explorer. He acknowledges the futility of the search, and yet, like Browning, he sees the unknown as finally accessible through the partial revelation that can achieve radiance in certain powerfully realized images:

> We shall not cease from exploration
> And the end of all our exploring
> Will be to arrive where we started
> And know the place for the first time.
> Through the unknown, remembered gate
> When the last of earth left to discover
> Is that which was the beginning;
> At the source of the longest river
> The voice of the hidden waterfall
> And the children in the apple-tree
> Not known, because not looked for
> But heard, half-heard, in the stillness
> Between two waves of the sea.
> ["Little Gidding," 5]

The revelation comes unsought and only partially heard, distinct from desire and incompletely understood. Eliot, like Hopkins, wants to interpret the source of inspiration as divine, yet his revelatory images retain the characteristics of the literary epiphany. Unwilling to lie down in Yeats's "foul rag-and-bone shop of the heart,"

Eliot is nevertheless willing to ground meaning in a life of "significant soil" that includes "the hidden waterfall," "the children in the apple-tree," and the failing light on "a winter's afternoon." In this tendency to emphasize the revelatory quality of the details of ordinary experience, Eliot not only continues the theophanic tradition of Hopkins but also advances the development of the secular epiphany in the twentieth century.

STEVENS: "MOMENTS OF AWAKENING"

> Against the gateway, against some cedar tree I saw blaze bright . . . our life, our identity . . . we six, out of how many million millions, for one moment out of what measureless abundance of past time and time to come, burnt there triumphant. The moment was all; the moment was enough.
> —Virginia Woolf, *The Waves*

For Wallace Stevens, unlike Eliot, the epiphany is always achieved in the secular sphere, when the imagination succeeds in "pressing back against the pressure of reality." The nobility of the poet derives not from what Yeats had called service to "life in its nobler forms" but from an ability to remain noble in the face of uncertainty—in Stevens's image, to maintain nobility while riding a horse the poet knows does not exist. The image appears in the essay "The Noble Rider and the Sound of Words," where Stevens argues that the "supreme fictions" with which the poet helps us to live our lives are not false; rather, they are neither true nor false but simply the testimony of "whatever the imagination and senses have made of the world." This nobility derives from the ability to see in experience something more than the bare, mechanistic details described by modern science.

For Stevens, the momentary manifestation of significance in the mind is like a wave. Meaning moves through experience, not identified with experience, but transforming perception into imaginative creations that help us to live our lives.[20] The process of poetic creation is not merely therapeutic wish fulfillment for Stevens, however; each valid metaphor participates in a reality that is somehow beyond the mind. The way such levels of understanding are achieved is important to Stevens and allies him with the tradition of the literary epiphany. For Stevens, the nature of the object of perception always remains mysterious: "Experience, at least in the case of a poet of any scope, is much broader than reality." At the same time, the essence of experience is conveyed in a revelation that is firmly anchored in the world of sense: "Poetry has to be something more than a conception of the mind. It has to be a revelation of nature. Conceptions are artificial. Perceptions are essential."[21]

Stevens's notion of epiphany, like Yeats's, involves more than the purely aesthetic moments posited by Pater. This emphasis becomes clear when Stevens attacks imagism because it assumes that "all objects are equal." Stevens does not suggest that we make experience meaningful only on the basis of a conscious decision to value certain objects which otherwise have no intrinsic value. Using a related argument, he finds a destructive fault in surrealism, which "invents without discovering."[22] According to the surrealists, the mind is able to conjoin *any* set of objects and extract meaning. Thus any series of thoughts, ideas, or images can be held in an association that produces aesthetic value. For Stevens, however, the association only makes sense if it reflects some real, external relation, not an arbitrary relation between an object and any description, but an essential link between poetic creation and the object of that creation. The relation between the poem and the poem's subject can always reveal a new significance.

In a skeptical age like ours, says Stevens, the mind, "in the absence of a belief in God . . . turns to its own creations and examines them, not alone from the aesthetic point of view, but for what they reveal, for what they validate and invalidate, for the support that they give." The achievement is not a simple correspondence between the mind and external nature but an elevation of consciousness to a point where the relation between mind and the world is acknowledged in all its complexity. Such an elevation is always achieved through emotion. "We never arrive intellectually," he concludes in "Adagia," "but emotionally we arrive constantly (as in poetry, happiness, high mountains, vistas)." Epiphany, for Stevens, records emotional elevations which possess a completeness and self-sufficiency that is lacking in moments of purely intellectual insight.

Stevens often "arrives" in a poem in the terms I have been calling epiphanic. His imagination is epiphanic because it seeks to transform the ordinary by an act of purified consciousness of the object—"In the presence of extraordinary actuality, consciousness takes the place of imagination." In "An Ordinary Evening in New Haven," for example, Stevens speaks of our search for

The Poetics of Epiphany

> 9
> . . . .
> The poem of pure reality, untouched
> By trope or deviation, straight to the word,
> Straight to the transfixing object, to the object
>
> At the exactest point at which it is itself,
> Transfixing by being purely what it is. . . .[23]

Stevens often accomplishes just such a vision of an object that transfixes the mind, of the one illuminated instant that is able, via epiphany, to put pattern and order into the world.

In "The Idea of Order at Key West," the light from the fishing boats seen by the speaker becomes the physical illumination that parallels an illumination of order in the mind. This light, by acting on the mind, "Mastered the night and portioned out the sea, / Fixing emblazoned zones and fiery poles." The result is not an intellectual ordering of the objects of experience but an emotion expressed in the narrator's cry—"Oh! Blessed rage for order, pale Ramon"—and in the penultimate stanza's final line, which merges the patterned scene and the elevated consciousness into one image of "Arranging, deepening, enchanting night." Like Wordsworth's leech-gatherer "wandering" in the mind's eye, Stevens's use of the gerund forms is essential. The epiphany of the poem describes an ongoing mental process, not a static achievement. It is telling that the critic Ramon Fernandez, who is addressed by name in "The Idea of Order at Key West," provides in his own work a very Wordsworthian description of the action of the mind. "Creation incessantly modifies reality without betraying it," Fernandez wrote: "the known depends greatly on the nature of the act of knowing."[24] For Stevens, who adopts this notion almost word for word, the sense of revelation always passes suddenly, but the mind's ability to transform the objects of experience continues. Epiphany can denote an absolute experience which, in turn, applies connotatively to numerous associations and meanings.

"Notes toward a Supreme Fiction" represents Stevens's clearest statement of the way a new form of inspiration replaces an older form in the modern world. The God of the old world is gone, replaced by revelations that originate in the ordinary:

> 7
> It feels good as it is without the giant,

> A thinker of the first idea. Perhaps
> The truth depends on a walk around a lake,
>
> A composing as the body tires, a stop
> To see hepatica, a stop to watch
> A definition growing certain and
>
> A wait within that certainty, a rest
> In the sway of pine trees bordering the lake.

Specific moments allow certainty to grow, providing a vehicle for understanding. Revelation as a process involves growth and waiting. The new form of inspiration comes not as a thunderbolt or a voice from the clouds but by way of an image—lake, hepatica, pine trees—that allows composition to begin and definition to develop. "Perhaps there are times of inherent excellence," Stevens continues, "incalculable balances." Such ultimately unknowable resolutions are

>   not balances
> That we achieve but balances that happen,
>
> As a man and woman meet and love forthwith.
> Perhaps there are moments of awakening,
> Extreme, fortuitous, personal, in which
>
> We more than awaken, sit on the edge of sleep
> As on an elevation. . . .

In this critique of epiphany, Stevens suggests that epiphany provides a way of organizing moments of emotional fulfillment—which in and of themselves are neither fully rational nor completely explicable—into complexes of meaning that emerge from a particularly vivid perception of the world.

Stevens's poem "Martial Cadenza" is a complete and self-analyzing version of such an epiphany, in which Stevens records the experience that gives rise to the epiphany and describes the way experience is transformed in a poem. The image of revelation, as in Wordsworth and Browning, is a star—in Stevens's case, the evening star seen low on the horizon in 1942. Critics have tended to see "Martial Cadenza" as a poem about World War II, a statement about enduring emotional time in a world beyond historical human time, Stevens's version of Hardy's "In Time of 'The Breaking of Nations'" or Browning's "Love among the Ruins." Others have noted the poem's emphasis on the mental catalyst—the star— and its role in focusing consciousness. Henry Wells sees the poem moving from "despairing melancholy" to "brilliant joy" through the mediation of the star, which transforms the poet's surroundings: "A world without spiritual meaning suddenly becomes a world of the most intense meaning."[25] Yet Wells anchors the poem finally in a response to social and political events. Joseph Riddel calls the poem a "longing of man for knowledge of the first idea, for the fixed and changeless 'evening star.'"[26]

Critics have failed to note the poem's real subject; the ability of the mind to dwell on a powerful image and draw from that image not only strength but also an enduring sense of revelation, a sense of a temporal cycle that establishes continuity in the mind:

1

Only this evening I saw again low in the sky
The evening star, at the beginning of winter, the star
That in spring will crown every western horizon,
Again . . . as if it came back, as if life came back. . . .

The star is permanent; Stevens sees it again because he has seen it before and because it has remained, in one sense, in the same place. The mind is able to return to the past and to bring life back to the present. In the process, the mind shatters the ordinary features of time, ushering in the feeling of aionic timelessness that characterizes epiphany:

2

It was like sudden time in a world without time,
This world, this place, the street in which I was,
Without time: as that which is not has no time. . . .

The mind, via imagination, moves out beyond the sense of a particular time and place, leaving behind the warring armies—drums, commanders, and arms—"fixed fast in a profound defeat." The armies are all defeated because they are caught in a chronological time that demands distinctness and separates them from eternity.

The star indicates the mind's imaginative ability to project itself into a realm of changelessness through a powerful perception of the present; according to Stevens, we must "find the spiritual in reality." The contents of such an elevation of the ordinary are not described in Stevens's poem; if Hopkins or Eliot had described them, the poem might have become theophanic. Instead, like

Wordsworth in "A Night-Piece" or Browning in "By the Fireside," Stevens is willing to let the star simply stand "apart" from the world that includes England, France, and the "German Camps." In its unrestricted expansiveness, this image of the star is finally able to unite with the Heraclitean flux:

3

....
Yet it is this that shall maintain—Itself
Is time, apart from any past, apart
From any future, the ever-living and being,
The ever-breathing and moving, the constant fire. . . .

Like the star that is its symbol, this imagined fire describes an eternity beyond consciousness but nonetheless clearly felt in the revivifying repetitions of the poem's closing stanza.

Epiphany for Stevens always involves emotion: "Insight is bound to be accompanied by remarkable emotions. A poem would be nothing without some meaning. The truth is that meaning, is an awareness and a communication. But it is no ordinary awareness, no ordinary communication."[27] In moments of extraordinary awareness the mind is renovated by its ability to repeat an experience and thereby enter into a cycle that hints at endurance. The "flashing" image then focuses the intensely realized present and the sense of eternity into an epiphany:

4

The present close, the present realized,
Not the symbol but that for which the symbol stands,
The vivid thing in the air that never changes,
Though the air change. Only this evening I saw it again,
At the beginning of winter, and I walked and talked
Again, and lived and was again, and breathed again
And moved again and flashed again, time flashed again.

The stately, pulsing, last lines achieve that Wordsworthian intermingling of sense and the objects of sense so often found in Stevens. The poem is not about war but about renovation, about an "I" who feels paralysis and is suddenly able to walk and talk and live and *be* again. This return to life is accomplished by a simple act of the epiphanic imagination, the same imagination of which Stevens said, "God and the imagination are one." Once the self achieves this restoration by having truly seen a star, the image of

The Poetics of Epiphany

the star is transformed, becoming also a manifest image of the self ("I . . . flashed again") and of a time that will never change ("time flashed again"). The mind focuses on a star and transforms the star into a poetic image which radiates significance. Life is made manifest not only in the experience but in the poem. Or rather, as Stevens suggests, "To read a poem should be an experience like experiencing an act." The poem as an experience reveals glory by an act of creative imagination. In such modern epiphanies, for Stevens, "The glory of God is the glory of the world."

HEANEY: "DESCRIPTION IS REVELATION!"

> As a child then, my days, just as they do now, contained a large proportion of this cotton-wool, this non-being. Week after week passed at St Ives and nothing made any dint upon me. Then, for no reason that I know about, there was a sudden, violent shock; something happened so violently that I have remembered it all my life.
> —Virginia Woolf, "A Sketch of the Past"

In contemporary poetry the tradition of the literary epiphany is receiving perhaps its fullest treatment in the work of Seamus Heaney. In both his poetry and prose criticism, Heaney has elevated the sense of a privileged moment to the status of a poetic touchstone. In fact, Heaney's poetics is based on the idea that the mind can transform ordinary experience into revelation by an act of imaginative description. He thus begins his essay "Feeling into Words" with a quotation from Wordsworth that suggests the extent to which Heaney's view of poetry derives from the tradition I have been tracing. He says he intends to "retrace some paths into what William Wordsworth called in *The Prelude* 'the hiding places.'" He quotes from Wordsworth:

> The hiding places of my power
> Seem open; I approach, and then they close;
> I see by glimpses now; when age comes on,
> May scarcely see at all, and I would give,
> While yet we may, as far as words can give,
> A substance and a life to what I feel:
> I would enshrine the spirit of the past
> For future restoration.

204

Epiphany in Twentieth-Century Poetry

Heaney then connects this passage with his own work as a poet:

> Implicit in those lines is a view of poetry which I think is implicit in the few poems I have written that give me any right to speak: poetry as divination, poetry as revelation of the self to the self, as restoration of the culture to itself; poems as elements of continuity, with the aura and authenticity of archaeological finds, where the buried shard has an importance that is not diminished by the importance of the buried city; poetry as a dig, a dig for finds that end up being plants.[28]

Heaney's opening paragraph suggests the relationship between modern poetics and the literary epiphany. By allying poetry with a process of divination that points toward the "hiding places," Heaney emphasizes the mind's power to turn the unknown into the known, the deeply felt and partially understood into the memorable and significant. Poetry reveals the self to itself by hinting at those sources of imaginative order that can transform the accidents of experience into moments of literary significance. Yeats had described the poet as the one who can turn the self, a "bundle of accident and incoherence," into "an idea, something intended, complete." For Heaney, the result of this intention on the poet's part is a poem with an "aura," a poem surrounded by a mysterious force field that is at once radiant and radiating. At the same time, however, such a poem derives not from the complexity of the "buried city" but from the simplicity of a single "shard," a fragment that can be turned by the poet to useful and meaningful account. The poet achieves this goal not by inventing a meaning but, as Heaney suggests, by discovering the role this fragment plays in the development of an individual life, a particular vision. Finally, in an image taken from one of his earliest poems, Heaney suggests that poetry is a "dig," a process that uncovers living plants rather than static objects. The poem that results is capable of growth, development, exfoliation.

For Heaney, this process is a matter not simply of choice, as it is for Hopkins and Eliot, but of a personal viewpoint confirmed by an experience of the world. As Heaney notes, his earliest attempts at poetry failed because of an absence. The process of acquiring formal poetic skill was straightforward: "But nothing happened inside me. No experience. No epiphany. All craft—and not much of that—and no technique." Heaney distinguishes craft from technique, suggesting that the latter allows the poet to discover "ways

The Poetics of Epiphany

to go out of his normal cognitive bounds and raid the inarticulate." This ability distinguishes epiphany as experience from epiphany as literary technique. Technique involves "a dynamic alertness that mediates between the origins of feeling in memory and experience and the formal ploys that express these in a work of art." The poem, he concludes, "always has elements of accident about it."[29] In Heaney's epiphanic poems, these accidents give way to significance when acted on by the image-making, or symbol-making, mind.

In this context, Heaney quotes Robert Graves, who suggests a connection between the blinding yet vague source of a poem and its imaginative transformation into significant structure. Of words themselves, Graves says,

> To make them move, you should start from lightning
> And not forecast the rhythm: rely on chance
> Or so-called chance for its bright emergence
> Once lightning interpenetrates the dance.
>
> Grant them their own traditional steps and postures
> But see they dance it out again and again
> Until only lightning is left to puzzle over—

For Graves, chance is "so-called chance" because the active mind is always working to create an order (a rhythm) out of the uncontrolled energy (the lightning) of pure experience. This lightning is like the source of all literary epiphanies; Heaney calls it "puzzling and brilliant." He suggests that there is "nearly always an element of the bolt from the blue about a poem's origin."[30]

This line of thought derives from the Wordsworthian spot of time as well as from Joyce's notion of epiphany. Heaney admits "a good bit of symbolist theory" behind the modern production of meaningful images out of ordinary experience but makes a very Wordsworthian and nonsymbolist claim about the relationship between poetic theory and the actual writing of poetry: "You survive in your own esteem not by the corroboration of theory but by the trust in certain moments of satisfaction which you know intuitively to be moments of extension." Behind all literary talk about what a poem means or how it comes to have meaning or whether it means anything lies the simple fact that certain experiences in life rise to a position of psychic prominence. Numerous more or less related associations cluster around these moments and give rise to a powerful sense of ordered significance, even if this significance initially applies only to the context of a single personal identity. Of his poems "Digging" and "Bogland," Heaney says that the "seminal influence" was "unconscious." He then allows for a "something lying beneath the floor of memory, something I only connected with the poem months after it was written." At this point we move beyond the personal and are drawing close to Joyce's sense of a "spiritual manifestation" that emerges *from* experience and occurs *in* the mind and Wordsworth's sense of a hiding place of power, a place seen only "by glimpses" but which nevertheless can give a "substance and a life" to the poet's feelings.

In his "Glanmore Sonnets," Heaney attributes the source of his own epiphanies to the emotions that accompany certain experiences:

> 2
> Sensings, mountings from the hiding places,
> Words entering almost the sense of touch
> Ferreting themselves out of their dark hutch—
> "These things are not secrets but mysteries,"
> Oisin Kelly told me years ago
> In Belfast, hankering after stone
> That connived with the chisel, as if the grain
> Remembered what the mallet tapped to know.[31]

Each of the Glanmore sonnets records a mystery that is not a secret, something not known so much as felt and then transformed into meaning by the mind. Several of the sonnets refer directly to Wordsworth: 3, with its conversation, "Dorothy and William— She interrupts: / 'You're not going to compare us two . . . ?' "; 4, with its description of the poet lying, like Wordsworth listening on the Keswick road, with his "ear to the line" of the railroad track, struck suddenly by an unexpected sound of cars coupling and shunting in the distance; 6, describing a man who lived in "the unsayable lights" like someone "Sudden and sure," a version of the Wordsworthian iceskater who "dared the ice / And raced his bike across the Moyola River"; and 10, where the poet and his lover lie like William and Dorothy in their "graves" in the woods: "we were laid out / Like breathing effigies on a raised ground." The sonnet sequence echoes the diction of epiphany at points: "Thunderlight on the split logs," "My all of you birchwood in lightning," "your face / Haunts like a new moon glimpsed through tangled glass." In Heaney, the illuminated focus of epiphany is not the exception but the rule that produces poems.

"Description is revelation!" cries the protagonist in "Fosterage." Heaney has said that such revelation is always derived from a source of power located in the memory and made manifest in the lyric poem's ability to be a "condensed, nondiscursive conductor of energy, a pebble that would stir the consciousness in pleasurable and suggestive ways."[32] Description becomes revelation whenever it is able to serve the object it describes, whenever it manifests the object's power. The object may be a wet swamp, "The bogholes might be Atlantic seepage. / The wet centre is bottomless"; primitive fire builders, "What could strike a blaze / From our dead igneous days?"; or a jack-o'-lantern,

> Death mask of harvest, mocker at All Souls
> With scorching smells, red dog's eyes in the night—
> We ring and stare into unhallowed light.

In countless similar images, what Heaney "had taken as a matter of fact as a youngster became a matter of wonder in memory."[33] In just this way, Emerson's facts become signs of wonder because they can take on the radiance of epiphany. Likewise in Wordsworth, a woman carrying water on her head or a child waiting for horses or a drowned man rising to the surface of a lake can be transformed in the mind in various ways until it manifests a sense of wonder and mystery.

Discussing Wordsworth's poem "The Thorn," Heaney reveals how epiphanies emerge from emotions that find a way of transforming themselves into words. Wordsworth described the genesis of "The Thorn" by saying that he sought a means of transforming his own almost superstitious sense of recognition of a thorn seen during a storm into a permanently "impressive object." As a poet he longed to do for others what the storm had done for him; he longed to make the thorn stand out in the reader's mind. Just as the storm, says Heaney, "was nature's technique for granting the thorn-tree its epiphany," so Wordsworth produced a poetic epiphany that would stir in his readers the same elevation of consciousness that he felt when confronted with this otherwise undistinguished natural object. Wordsworth's "technical triumph," says Heaney, "was to discover a means of allowing his abnormal, slightly numinous vision of the thorn to 'deal out its being.'" Wordsworth can make the thorn into a permanent and impressive object because "images and ideas from different parts of his conscious and unconscious mind were attracted by almost magnetic power." The result is the power found whenever an object like the thorn achieves its epiphany in the poet's mind. Once transformed by the "storm" of the mind, Heaney concludes, "the thorn in its new, wind-tossed aspect had become a field of force."[34] The ordinary object now has the power to radiate significance, to impress itself permanently on the mind of all those who read the poem.

Many of Heaney's most powerful poems suggest the importance of emphasis on the commonplace. Often he describes a loss of one kind of vision, which nevertheless represents an ultimate widening of vision. In "Girls Bathing, Galway 1965," for example, he claims that the myth of the goddess of love need not involve another world. Instead, the image of Venus Aphrodite can be appreciated in its ordinary origins, in a description that achieves revelatory status in terms of Irish girls at the seaside in the second half of the twentieth century:

> Bare-legged, smooth-shouldered and long-backed
> They wade ashore with skips and shouts.
> So Venus comes, matter-of-fact.[35]

These lines do not achieve an epiphany but suggest how epiphanies can arise from the most matter-of-fact circumstances. Like Stephen Dedalus's epiphany of the bird-girl of Sandymount Strand, the significance of an event is often out of proportion to the actual perception. For Heaney, the origins of the goddess Venus are repeated in the world of sense. Matters of fact, as Yeats noted, have the power, when acted upon by the imagination, to bring a "god" among us.

The dark side of epiphany, explored so powerfully in many of Wordsworth's childhood "spots of time," is evident in Heaney as early as his first volume, *Death of a Naturalist*. The title poem records a moment of powerfully transformed vision in which the ordinary gives way to the extraordinarily fearful. The young boy in the poem is an aspiring natural historian, delighted with the "warm thick slobber / Of frogspawn" and the "nimble- / Swimming tadpoles" that emerge from the "jampotfuls of the jellied / Specks." But the same child is horrified one hot day when he suddenly hears the sound of frogs in a new way:

> I ducked through hedges
> To a coarse croaking that I had not heard

> Before. The air was thick with a bass chorus.
> Right down the dam gross-bellied frogs were cocked
> On sods; their loose necks pulsed like sails. Some hopped:
> The slap and plop were obscene threats.

The childlike, schoolroom sense of frogs as harmless creatures is startlingly overwhelmed by a dark underside of nature; the frogs are allied to forces so dark they threaten to destroy:

> I sickened, turned, and ran. The great slime kings
> Were gathered there for vengeance and I knew
> That if I dipped my hand the spawn would clutch it.

The images convey an almost physical sense of the sudden maturation from young boy into adolescent. The child's increasing fear is focused on the obscene and grotesquely transformed frogs. Like the young Wordsworth, who was pursued in his mind by "huge and shadowy forms," the boy in "Death of a Naturalist" flees from his sudden insight into the nature of things; a force wants to drag him down. At the same time, however, the poem suggests that a deepening of vision has occurred. As in so many of Wordsworth's spots of time, the fear is turned into an ultimately beneficent emotion because it signals that something has been revealed. But this revelation occurs only in the mind. The frogs themselves are no more changed in the course of the poem than is Wordsworth's humble leech-gatherer; only the poet's vision alters. Once such transformed images impress themselves upon the mind, however, they can become a continuing source of renovation.

A Wordsworthian sense of the power of epiphany is likewise evident in Heaney's poem "Vision," in which the poet returns to the banks of a river where adults had frightened him as a child:

> Unless his hair was fine-combed
> The lice, they said, would gang up
> Into a mealy rope
> And drag him, small, dirty, doomed
>
> Down to the water. He was
> Cautious then in riverbank
> Fields. Thick as a birch trunk
> That cable flexed in the grass
>
> Every time the wind passed. Years
> Later in the same fields

Epiphany in Twentieth-Century Poetry

> He stood at night when eels
> Moved through the grass like hatched fears
>
> Towards the water. To stand
> In one place as the field flowed
> Past, a jellied road,
> To watch the eels crossing land
>
> Re-wound his world's live girdle.
> Phosphorescent, sinewed slime
> Continued at his feet. Time
> Confirmed the horrid cable.

The fears have been incubating for years. They hatch in the Coleridgean image of eels, an image of childhood fear now embodied in the mind of the adult. The mind manifests a mystery remembered for years in a fleeting instant of epiphanic recognition. The mental ability to unite past and present in such an image becomes a way of holding the world together. Time establishes a "horrid" cable that drags consciousness into the world, into that same darkness and mystery hinted at by the frogs transformed into slime kings in "Death of a Naturalist."

The images of darkness in these poems are analogues to the light imagery used in other epiphanies I have discussed. For Heaney, darkness realized in a fearful epiphany can actually defeat darkness by being acknowledged. "I rhyme," Heaney says in "Personal Helicon," "To see myself, to set the darkness echoing." Just as the epiphanic images of Wordsworth, Coleridge, and Browning radiate verbal light that points beyond the images themselves, so Heaney's rhymes radiate echoing sounds through the silent darkness.

Heaney's poem "Exposure" concludes that the poet is never certain if he has achieved the goal he has set for himself, namely, to make life manifest in the poem. Heaney has seen a falling star but wants more:

> A comet that was lost
> Should be visible at sunset,
> Those million tons of light
> Like a glimmer of haws and rose-hips,
>
> And I sometimes see a falling star.
> If I could come on meteorite!

The falling star is what can be seen from this world; it represents the revelation available here and now—Wordsworth's starry sky in "A Night-Piece," Coleridge's quietly shining moon, Browning's radiant star. Heaney wonders, however, if the poet can expect further revelation. Is it possible to achieve the other-worldly source of the falling star; is it possible to "come on meteorite"? At this point, Heaney thinks not. In the end it is only poets

> Who, blowing up these sparks
> For their meagre heat, have missed
> The once-in-a-lifetime portent,
> The comet's pulsing rose.

The mind's ability to blow the sparks of experience into an epiphany is not doubted by Heaney at this point, but he recognizes the limitations of this new form of inspiration. Beyond the falling star, which we can perceive, lies the invisible meteorite, denied to us only because of our human limitations. The invisible meteorite is the actual source of the visible falling star. From earth the human eye sees only a fleeting streak of light. In the atmosphere, however, a mountain-sized chunk of stone is burning up as it races through the sky. Heaney's image is a version of Shelley's vision of power in "Mont Blanc." The eye can see only the visible effects of the invisible workings of the world.

Epiphany, in all of the poets I have discussed, transforms the details of ordinary experience and yields up visible manifestations of meaning out of the invisible workings of the mind. The only ghosts are ghosts given shape by language. For Wordsworth, Browning, and Tennyson, no less than for Yeats, Stevens, and Heaney, epiphany is one of the most direct ways of moving beyond the self and into the world. The poetics of epiphany allows poets to produce their own versions of the isolated moment of power that widens out onto an open-ended series of associative meanings. In epiphany, words may manifest power in equivocal, multifarious ways, but they manifest power nevertheless. Over the past two centuries, literary epiphanies have continually suggested the limits of human vision and the unlimited powers of the human imagination. From the spots of time of Wordsworth to the revelatory moments of Heaney, epiphany serves as a fleeting buttress against forms of experience and uses of language that seem increasingly uncertain, indefinite, and problematic.

Notes

1 The New Epiphany

1. See *Agenda* 21, no. 1 (1983): 68–71; *New York Times Book Review,* August 21, 1983, p. 12; "The Structure of Epiphanic Imagery in Ten Coleridge Lyrics," *Studies in Romanticism* 22, no. 1 (1983): 29–40. Bidney offers a phenomenological reading of Coleridge's imagery, based on the model of Gaston Bachelard.

2. Roger Cardinal, *Figures of Reality: A Perspective on the Poetic Imagination* (Totowa, N.J.: Barnes & Noble, 1981), p. 224. Cardinal quotes Coleridge, "Poetry gives most pleasure when only generally and not perfectly understood." For Culler, see *Structuralist Poetics: Structuralism, Linguistics, and the Study of Literature* (London: Routledge & Kegan Paul, 1975), p. 175.

3. Robert Langbaum, *The Poetry of Experience,* rev. ed. (New York: Norton, 1971), p. 46. Langbaum has recently expanded this point and analyzed the importance of Wordsworth to the tradition of epiphany, in "Wordsworth and the Epiphanic Mode in Modern Poetry," *New Literary History* 14, no. 2 (1983): 335–58.

4. Northrop Frye, *A Study of English Romanticism* (Brighton, Sussex: Harvester Press, 1983), p. 158. Frye entitles his chapter on Keats, "Endymion: The Romantic Epiphanic."

5. Northrop Frye, *Anatomy of Criticism* (Princeton: Princeton University Press, 1971), p. 223. Frye compares Joyce's "nontheological use of the theological term epiphany" with Valéry's notion of "total intelligence," Yeats's conception of "the artifice of eternity," and Dylan Thomas's "hymns to a universal human body" (pp. 122, 203, 299).

6. Morris Beja, *Epiphany in the Modern Novel* (Seattle: University of Washington Press, 1971), p. 32. See particularly Beja's chapter "The Present of Things Past."

7. M. H. Abrams, *Natural Supernaturalism: Tradition and Revolution in Romantic Literature* (New York: Norton, 1971), p. 421. Abrams analyzes the Romantic desire to find vivid sensations that can "make the world new." He sees such instantaneous perceptions

being described in Proust's *moments privilégiés*, Henry James's imaginative acts which derive "revelations" from the "very pulses of the air," Conrad's "moments of vision," Virginia Woolf's "moments of vision," Thomas Wolfe's "single moment," and Faulkner's "instant of sublimation. . . . a flash, a glare" (p. 419). For a related discussion see Kenneth Clark, *Moments of Vision* (Oxford: Clarendon Press, 1954), particularly pp. 1–24. Clark describes "moments of vision" in which "the brooding troubled mind and the eye perpetually [dwell] on an irrelevant object, till unconsciously thought and perception are merged" (p. 3).

8. Geoffrey Hartman, "Toward Literary History," in *Beyond Formalism: Literary Essays, 1958–1970* (New Haven: Yale University Press, 1970), pp. 356–86. See also Hartman's discussion of transitional eighteenth-century poets (p. 291).

9. Geoffrey Hartman, *Wordsworth's Poetry, 1787–1814* (New Haven: Yale University Press, 1964), p. 184. Hartman notes that, "because modern lyric poetry is essentially occasional, and takes for granted the celebration of ordinary things and private moods, one can easily overlook the significance of Wordsworth's interest in the moods of his mind" (pp. 163–64).

10. A. D. Nock, *Conversion: The Old and the New in Religion from Alexander the Great to Augustine of Hippo* (Oxford: Oxford University Press, 1933), pp. 87, 90. See also Sante de Sanctis, *Religious Conversion*, trans. Helen Augur (New York: Harcourt, Brace, 1927).

11. James Frazer, *The Golden Bough: A Study in Magic and Religion*, abr. ed. (New York: Macmillan, 1958), p. 106.

12. Ibid, p. 108.

13. The feast was originally celebrated on the same day as Christmas but was later separated by twelve days in order to make the date of the birth of Jesus coincide with certain pagan practices. An early Syrian commentator, quoted by Frazer, explained this change: "The reason why the fathers transferred the celebration of the sixth of January to the twenty-fifth of December was this. It was a custom of the heathen to celebrate on the same twenty-fifth of December the birthday of the Sun, at which they kindled lights in token of festivity. In these solemnities and festivals the Christians also took part. Accordingly, when the doctors of the Church perceived that the Christians had a leaning to this festival, they took Counsel and resolved that the true Nativity should be solemnized on that day and the festival of Epiphany on the sixth of January."

The twelve days of Christmas were created when the separation of these two festivals took place (Frazer, *Golden Bough*, pp. 416–17).

14. James Joyce, *Stephen Hero* (New York: New Directions, 1963), p. 211.

15. Abrams cites Emerson's journal entry for June 21, 1838. At points the lecture quotes the journal word-for-word, but six months had allowed Emerson to develop the idea into a full-fledged theory of value. The lecture was delivered at the Masonic Temple in Boston and was never repeated. See *The Early Lectures of Ralph Waldo Emerson*, vol. 3, *1838–1842*, ed. Robert E. Spiller and Wallace E. Williams (Cambridge, Mass.: Harvard University Press, Belknap Press, 1972), p. 47.

16. Ibid., pp. 48–49. Compare Thoreau's emphasis on "the harvest of my daily life," which he calls "a little star-dust caught, a segment of the rainbow which I have clutched." Emerson's notion of facts as an epiphany of God is clearly related to Thoreau's contention that experience is meaningful because of the role it plays in a particular mind—the poet "sees a flower or other object, and it is beautiful or affecting to him because it is a symbol of his thought, and what he indistinctly feels or perceives is natural in some other organization. The object I behold corresponds to my mind." See Frederick Garber, *Thoreau's Redemptive Imagination* (New York: New York University Press, 1977), pp. 20, 27.

17. Emerson's 1850 essay "Shakespeare; or, The Poet," reprinted in *English Critical Essays: Nineteenth Century*, ed. Edmund D. Jones (Oxford: Oxford University Press, 1971), p. 474. Joyce quotation is from *A Portrait of the Artist as a Young Man* (New York: Viking Penguin, 1964), p. 217.

18. William T. Noon, *Joyce and Aquinas* (New Haven: Yale University Press, 1957), pp. 60–62. Noon compares epiphany as an aspect of experience with Hopkins's "inscape." Joyce's notion of epiphany as a verbal strategy, Noon argues, bears comparison with Hopkins's description of "poetic clarity" as "an explosion out of darkness." See also C. H. Peake, *James Joyce: The Citizen as Artist* (London: Arnold, 1977), who notes that moments of epiphany can come for the reader or for the character in the story. He cites Stanislaus Joyce's claim in *My Brother's Keeper* (New York: Viking, 1958), p. 124, that epiphanies were "manifestations or revelations . . . ironical observations of slips, and little errors and gestures . . . by which people betrayed the things they were most

careful to conceal." Warren Beck, in *Joyce's Dubliners: Substance, Vision, and Art* (Durham: Duke University Press, 1969), p. 23, notes that, "as there are in Joyce's early experimental fragments two kinds of epiphany, the naturalistic-objective and the subjective-psychological, so too with *Dubliners*." In some stories, that is, "Epiphany must accrete in the reader's recognition." In others, "Characters themselves experience a crisis of emotion under stress of a further realization which they demonstrate."

19. Irene Hendry, "Joyce's Epiphanies," *Sewanee Review* 54 (1946): 449–67. For another early view see Theodore Spencer's *"Stephen Hero:* The Unpublished Manuscript of James Joyce's *Portrait of the Artist as a Young Man," Southern Review* 7, no. 1 (1941): 186, where Spencer argues that Joyce's literary theory of epiphany "is a theory which implies a lyrical rather than a dramatic view of life. It emphasizes the radiance, the effulgence, of the thing itself revealed in a special moment, an unmoving moment, of time."

20. Noon, *Joyce and Aquinas*, p. 73.

21. The letter is quoted in *The Workshop of Daedalus: James Joyce and the Raw Materials for "A Portrait of the Artist as a Young Man,"* ed. Robert Scholes and Richard M. Kain (Evanston, Ill.: Northwestern University Press, 1965), p. 247.

22. Joyce, *Stephen Hero*, p. 213.

23. See Strauss's *Life of Jesus* (1835), translated by George Eliot. This passage is quoted by Bernard M. G. Reardon in *Religious Thought in the Nineteenth Century* (Cambridge: Cambridge University Press, 1966), p. 120.

24. My quotations come from the Everyman edition of the *Confessions*, trans. E. B. Pusey (London: Dent & Sons, 1907), pp. 170–71.

25. Ibid., p. 171.

26. Both quotations are from Abrams, *Natural Supernaturalism*, pp. 383–84.

27. John Bunyan, *Grace Abounding to the Chief of Sinners*, Everyman edition (London: Dent & Sons; New York: Dutton, 1976), sec. 229, p. 72.

28. Ibid., p. 102.

29. George Trosse, *The Life of the Reverend Mr. George Trosse: Written by Himself and Published Posthumously according to His Order in 1714*, ed. A. W. Brink (Montreal: McGill-Queen's University Press, 1974), p. 86.

30. Ibid., pp. 87–88.

31. Wesley's *Journal*, ed. Nehemiah Curnock, 8 vols. (London: Epworth Press, 1909–16), 1:475–76.

32. Quoting Umphrey Lee in *John Wesley and Modern Religion* (Nashville: Cokesbury Press, 1936), pp. 89–90.

33. *The Letters of John Wesley,* ed. John Telford, 8 vols. (London: Epworth Press, 1931), 5:16. Brackets in edited version.

34. In a letter to George and Tom Keats of December 1817 (*Letters of John Keats,* ed. Robert Gittings [Oxford: Oxford University Press, 1970], p. 43).

35. Georges Poulet, *Studies in Human Time,* trans. Elliott Coleman (Baltimore: Johns Hopkins University Press, 1956), p. 23. See also H. G. Schenk, *The Mind of the European Romantics,* rev. ed. (Oxford: Oxford University Press, 1979), p. 20, who notes that the Romantic emphasis on "'singularity' applied not only to each distinctive stage in a person's development, but even to much shorter units of time, and in the last analysis to each single moment in life. This was one of the reasons why the Romantics abandoned themselves wholeheartedly, or so it seemed, to the most fleeting emotions."

36. David Hume, *A Treatise of Human Nature,* ed. L. A. Selby-Bigge (Oxford: Clarendon Press, 1888), p. 31, in the chapter entitled "Of the Infinite Divisiblity of Space and Time."

37. See ibid., bk. 1, sec. 6, "Of Personal Identity," pp. 251–53.

38. Frank Kermode, *The Sense of an Ending: Studies in the Theory of Fiction* (New York: Oxford University Press, 1967), p. 169.

39. John Beer, *Wordsworth in Time* (London: Faber & Faber, 1979), p. 60. See particularly chapter 2, "Cycles and Occasions," where Beer notes the current use of the term "kairos" in Paul Tillich's "theology of crisis." Beer adds that such modern theological uses "do not correspond to the demonstrable biblical usages of those words" (p. 214).

40. Ibid., pp. 31–32. Beer derives the distinction from E. Panofsky's *Studies in Iconology* and connects Wordsworth's most powerful visions with both kairos and aiōn: "The one commemorates moments when a human being feels himself to be actively and totally fitted to the world about him, the other those when he or she is so possessed by inward imagination as to feel no transience in the passing of time" (p. 32).

41. Samuel Taylor Coleridge, *Poetical Works,* ed. Ernest Hartley Coleridge (Oxford: Oxford University Press, 1969), pp. 419–20. He also refers to these two senses of time as "time objective and subjective" (p. 420n).

42. Virginia Woolf, *Orlando* (New York: Harcourt Brace, 1928), p. 98. See also C. A. Patrides in *Aspects of Time* (Manchester: Man-

chester University Press, 1976), p. 1. These two senses of time have been discussed by numerous contemporary authors and critics. Sartre, in his essay "On *The Sound and the Fury:* Time in the Work of Faulkner," notes that the key to understanding the novel lies in abandoning "chronology" for "temporality." He quotes Faulkner, "Time is dead as long as it is being clicked off by little wheels; only when the clock stops does time come to life," and concludes, "In order to arrive at real time, we must abandon this invented measure which is not a measure of anything" (*Literary and Philosophical Essays,* trans. Annette Michelson [New York: Criterion, 1955], p. 80.

43. Abrams, *Natural Supernaturalism,* pp. 386–87.

44. Note 8 in *Poetical Works,* ed. Thomas Hutchinson, corr. G. M. Matthews (Oxford: Oxford University Press, 1970), p. 825.

45. Consider also Blake's call for a heightened imaginative response to perception. Blake, however, is difficult to categorize. In terms of epiphany, this problem is compounded by Blake's suggesting that he lived in this transformational state of imaginative consciousness all of the time, rather than for fleeting moments of revelation. In addition, many of his prophecies adopt the rhetorical posture of traditional inspiration—"Isaiah and Ezekiel dined with me," "An Angel came to me and said"—without ever suggesting that these descriptions refer to anything more than hypostatized imaginative entities. Applying my argument to Blake would lead us to conclude that Blake saw his entire poetic output as a single epiphany.

46. Numerous modern theologians suggest that revelation need not be understood in the strict terms of traditional God-language. The general problem for the contemporary theologian centers on the status and validity of all claims about God. What continues to distinguish the literary epiphany from modern theological revelations—Langdon Gilkey calls them "hierophanies," that is, manifestations of the sacred—is the question of content. The content of the literary epiphany need not be, in any sense, sacred or divine or indicative of any "otherness" beyond consciousness. Formally, of course, such theological elevations of consciousness can be described in terms of their suddenness, power, or revelatory quality. See Langdon Gilkey, *Naming the Whirlwind: The Renewal of God Language* (New York: Bobbs-Merrill, 1969); James Loder, *The Transforming Moment: Understanding Convictional Experiences* (San Francisco: Harper & Row, 1981); Owen Chadwick, *The Secularization of the Eu-*

ropean Mind in the Nineteenth Century (Cambridge: Cambridge University Press, 1975); Sallie McFague, *Metaphorical Theology: Models of God in Religious Language* (Philadelphia: Fortress Press, 1982); and John Macquarrie, *God-Talk: An Examination of the Language and Logic of Theology* (New York: Harper & Row, 1967).

47. Carol T. Christ, *Victorian and Modern Poetics* (Chicago: University of Chicago Press, 1984), p. 4. See particularly Christ's chapters "Dramatic Monologue, Mask, and Persona" and "The Picturesque and Modernist Theories of the Image."

48. J. Hillis Miller, *The Linguistic Moment: From Wordsworth to Stevens* (Princeton: Princeton University Press, 1985), p. 55.

49. M.-L. von Franz, "Time and Synchronicity in Analytic Psychology," in *The Voices of Time,* ed. J. T. Fraser (Amherst: University of Massachusetts Press, 1981), pp. 218–32. See also Jung's *Structure and Dynamics of the Psyche,* which is volume 8 of *Collected Works* (Princeton: Princeton University Press, 1960). See the comments of Edward F. Edinger in *Ego and Archetype* (Middlesex: Penguin Books, 1973), p. 101: "Jung is calling 'God' what most people call chance or accident. He experiences apparently arbitrary happenings as meaningful rather than meaningless. This is precisely how the primitive experiences life. . . . For the Self-connected man, as for the child and the primitive, chance does not exist."

50. Thomas De Quincey, *The Collected Writings,* ed. David Masson (London: Black, 1897), 13:347. See also Christopher Salvesen in *The Landscape of Memory: A Study of Wordsworth's Poetry* (Lincoln: University of Nebraska Press, 1965), p. 171.

51. Ricoeur's discussion of poetic symbols occurs in his introduction to *The Symbolism of Evil,* trans. Emerson Buchanan (Boston: Beacon Press, 1967), pp. 11, 14. This passage includes a quotation drawn from Gaston Bachelard's *The Poetics of Space,* trans. Maria Jolas (Boston: Beacon Press, 1969).

52. Ricoeur, *Symbolism of Evil,* p. 11.

53. James Joyce, *Ulysses* (New York: Random House, 1961), p. 34.

2 WORDSWORTH AND THE ORIGINS OF EPIPHANY

1. Samuel Taylor Coleridge, *Biographia Literaria,* ed. J. Shawcross, 2 vols. (Oxford: Oxford University Press, 1965), 2:124.

2. De Quincey, *Collected Writings* 11:315, quoted by Robert Rehder in *Wordsworth and the Beginnings of Modern Poetry* (Totowa, N.J.: Barnes & Noble, 1981), p. 202. Rehder points out that every major

English poet after Wordsworth—"Byron, Shelley, Keats, Tennyson, Browning, Hardy, Hopkins, Yeats and Stevens"—had to come to terms with Wordsworth's "new mode of interpreting reality."

3. *Eclectic Review* 28 (1850): 550. Reprinted in *The Prelude: 1799, 1805, 1850,* ed. Jonathan Wordsworth, M. H. Abrams, and Stephen Gill (New York: Norton, 1979), p. 548. All of my references to *The Prelude* will be taken from this edition and will specify the date of the text.

4. "The Prelude," *Eclectic Review* 28 (1850): 550–62; *Tait's Edinburgh Magazine* 17 (1850): 521–27; *Graham's Magazine* (Philadelphia) 37 (1850): 322–23; *British Quarterly Review* 12 (1850): 549–79; all reprinted in the Norton edition of *The Prelude,* pp. 547–55.

5. Dorothy's comments can be found in her *Journals,* ed. Mary Moorman (Oxford: Oxford University Press, 1971). The journals list thirty-three poems by Wordsworth that Dorothy relates to immediate autobiographical circumstances. The majority of Wordsworth's comments on the circumstances surrounding poetic composition are to be found in the Fenwick notes to the poems in *The Poetical Works of William Wordsworth,* ed. E. de Selincourt and Helen Darbishire, 5 vols. (Oxford: Clarendon Press, 1940–49). My subsequent quotations from Wordsworth, with the exception of *The Prelude,* will be taken from this edition.

6. J. J. Rousseau, *The Reveries of a Solitary Walker,* trans. Charles E. Butterworth (New York: New York University Press, 1979), p. 71.

7. *The Confessions of J. J. Rousseau,* trans. W. Conyngham Mallory (New York: Tudor Publishing, 1935), p. 28. Cecil Lang comments on the role of "life-enhancing epiphany" in Rousseau and "the poet of *The Prelude*" in his introduction to *The Pre-Raphaelites and Their Circle* (Chicago: University of Chicago Press, 1975), p. xxix.

8. Quoted by Poulet in *Studies in Human Time,* p. 21. Poulet also quotes Rousseau's comment, "Have you never experienced those involuntary transports which sometimes seize hold of a mind . . . and carry us up into the empyrean?" p. 173. This image is adopted by Shelley in the closing lines of "Adonais." The process reverses traditional inspiration in another way, by describing a soul that goes out toward the truth rather than a soul that has the truth breathed into it.

9. Both quotations are from McDowell's translation, *La Nouvelle Héloïse: Julie, or the New Heloise* (University Park: Pennsylvania State University Press, 1968), pp. 16, 286. For a useful discussion of the

connection between memory and the value of the present in Wordsworth, see Salvesen's *Landscape of Memory*. Salvesen cites Irving Babbitt's comment that "Rousseau's great discovery was revery . . . the imaginative melting of man into nature" (*Rousseau and Romanticism* [Boston: Houghton Mifflin, 1919], p. 269). In Salvesen, see particularly pp. 170–98.

10. Gaston Bachelard, *The Poetics of Reverie: Childhood, Language, and the Cosmos,* trans. Daniel Russell (Beacon Press: Boston, 1969), p. 8. Bachelard applies the notion of reverie to his own phenomenological approach to experience: "I have chosen phenomenology in hopes of reexamining in a new light the faithfully beloved images which are so solidly fixed in my memory that I no longer know whether I am remembering or imagining them when I come across them in my reveries" (p. 2). The goal of all phenomenology, Bachelard claims, "is to situate awareness in the present, in a moment of extreme tension."

11. Ibid., p. 116.

12. Wordsworth, *Poetical Works* 1:318–19. See also Charles Sherry, *Wordsworth's Poetry of the Imagination* (Oxford: Clarendon Press, 1980). Sherry points out that, for Wordsworth, revelation is not continual but momentary. Wordsworth's "Preface" appears in *Poetical Works* 2:384–404.

13. James Engell, *The Creative Imagination: Enlightenment to Romanticism* (Cambridge: Harvard University Press, 1981), p. 31. "We greet nature," Engell adds, "and even as we do so, we are creating it, as well as our own identities." See also Engell, pp. 267–76.

14. Donald H. Reiman, "Wordsworth, Shelley, and Romantic Inheritance," *Romanticism Past and Present* 5, no. 2 (1981): 8–9.

15. *The Autobiography of Mark Rutherford, Dissenting Minister,* ed. Reuben Shapcott (New York: Garland Publishing, 1976), chap. 2, p. 24.

16. William Hazlitt, *Complete Works,* ed. P. P. Howe, 21 vols. (London: J. M. Dent, 1930–34), 11:93.

17. Poulet, *Studies in Human Time,* p. 20.

18. James Olney, *Metaphors of Self: The Meaning of Autobiography* (Princeton: Princeton University Press, 1972), pp. 29, 48. See Olney's preface and chap. 1, "A Theory of Autobiography." See also Olney, ed., *Autobiography: Essays Theoretical and Critical* (Princeton: Princeton University Press, 1980), particularly Olney's "Autobiography and the Cultural Moment," and Georges Gusdorf's "Conditions and Limits of Autobiography."

19. W. B. Yeats, *Essays and Introductions* (New York: Collier Books, 1968), p. 260.

20. Wordsworth, *Poetical Works* 1:244. Wordsworth notes that such stone men were common in the Lake District. Wallace Stevens recalls this poem when he says, "Piece the world together, boys, but not with your hands."

21. In a letter to Charles Kingsley of 1851, quoted in the Norton edition of *The Prelude*, p. 560. Compare Hegel's notion of "secular spirituality," in *Philosophy of History*. Hegel argues that, in the modern world, spirituality can emerge only out of the secular details of ordinary experience.

22. Keats, *Letters*, p. 38, November 22, 1817, to Benjamin Bailey.

23. Ibid., p. 250, March 17, 1819, to George and Georgiana Keats.

24. Ibid., p. 43, December 22, 1817, to George and Tom Keats.

25. A. D. Nuttall, *A Common Sky: Philosophy and the Literary Imagination* (London: Chatto & Windus, 1974), p. 172. Nuttall says we "even find persisting in Sartre the Wordsworthian 'nostalgia for thinghood.'"

26. *Letters of William and Dorothy Wordsworth*, ed. E. de Selincourt, rev. Chester L. Shaver, 3 vols. (Oxford: Clarendon Press, 1967), 1:586–87, 594.

27. J. R. MacGillivray, "The Three Forms of *The Prelude*, 1798–1805," in *Wordsworth, The Prelude*, ed. W. J. Harvey and Richard Gravil (London: Macmillan, 1972), pp. 99–115. For the 1799 version see also *The Prelude, 1798–99*, ed. Stephen Parrish (Ithaca: Cornell University Press, 1977), vol. 2 of the Cornell edition of Wordsworth's poetry. The poem was first published by Jonathan Wordsworth and Stephen Gill in the third edition of *The Norton Anthology of English Literature* (1974) and subsequently in the Norton edition of *The Prelude* (1979) from which my citations are drawn. See also Jonathan Wordsworth's essay "The Two-Part *Prelude* of 1799," reprinted in the Norton edition, pp. 567–85.

28. Jonathan Wordsworth, *William Wordsworth: The Borders of Vision* (Oxford: Clarendon Press, 1982), p. 2. Jonathan Wordsworth also notes that "the sense of 'something evermore about to be' is infinitely valuable but not a religious experience" (p. 34). He argues that Wordsworth's "border impulse" bears comparison to Shelley's state of mind in "Mont Blanc" and Browning's "moment, one and infinite."

29. "Lake Reminiscences from 1807 to 1830, in *Tait's Edinburgh Magazine* 6 (1839): 94.

30. See Kenneth Johnston's important discussion of this poem, "The Idiom of Vision," in *New Perspectives on Coleridge and Wordsworth*, ed. Geoffrey H. Hartman (New York: Columbia University Press, 1972). According to Johnston, "Wordsworth tells us that the fall into the quotidian is not a Fall but the occasion for ascent and vision" (p. 2). For a related discussion see Karl Kroeber, *Romantic Narrative Art* (Madison: University of Wisconsin Press, 1960), pp. 51–63. Kroeber cites "A Night-Piece" as a "visionary lyric," in which the vision "does not reveal eternal truth, either of Nature or of God, but is presented . . . rather as a random personal experience, one memorable for the emotions aroused" (p. 56).

31. Wordsworth, *Letters* 2:705.

32. Note to "The Thorn" in the 1800 edition of *Lyrical Ballads*.

33. See John L. Phillips, Jr., *Piaget's Theory: A Primer* (San Francisco: Freeman, 1981), pp. 22–28. For Piaget's own works see *The Child's Conception of Space*, trans. F. J. Langdon and J. L. Lynyer (New York: Norton, 1956); and *Memory and Intelligence*, trans. A. J. Pomerans (New York: Basic Books, 1972).

34. See Edinger, *Ego and Archetype*, p. 295; Rudolf Otto, *The Idea of the Holy*, trans. John W. Harvey (London: Oxford University Press, 1957), chaps. 4 and 5; and G. van der Leeuw, *Religion in Essence and Manifestation*, trans. J. E. Turner, 2 vols. (Gloucester, Mass.: Peter Smith, 1967), 1:43.

35. Michael Paffard has empirically analyzed this kind of experience. His research, including numerous interviews with young adults, suggests that experiences like those described by Wordsworth and later by Joyce are a commonplace. Paffard also suggests that, "in countless autobiographies and memoirs, and even in fiction, one encounters descriptions of 'Wordsworthian' moments in childhood or adolescence. . . . the writer looks back, often over a group of several decades, and certain fleeting memories of the past, certain events and experiences, in themselves apparently trivial and inconsequential, stand out with peculiar vividness and insistently proclaim an obscure significance" (*Inglorious Wordsworths* [London: Hodder & Stoughton, 1973], p. 20). Robert Nichols connects such experiences with the production of poems. In "The Birth of a Poem," he describes how a sunrise at sea became the source of poetry: "The newly risen sun sent flickering over the long, low, smooth, glassy mounds of the rolling swells a series of elastic reflections. . . . I became aware of an extraordinary physical exhilaration. . . . It was at that moment, as I now discern, that I

had only to yield to the emotion evoked by what I beheld to discover a poem.... My eye dwelled upon the scene and the longer it dwelled—though but a moment passed—the more I was filled with an immense and pure emotion *which was the reflection of what I saw,* that is to say I was conscious of a regular and growing central excitement surrounded by an area of deep, tranquil and joyful satisfaction." Nichols's essay appears as the appendix to Rosamond E. M. Harding, *An Anatomy of Inspiration* (Cambridge: Cambridge University Press, 1940), pp. 151–53. Joseph Chiari extends this experience into the realm of the scientific in *Realism and Imagination* (London: Barrie & Rockliff, 1960), p. 195, where he describes "moments of illumination" which "emerge from a background of sustained conscious and subconscious tension toward a goal. They imply a capacity for detecting hitherto unsuspected relationships and fusing them into organic wholes or into physical laws.... The greatest scientific discoveries have been made through such unexplainable moments."

36. See Baker's introduction to the Rinehart edition. He says that in Wordsworth's poetry we learn "through the sudden leap of intuition, the unlooked-for epiphany by which one impulse . . . from a springtime woodland *may* . . . teach the man of sensibility more about how men's minds work than a reading of all the sages" (*William Wordsworth: The Prelude, Selected Poems and Sonnets,* rev. ed. [New York: Holt, Rinehart & Winston, 1954], p. xiv).

37. T. S. Eliot, "Hamlet," in *Selected Prose of T. S. Eliot,* ed. Frank Kermode (New York: Harcourt, Brace, Jovanovich; Farrar, Straus & Giroux, 1975), p. 48.

38. Hartman, *Wordsworth's Poetry,* p. 49.

3 FLASHES OF INTERNAL INSPIRATION

1. "Sonnet: Composed on a Journey Homeward; the Author Having Received Intelligence of the Birth of a Son, Sept. 20, 1796," in Coleridge, *Poetical Works,* p. 153. All Coleridge quotations are from this edition.

2. Basil Willey, *The Seventeenth-Century Background: Studies of the Thought of the Age in Relation to Poetry and Religion* (New York: Doubleday, 1934), p. 299. See Willey's discussion of "Wordsworth and the Locke Tradition," pp. 298–305. For more recent discussions see Herbert Lindenberger, *On Wordsworth's "Prelude"* (Princeton: Princeton University Press, 1963); and Jeffrey Baker, *Time and Mind in Wordsworth's Poetry* (Detroit: Wayne State University Press, 1980).

3. Willey, *Seventeenth-Century Background*, p. 300.

4. Edmund Burke, *A Philosophical Enquiry into the Origin of Our Ideas of the Sublime and Beautiful*, ed. J. T. Boulton (London: Routledge & Kegan Paul, 1958), p. 39. On the connection between the sublime and the Wordsworthian spot of time, see Thomas Weiskel, *The Romantic Sublime: Studies in the Structure and Psychology of Transcendence* (Baltimore: Johns Hopkins University Press, 1976), particularly chapter 7, "Wordsworth and the Defile of the Word."

5. See Bertram D. Lewin, *The Image and the Past* (New York: International Universities Press, 1968), pp. 9–26. Lewin comments on Freud's claim that the adult fills in gaps in memory in order to fulfill mental expectations (p. 10). See also Brian Smith, *Memory* (London: Allen & Unwin, 1966). Dostoevsky says that a man "is inclined to mark points in his past, so that later he can orient himself, and deduce from them something whole, for the sake of order and self-edification" (quoted by Esther Salaman in *A Collection of Moments: A Study of Involuntary Memories* [London: Longmans, 1970], p. 138).

6. Stephen Prickett, *Coleridge and Wordsworth: The Poetry of Growth* (Cambridge: Cambridge University Press, 1970), p. 18.

7. Miller, *Linguistic Moment*, p. 44.

8. Letter from Wordsworth to Sara Hutchinson in *Letters* 1:366.

9. "Preface to Lyrical Ballads," in Wordsworth, *Poetical Works* 2:393.

10. Note in Coleridge, *Poetical Works*, p. 393.

11. Ibid., p. 153.

12. In a letter to his brother, quoted in Charles Ryskamp, "Wordsworth's Lyrical Ballads in Their Time," in *From Sensibility to Romanticism*, ed. Frederick W. Hilles and Harold Bloom (New York: Oxford University Press, 1965), p. 372.

13. Coleridge, *Poetical Works*, p. 429.

14. September 22, 1800, in *Unpublished Letters of Samuel Taylor Coleridge*, ed. E. L. Griggs (New Haven: Yale University Press, 1932–33), 1:154. See also Clarence DeWitt Thorpe in "Coleridge on the Sublime," in *Wordsworth and Coleridge*, ed. Earl Leslie Griggs (New York: Russell & Russell, 1962), pp. 192–219. Thorpe notes that "almost any object, however mean, provided it may occur in such a circumstance as to become a symbol for that which is great or eternal, may excite the mind to sublimity" (pp. 199–200).

15. Oscar Campbell, "Wordsworth's Conception of the Esthetic Experience," in *Wordsworth and Coleridge*, ed. Griggs, p. 30.

16. John Livingston Lowes, *The Road to Xanadu: A Study in the*

Ways of the Imagination (Boston: Houghton Mifflin, 1927), pp. 163–64. Lowes's study is still a useful source of information on the details of Coleridge's remarkable imaginative transformations.

17. Moonlight is an apt romantic symbol for mental activity because its light is derivative. Yeats notes the Romantic fear of a light so pure it would be blinding. He quotes Coleridge:

> Resembles life what once was deemed of light,
> Too ample in itself for human sight?
> An absolute self—an element ungrounded—
> All that we see, all colours of all shade,
>   By encroach of darkness made?
> [Yeats, *Essays and Introductions*, p. 463]

In the poem, entitled "What Is Life?" Coleridge follows these lines by asking, "Is very life by consciousness unbounded?"

18. Harold Bloom, *The Visionary Company* (Ithaca: Cornell University Press, 1971), pp. 204–5. Bloom compares the "fierce epiphanies of Wordsworth" to Coleridge's "naive sweetness."

19. See Stauffer's introduction to *Selected Poetry and Prose of Coleridge* (New York: Random House, 1951), pp. ix–xxiv.

20. *Shelley's Poetry and Prose*, ed. Donald H. Reiman and Sharon B. Powers (New York: Norton, 1977), pp. 96–97. All my quotations are from this edition.

21. Bloom, *Visionary Company*, p. 291.

22. Earl R. Wasserman, *Shelley: A Critical Reading* (Baltimore: Johns Hopkins University Press, 1971), pp. 187–88. Wasserman connects this passage with the quasi-Berkeleyan idea that "matter has no essence independent of mental perception."

23. Other editors (Ingpen, Peck, Clark) read "ineffectual" for "inefficient."

24. Shelley, *Poetry and Prose*, p. 504.

25. Wasserman, *Shelley*, p. 198.

26. See Donald H. Reiman, "Structure, Symbol, and Theme in 'Lines Written among the Euganean Hills,'" *PMLA* 77 (1962): 404–13, reprinted in the Norton edition. Reiman quotes Oliver Elton, who cited, in 1920, "the rapid, impassioned, shimmering brilliancy of the imagery, which resolves itself into the emotions of the poet." In connection with Shelley's concerns about this power of mind, see Charles Schug, *The Romantic Genesis of the Modern Novel* (Pittsburgh: University of Pittsburgh Press, 1979), p. 85. Discussing Henry James's "germ" of artistic creation, Schug compares this idea

to a "Shelleyan disregard for the actual in the face of the imaginative" and sees this tendency operating in Wordsworth's spots of time. He says that Virginia Woolf's "moments of being" and Joyce's epiphanies can be seen as aestheticized versions of the spot of time. Anne K. Mellor has described certain Romantic works as possessing "an all-important liminal experience of unstructured openness, a sacred participation in the process of life" (*English Romantic Irony* [Cambridge: Harvard University Press, 1980], p. 6). Mellor's anthropological emphasis emerges from the conviction that Romantic irony "posits a universe founded on chaos and incomprehensibility." The Romantic thus strives to order this world in the mind.

27. Harold Bloom, "The Witch of Atlas," in *Shelley: Modern Judgments*, ed. R. B. Woodings (London: Macmillan, 1968), pp. 93–101.

28. All of these passages are taken from "A Defence of Poetry."

29. In *Portrait of the Artist*, pp. 212–20; and *Stephen Hero*, pp. 211–13.

30. "Preface to Lyrical Ballads," in Wordsworth, *Poetical Works* 2:384–404. Richard Guggenheimer uses similar language to describe the productions of a whole class of modern artists. Such "spontaneous artists," he says, accomplish "that attention to totality which becomes revelatory." In such cases, both artist and audience "become charged with a conviction of meaningfulness, of almost mysterious sufficiency." He concludes that such art produces increasing emotion until a "sense of unutterable rightness glows around the entire structure. . . . This kind of seeing is stirring because all the trivialities are gone" (*Creative Vision in Artist and Audience* [New York: Harper, 1950], pp. 3, 74–77).

4 Browning's Modernism

1. For the details of this discussion see particularly Langbaum, *Poetry of Experience*, chap. 2, and the preface to the 1971 edition; William Cadbury, "Lyric and Anti-Lyric Forms: A Method for Judging Browning," in *Browning's Mind and Art*, ed. Clarence Tracy (London: Oliver & Boyd, 1968); Loy D. Martin, "The Inside of Time: An Essay on the Dramatic Monologue," in *Robert Browning: A Collection of Critical Essays*, ed. Harold Bloom and Adrienne Munich (Englewood Cliffs, N.J.: Prentice-Hall, 1979), pp. 75–78; and Park Honan, *Browning's Characters* (New Haven: Yale University Press, 1961), chaps. 4 and 5. See also the recent discussion of "The Dra-

matic 'I' Poem" in *Victorian Poetry* 22, no. 2 (1984), guest-edited by Linda M. Shires.

2. William O. Raymond, *The Infinite Moment and Other Essays in Robert Browning* (Toronto: University of Toronto Press, 1950), p. 7.

3. Carol T. Christ, *The Finer Optic: The Aesthetic of Particularity in Victorian Poetry* (New Haven: Yale University Press, 1975). Christ's chapter "The Good Moment: The Mastery of Accident" contains a thorough discussion of the importance of the particular in Browning's moments.

4. All Browning quotations are from *The Works of Robert Browning*, Centenary Edition, ed. F. G. Kenyon (New York: Barnes & Noble, 1966).

5. *The Letters of Robert Browning and Elizabeth Barrett Browning*, ed. Elvan Kintner, 2 vols. (Cambridge: Harvard University Press, Belknap Press, 1969), 1:17.

6. *Robert Browning and Julia Wedgwood: A Broken Friendship Revealed in Their Letters*, ed. Richard Curle (New York: Stokes, 1937), p. 7. See also Herbert F. Tucker, Jr., *Browning's Beginnings: The Art of Disclosure* (Minneapolis: University of Minnesota Press, 1980), p. 184. Tucker points out that the words "infinity, endlessness, incompleteness, unfulfillment, imperfection" are important to Browning because he prefers "transition and movement" to stasis (p. 14).

7. Hans Robert Jauss, *Aesthetic Experience and Literary Hermeneutics*, trans. Michael Shaw (Minneapolis: University of Minnesota Press, 1982), p. xxix.

8. Jerome H. Buckley, *The Triumph of Time: A Study of the Victorian Concepts of Time, History, Progress, and Decadence* (Cambridge: Harvard University Press, 1966), p. 147.

9. Roma A. King, Jr., *The Focusing Artifice: The Poetry of Robert Browning* (Athens: Ohio University Press, 1968), p. xxiii.

10. William Clyde DeVane, *A Browning Handbook*, 2d ed. (New York: Appleton, 1955), pp. 222–23.

11. Walter Pater, "The School of Giorgione," in *The Renaissance: Studies in Art and Poetry*, ed. Donald L. Hill (Berkeley: University of California Press, 1980), p. 118. This idea of overcoming temporal restrictions is more important to Browning's epiphanies than are Pater's moments "lived only for their own sake," which point toward the purely aesthetic instants of the Decadents.

12. All Arnold quotations are from *The Poems of Matthew Arnold*, ed. Kenneth Allott, 2d. ed. Miriam Allott (London: Longman, 1979).

13. Christ, *Finer Optic*, p. 108. She is here commenting on Ker-

mode's discussion of the "end-feeling" in *The Sense of an Ending,* pp. 24–25.

14. See the closing paragraphs of "The Everlasting Yea," in Thomas Carlyle, *Sartor Resartus* (New York: Odyssey Press, 1937), p. 196.

15. Joyce, *Portrait of the Artist,* p. 206.

16. Buckley, *Triumph of Time,* p. 148.

17. Christopher Clausen, "Poetry in a Discouraging Time," *Georgia Review* 35, no. 4 (1981): 703–16.

18. See Mary Shelley's introduction to the 1831 edition of *Frankenstein:* "Perhaps a corpse would be reanimated; galvanism had given token of such things" ([New York: Macmillan, 1961], p. 10).

19. Walter E. Houghton, *The Victorian Frame of Mind: 1830–1870* (New Haven: Yale University Press, 1957), p. 15. William E. Buckler, *The Victorian Imagination: Essays in Aesthetic Exploration* (New York: New York University Press, 1980), p. 288.

20. See Henri Bergson, *Time and Free Will: An Essay on the Immediate Data of Consciousness,* trans. F. L. Pogson (New York: Macmillan, 1911); and *Matter and Memory,* trans. Nancy Margaret Paul and W. Scott Palmer (New York: Macmillan, 1911).

21. Betty S. Flowers, *Browning and the Modern Tradition* (London: Macmillan, 1976), p. 173. Flowers suggests that Browning is an exemplar of those writers of both poetry and prose who are "concerned with life as experienced rather than life as seen." She cites Joyce, Woolf, and Proust, all writers for whom "the significant moment may, from the outside, seem very insignificant."

22. Stephen Toulmin and June Goodfield, *The Discovery of Time* (New York: Harper & Row, 1965), p. 235. Natural history began, according to the authors, with a sense of specific moments in the past which had determined vast amounts of subsequent history. In addition to these moments, fragmentary traces had been left as a fossil record that could reveal large-scale truths about the past. These fragments could prove "as direct and reliable as any human tradition" (p. 142).

23. In James's *Pragmatism,* quoted by Robert Langbaum in "Hardy, Frost, and the Question of Modern Poetry," *Virginia Quarterly Review* 58, no. 1 (1982): 69–80. See also George Roppen, *Evolution and Poetic Belief* (Oxford: Blackwell, 1978). Roppen discusses progressivism and perfectionism, two movements connected with evolutionary thinking and its emphasis on randomness, accidental change, and meaning which changes as circumstances change.

24. Hans Myerhoff, *Time in Literature* (Berkeley: University of California Press, 1960).

25. Ibid., p. 25. See Loy D. Martin, *Browning's Dramatic Monologues and the Post-Romantic Subject* (Baltimore: Johns Hopkins University Press, 1985). Martin's Marxist reading argues that the "ideological goal" of the dramatic monologue is the transformation of the Romantic lyric into an open-ended dynamic form (p. 25).

26. David Newsome, *Two Classes of Men: Platonism and English Romantic Thought* (London: Murray, 1974), p. 89. Newsome quotes Blake in "The Last Judgment": "He who wishes to see a vision, a perfect whole, / Must see it in its Minute Particulars, Organized."

27. Richard D. Altick and James F. Loucks, II, *Browning's Roman Murder Story: A Reading of "The Ring and the Book"* (Chicago: University of Chicago Press, 1968), p. 111. Browning's effort, according to Altick and Loucks, is "to reveal the timeless in the temporal, the universal in the individual, the abstract in the circumstantial—in short, to derive philosophy from crude earthly material."

28. William Clyde DeVane, in *The Victorian Poets: A Guide to Research*, ed. Frederick E. Faverty (Cambridge: Harvard University Press, 1956), p. 58.

29. Thomas Pynchon, *Gravity's Rainbow* (New York: Bantam Books, 1974), p. 33.

5 Victorian Versions of Epiphany

1. Alan Sinfield, "*In Memoriam* and the Language of Modern Poetry," in *The Language of Tennyson's "In Memoriam"* (Oxford: Blackwell, 1971), pp. 196–210, reprinted in the Norton edition of *In Memoriam* (New York, 1973), p. 251. The earlier comments on Tennyson's mysticism can be found in Carlisle Moore, "Faith, Doubt, and Mystical Experience in 'In Memoriam,'" *Victorian Studies* 7 (1963): 155–69. Moore quotes Sir Charles Tennyson from *Six Tennyson Essays* (London: Cassell, 1954), p. 96; and Sir Harold Nicolson from *Tennyson* (London: Constable, 1923), p. 27. For Willey, see Basil Willey, "In Memoriam," in *More Nineteenth-Century Studies: A Group of Honest Doubters* (London: Chatto & Windus, 1956), reprinted in the Norton edition, pp. 153–64. Coleridge noted the problem with the term "mystical" when he described Wordsworth's "vague, misty rather than mystic, confusion of God with the world." See Allsop, *Letters, Conversations, and Recollections of S.T.C.* (1836), quoted in Schenk, *Mind of the European Romantics*, p. 171.

2. In Tennyson, *In Memoriam*, p. 167.

3. Hallam Tennyson, *Alfred, Lord Tennyson: A Memoir*, 2 vols. (London: Macmillan, 1897), 1:320. See also D. J. Palmer, "Tennyson's Romantic Heritage," in *Tennyson*, ed. Palmer (London: G. Bell, 1973), p. 32. Palmer connects Tennyson's self, realized beyond the self, with the Romantics: "Wordsworth's belief in the organic sympathy between nature and the mind, Coleridge's theory of imagination, which held that the act of perception was essentially creative, and Keat's quest for poetic identity through sensuous involvement with the plurality of being outside himself, formulate in different ways the Romantic ideal of the mind's capacity to realize itself through imaginative experience of a world-beyond-self" (p. 24).

4. Robert Preyer, "Tennyson as an Oracular Poet," *Modern Philology*, 55 (1958): 250.

5. A. Dwight Culler, *The Poetry of Tennyson* (New Haven: Yale University Press, 1977), chap. 1 and pp. 182–83.

6. Robert Bernard Martin, *Tennyson: The Unquiet Heart* (Oxford: Clarendon Press, 1980), p. 279.

7. R. C. Zaehner, *Mysticism, Sacred and Profane: An Inquiry into Some Varieties of Praeternatural Experience* (Oxford: Clarendon Press, 1957), pp. 31, 37. In his famous definition of mystical experience, William James is careful to point out that the first characteristic of the mystical event is that it is "ineffable," that is, it cannot be put into words or imparted to others or shared. The literary epiphany, conversely, is always put into words as a poem or prose narrative, and a major part of its function is the sharing of the experience with the author's readers. See *The Varieties of Religious Experience* (New York: Longmans, Green, 1902), pp. 380–81.

8. Tennyson, *Alfred, Lord Tennyson* 1:312, excerpted in Norton edition, p. 118.

9. Jerome Buckley, *Tennyson: The Growth of a Poet* (Cambridge: Harvard University Press, 1960), pp. 123, 126–27.

10. All Tennyson quotations are from *The Poems of Tennyson*, ed. Christopher Ricks (London: Longmans, 1969).

11. See Søren Kierkegaard, *Concluding Unscientific Postscript*, trans. David F. Swenson and Walter Lowrie (Princeton: Princeton University Press, 1944); and Paul Tillich, *Dynamics of Faith* (New York: Harper & Row, 1958), particularly chapter 2, "What Faith Is Not."

12. James R. Kincaid, *Tennyson's Major Poems* (New Haven: Yale University Press, 1975), pp. 226–27.

13. Northrop Frye, *Fearful Symmetry: A Study of William Blake* (Princeton: Princeton University Press, 1947), pp. 114–15. Frye suggests one of the consequences of epiphany in describing the way that all poems mean: "In a poem the sounds and rhythms of words are revealed more clearly than in ordinary speech, and similarly their meanings have an intensity in poetry that a dictionary can give no hint of."

14. Moore, "Faith, Doubt, and Mystical Experience," p. 165.

15. E. D. H. Johnson, "*In Memoriam:* The Way of the Poet," *Victorian Studies* 2 (1958): 139–48; John Jump, "Tennyson's Religious Faith and Doubt," in *Tennyson*, ed. Palmer, pp. 89–114.

16. Willey, "In Memoriam" p. 96.

17. Philip Collins, "Tennyson In and Out of Time," in *Studies in Tennyson*, ed. Hallam Tennyson (London: Macmillan, 1981), pp. 131, 153–154. Collins quotes Tennyson's letter to Emily in 1839, "Annihilate within yourself these two dreams of Space and Time" (H. Tennyson, *Alfred, Lord Tennyson* 1.171–72).

18. Moore, "Faith, Doubt, and Mystical Experience," p. 166.

19. The comment is noted by Hallam Tennyson. Tennyson himself suggested, in a note to this section in the Eversley Edition, that the phrase "his living soul" gave the "wrong impression." See also James Knowles, "Aspects of Tennyson: A Personal Reminiscence," *Nineteenth Century* 33 (1893): 164–88. Knowles quotes a comment by Tennyson which suggests that this heightened state did not always have implications beyond the self: "Sometimes . . . I get carried away out of sense and body, and rapt into mere existence, till the accidental touch or movement of one of my own fingers is like a great shock and blow and brings the body back with a terrible start" (reprinted in *Tennyson's Poetry,* ed. Robert W. Hill, Jr. [New York: Norton, 1971], p. 579).

20. Annotation to "In the Valley of Cauteretz," in Tennyson, *Poems*, p. 1123.

21. T. S. Eliot, "In Memoriam," in *Selected Essays* (New York: Harcourt, Brace & World, 1960), p. 292. Eliot's comment that Tennyson was one of those poets who "by some strange accident expresses the mood of his own generation, at the same time that he is expressing a mood of his own which is quite remote from that of his generation" reminds us of Eliot's own claim that "The Waste Land" was nothing more than a personal piece of "rhythmical grumbling."

22. Paull F. Baum, *Tennyson Sixty Years After* (Chapel Hill: University of North Carolina Press, 1948), pp. 306–7.

23. Tennyson, *Poems*, pp. 859–60. Ann C. Colley also notes this comment in *Tennyson and Madness* (Athens: University of Georgia Press, 1983), p. 133.

24. In "Tennyson as a Modern Poet," Arthur Carr points out that Tennyson "shows and hides, as if in embryo, a master theme of Joyce's *Ulysses*—the accentuated and moody self-consciousness and the sense of loss that marks Stephen Dedalus. He forecasts Yeats's interest in the private myth" (*Critical Essays on the Poetry of Tennyson*, ed. John Killham [London: Routledge & Kegan Paul, 1960], p. 42).

25. De Quincey, *Collected Writings* 13:347. From "Suspiria de Profundis."

26. Quoted by W. H. Gardner in *Gerard Manley Hopkins (1844–1889): A Study of Poetic Idiosyncrasy in Relation to Poetic Tradition*, 2 vols. (London: Oxford University Press, 1949), 2:61. Gardner connects Hopkins's idiosyncrasy with Wordsworth and also with Browning, because, as "the late Sir Henry Newbolt pointed out, Browning's technique . . . forced a new diction into the old metres, and thereby brought the everyday moods within the scope of poetry." Hopkins's letter to Baillie appears in *Further Letters of Gerard Manley Hopkins*, ed. C. C. Abbott (London: Oxford University Press, 1938), p. 69.

27. In *Comments on the Spiritual Exercises of St. Ignatius Loyola* (1880), quoted by Rehder, *Wordsworth and Modern Poetry*, p. 213.

28. Seamus Heaney, *The Fire i' the Flint: Reflections on the Poetry of Gerard Manley Hopkins*, Proceedings of the British Academy (London: Oxford University Press, 1974), p. 4. Heaney later quotes Laforgue on the internal source of a poem's meaning: "It cannot be too strongly stated that a poem is not the expression of a feeling that the poet had before he began to write" (p. 8).

29. Number 91 in *The Poems of Gerard Manley Hopkins*, ed. W. H. Gardner and N. H. MacKenzie, 4th ed., rev. and enl. (Oxford: Oxford University Press, 1970). All Hopkins quotations are from this edition.

30. *Sermons and Devotional Writings of Gerard Manley Hopkins*, ed. Christopher Devlin (Oxford: Oxford University Press, 1959), p. 195. See also note to "God's Grandeur" in the Oxford edition.

31. James Scully, ed., *Modern Poetics* (New York: McGraw-Hill, 1965), p. 74.

32. From Hopkins's notebooks, June 19, 1872, quoted by Gardner, *Hopkins* 1:12.

33. John Pick, *A Hopkins Reader*, (London: Oxford University Press, 1953), p. xvi. Pick, in his introduction, offers one of the best discussions of the relationship between "inscape" and "instress."

34. Ludwig Wittgenstein, *Philosophical Investigations*, trans. G. E. M. Anscombe (Oxford: Blackwell, 1972), no. 275, p. 96e.

35. *Letters of Gerard Manley Hopkins to Robert Bridges*, 2d ed., ed. C. C. Abbott (London: Oxford University Press, 1955), pp. 66–67.

36. Pater, "Conclusion" to *Renaissance*, pp. 189, 294n.

37. J. Hillis Miller, *The Disappearance of God: Five Nineteenth Century Writers* (Cambridge: Harvard University Press, Belknap Press, 1979), p. 346. Miller's definition of the Victorian notion of species can be applied to the literary epiphany: "In an evolutionary world species are not eternal types like beads on a string. They are momentary and accidental coagulations of universal matter" (p. 278).

6 Epiphany in Twentieth-Century Poetry

1. See Eliot's "The Perfect Critic," in *Selected Prose*, p. 52.

2. Arthur Symons, *The Symbolist Movement in Literature* (New York: Dutton, 1958), p. 5.

3. Ibid., p. 94.

4. Joyce, *Stephen Hero*, p. 213. Erwin R. Steinberg has recently connected the concept of epiphany with Symons's book. He also suggests that Joyce's use of the term "epiphany" can be compared to the use of the term "luminous" by impressionist painters to describe their attempts to capture evanescent effects of light in momentary visual perceptions. See his chapter "The Sources of the Stream" in *The Stream of Consciousness and Beyond in Ulysses* (Pittsburgh: University of Pittsburgh Press, 1973), pp. 257–76. Steinberg also notes the connection between epiphany and Eliot's "objective correlative," in which specific eternal details evoke a powerful emotion. See also S. L. Goldberg, *The Classical Temper* (London: Chatto & Windus, 1961), pp. 252–53: "The real artistic (and dramatic) unit of Joyce's 'stream of consciousness' writing is the epiphany. What he renders dramatically are minds engaged in the apprehension of epiphanies—the elements of meaning in apprehended life."

5. Ezra Pound, *Pavannes and Divisions* (New York: Knopf, 1918), p. 96. Pound emphasizes a simultaneity that captures a complex idea in an instant in time and renders it up as a single image. Roger

Cardinal has recently connected the concept of epiphany with the oriental forms of imagery which fascinated Pound. Cardinal compares a poem by the Sung Dynasty (A.D. 960–1280) poet Liu Tsung-Yuan to Apollinaire's Joycean claim, "A handkerchief falling to the ground may be for the poet the lever with which he will lift up the universe." Cardinal calls for a new kind of "transparent poetry," which "sees the world as intensified and renewed, not one in which the world is superceded" (*Figures of Reality*, pp. 68, 146–48, 208–24). See also Warner Allen, who quotes from the *Hui Ming Ching* (The Book of Consciousness and Life) to suggest the immediacy and transparency of certain poetic images (*The Timeless Moment* [London: Faber & Faber, 1946], p. 39).

6. Yeats, *Essays and Introductions*, pp. 156–57. Such perceptions, Yeats says, "call down among us certain disembodied powers, whose footsteps over our hearts we call emotions."

7. "William Blake and the Imagination," in ibid., p. 112.

8. W. B. Yeats, *Mythologies* (New York: Macmillan, 1959), pp. 364–65.

9. All references to poems are from *The Collected Poems of W. B. Yeats* (New York: Macmillan, 1956).

10. Yeats, *Mythologies*, p. 362.

11. "If I Were Four-and-Twenty," in *Explorations*, selected by Mrs. W. B. Yeats (London: Macmillan, 1962), p. 263.

12. Yeats, *Mythologies*, p. 361.

13. Yeats, *Collected Poems*, p. 449. Yeats once again cites Blake at this point: "Blake would have said, 'The authors are in eternity,' and I am quite sure they can only be questioned in dreams."

14. Yeats, *Essays and Introductions*, p. 524.

15. Ibid., p. 260.

16. Ibid., p. 494.

17. All citations to Eliot's poetry are from *T. S. Eliot: The Complete Poems and Plays, 1909–1950* (New York: Harcourt, Brace & World, 1971).

18. Denis Donoghue, "T. S. Eliot's *Quartets*: A New Reading," in *Twentieth-Century Poetry: Critical Essays and Documents*, ed. Graham Martin and P. N. Furbank (Milton Keynes: Open University Press, 1975), p. 303. Donoghue draws this phrase from a passage in *Middlemarch*: "If we had a keen vision and a feeling of all ordinary human life, it would be like hearing the grass grow and the squirrel's heart beat, and we should die of that roar which lies on the other side of silence."

19. See Donoghue's discussion of this debate, "Eliot's *Quartets*," pp. 315–19. Kenner's essay "Eliot's Moral Dialectic" first appeared in *Hudson Review* 2, no. 3 (1949): 421–48. Donald Davie's "T. S. Eliot: The End of an Era" can be found in *Twentieth Century* 159, no. 950 (1956): 350–62.

20. "The Noble Rider and the Sound of Words," in Wallace Stevens, *The Necessary Angel: Essays on Reality and the Imagination* (New York: Knopf, 1951), pp. 3–36.

21. "Adagia," in Wallace Stevens, *Opus Posthumous*, ed. Samuel French Morse (New York: Knopf, 1957), pp. 161, 164.

22. Stevens's comments on imagism and surrealism can be found in "Adagia," pp. 161, 177. See John T. Gage, *In the Arresting Eye: The Rhetoric of Imagism* (Baton Rouge: Louisiana State University Press, 1981), p. 132. See also Bergson's *Time and Free Will* (London: Allen & Unwin, 1910), p. 135: "Not all our ideas, however, are thus incorporated in the fluid mass of our conscious states. Many float on the surface, like dead leaves on the water of a pond."

23. All poetry quotations are from *The Collected Poems of Wallace Stevens* (New York: Knopf, 1954).

24. See Ramon Fernandez, *Messages: Literary Essays* (Port Washington, N.Y.: Kennikat Press, 1964), p. 50.

25. Henry W. Wells, *Introduction to Wallace Stevens* (Westport, Conn.: Greenwood Press, 1976), p. 190.

26. Joseph N. Riddel, *The Clairvoyant Eye: The Poetry and Poetics of Wallace Stevens* (Baton Rouge: Louisiana State University Press, 1965), p. 153.

27. "On Poetic Truth," in Stevens, *Opus Posthumous*, p. 238.

28. Seamus Heaney, *Preoccupations: Selected Prose, 1968–1978* (New York: Farrar, Straus & Giroux, 1980), p. 41.

29. All quotations from "Feeling into Words," Heaney, *Preoccupations*, pp. 41–60.

30. Ibid., p. 52.

31. "Glanmore Sonnets" in Seamus Heaney, *Field Work* (New York: Farrar, Straus & Giroux, 1979), p. 33. M. L. Rosenthal and Sally M. Gall have recently cited the Glanmore sonnets in their discussion of the modern poetic sequence. They describe modern lyrics as a new poetic form in which "human intensities are centered in moments of realization, shared in life and art, in which aesthetic conversion becomes possible" (*The Modern Poetic Sequence: The Genius of Modern Poetry* [New York: Oxford University Press, 1983], pp. 18, 327).

32. Letter to author from Seamus Heaney, September 4, 1983.
33. Heaney, "Feeling into Words," p. 48. Heaney quotes Frost on the importance of emotion to inspiration: "A poem begins as a lump in the throat, a homesickness, a lovesickness."
34. Ibid., p. 51.
35. *Seamus Heaney: Poems 1965–1975* (New York: Farrar, Straus & Giroux, 1980). All subsequent quotations are from this edition.

Bibliography

Abrams, M. H. *Natural Supernaturalism: Tradition and Revolution in Romantic Literature.* New York: Norton, 1971.
Allen, Warner. *The Timeless Moment.* London: Faber & Faber, 1946.
Altick, Richard D., and Loucks, James F., II. *Browning's Roman Murder Story: A Reading of "The Ring and the Book."* Chicago: University of Chicago Press, 1968.
Augustine. *Confessions.* Translated by E. B. Pusey. London: Dent & Sons, 1907.
Bachelard, Gaston. *The Poetics of Reverie: Childhood, Language, and the Cosmos.* Translated by Daniel Russell. Boston: Beacon Press, 1969.
———. *The Poetics of Space.* Translated by Maria Jolas. Boston: Beacon Press, 1969.
Baker, Jeffrey. *Time and Mind in Wordsworth's Poetry.* Detroit: Wayne State University Press, 1980.
Baum, Paull F. *Tennyson Sixty Years After.* Chapel Hill: University of North Carolina Press, 1948.
Beck, Warren. *Joyce's Dubliners: Substance, Vision, and Art.* Durham: Duke University Press, 1969.
Beer, John. *Wordsworth in Time.* London: Faber & Faber, 1979.
Beja, Morris. *Epiphany in the Modern Novel.* Seattle: University of Washington Press, 1971.
Bergson, Henri. *Matter and Memory.* Translated by Nancy Margaret Paul and W. Scott Palmer. New York: Macmillan, 1911.
———. *Time and Free Will: An Essay on the Immediate Data of Consciousness.* Translated by F. L. Pogson. London: Allen & Unwin, 1910.
Bidney, Martin. "The Structure of Epiphanic Imagery in Ten Coleridge Lyrics." *Studies in Romanticism* 22, no. 1 (1983): 29–40.
Bloom, Harold. *The Visionary Company.* Ithaca: Cornell University Press, 1971.
———. "The Witch of Atlas." In *Shelley: Modern Judgements,* edited by R. B. Woodings. London: Macmillan, 1968.

Brown, Merle E. *Wallace Stevens: The Poem as Act*. Detroit: Wayne State University Press, 1970.

Browning, Robert. *The Letters of Robert Browning and Elizabeth Barrett Browning*. Edited by Elvan Kintner. Cambridge: Harvard University Press, Belknap Press, 1969.

———. *Robert Browning and Julia Wedgwood: A Broken Friendship as Revealed by Their Letters*. Edited by Richard Curle. New York: Stokes, 1937.

———. *The Works of Robert Browning*. 1912. Centenary Edition, edited by F. G. Kenyon. New York: Barnes & Noble, 1966.

Buckler, William E. *The Victorian Imagination: Essays in Aesthetic Exploration*. New York: New York University Press, 1980.

Buckley, Jerome H. *Tennyson: The Growth of a Poet*. Cambridge: Harvard University Press, 1960.

———. *The Triumph of Time: A Study of the Victorian Concepts of Time, History, Progress, and Decadence*. Cambridge: Harvard University Press, 1966.

Bunyan, John. *Grace Abounding to the Chief of Sinners*. 1666. Everyman edition. London: Dent & Sons; New York: Dutton, 1976.

Burke, Edmund. *A Philosophical Enquiry into the Origin of Our Ideas of the Sublime and Beautiful*. 1759. Edited by J. T. Boulton. London: Routledge & Kegan Paul, 1958.

Cadbury, William. "Lyric and Anti-Lyric Forms: A Method for Judging Browning." In *Browning's Mind and Art*, edited by Clarence Tracy. London: Oliver & Boyd, 1968.

Cardinal, Roger. *Figures of Reality: A Perspective on the Poetic Imagination*. Totowa, N.J.: Barnes & Noble, 1981.

Carlyle, Thomas. *Sartor Resartus*. 1833. New York: Odyssey Press, 1937.

Carr, Arthur. "Tennyson as a Modern Poet." In *Critical Essays on the Poetry of Tennyson*, edited by John Killham. London: Routledge & Kegan Paul, 1960.

Chadwick, Owen. *The Secularization of the European Mind in the Nineteenth Century*. Cambridge: Cambridge University Press, 1975.

Chiari, Joseph. *Realism and Imagination*. London: Barrie & Rockliff, 1960.

Christ, Carol T. *The Finer Optic: The Aesthetic of Particularity in Victorian Poetry*. New Haven: Yale University Press, 1975.

———. *Victorian and Modern Poetics*. Chicago: University of Chicago Press, 1984.

Clark, Kenneth. *Moments of Vision*. Oxford: Clarendon Press, 1954.

Bibliography

Clausen, Christopher. "Poetry in a Discouraging Time." *Georgia Review* 34, no. 4 (1981): 703–16.

Coleridge, Samuel Taylor. *Biographia Literaria*. 2 vols. Edited by J. Shawcross. Oxford: Oxford University Press, 1965.

———. *Poetical Works*. Edited by Ernest Hartley Coleridge. Oxford: Oxford University Press, 1969.

Colley, Ann C. *Tennyson and Madness*. Athens: University of Georgia Press, 1983.

Collins, Philip. "Tennyson In and Out of Time." In *Studies in Tennyson*, edited by Hallam Tennyson. London: Macmillan, 1981.

Cornwell, Edith F. *The "Still Point": Theme and Variation in the Writings of T. S. Eliot, Coleridge, Yeats, Henry James, Virginia Woolf, and D. H. Lawrence*. New Brunswick: Rutgers University Press, 1962.

Culler, A. Dwight. *The Poetry of Tennyson*. New Haven: Yale University Press, 1977.

Culler, Jonathan. *Structuralist Poetics: Structuralism, Linguistics, and the Study of Literature*. London: Routledge & Kegan Paul, 1975.

Davie, Donald. "T. S. Eliot: The End of an Era." *Twentieth Century* 159, no. 950 (1956): 350–62.

De Quincey, Thomas. *The Collected Writings*. Edited by David Masson. London: Black, 1896–97.

de Sanctis, Sante. *Religious Conversion*. Translated by Helen Auger. New York: Harcourt, Brace, 1927.

DeVane, William Clyde. *A Browning Handbook*. 2d ed. New York: Appleton, 1955.

———. "Robert Browning." In *The Victorian Poets: A Guide to Research*, edited by Frederick E. Faverty. Cambridge: Harvard University Press, 1956.

Donoghue, Denis. "T. S. Eliot's *Quartets:* A New Reading." In *Twentieth-Century Poetry: Critical Essays and Documents*, edited by Graham Martin and P. N. Furbank. Milton Keynes: Open University Press, 1975.

Edinger, Edward F. *Ego and Archetype*. Middlesex: Penguin Books, 1973.

Eliot, T. S. *Selected Essays*. New York: Harcourt, Brace & World, 1960.

———. *Selected Prose of T. S. Eliot*. Edited by Frank Kermode. New York: Harcourt, Brace, Jovanovich; Farrar, Straus & Giroux, 1975.

_____. *T. S. Eliot: The Complete Poems and Plays, 1909–1950.* New York: Harcourt, Brace & World, 1971.

Emerson, Ralph Waldo. *The Early Lectures of Ralph Waldo Emerson.* Edited by Robert E. Spiller and Wallace E. Williams. Cambridge, Mass.: Harvard University Press, Belknap Press, 1972.

_____. "Shakespeare; or, The Poet." In *English Critical Essays: Nineteenth Century,* edited by Edmund D. Jones. Oxford: Oxford University Press, 1971.

Engell, James. *The Creative Imagination: Enlightenment to Romanticism.* Cambridge: Harvard University Press, 1981.

Flowers, Betty S. *Browning and the Modern Tradition.* London: Macmillan, 1976.

Frazer, James. *The Golden Bough: A Study in Magic and Religion.* 1922. Abr. ed. New York: Macmillan, 1958.

Frye, Northrop, *Anatomy of Criticism.* Princeton: Princeton University Press, 1971.

_____. *Fearful Symmetry: A Study of William Blake.* Princeton: Princeton University Press, 1947.

_____. *A Study of English Romanticism.* Brighton, Sussex: Harvester Press, 1983.

Gage, John T. *In the Arresting Eye: The Rhetoric of Imagism.* Baton Rouge: Louisiana State University Press, 1981.

Garber, Frederick. *Thoreau's Redemptive Imagination.* New York: New York University Press, 1977.

Gardner, W. H. *Gerard Manley Hopkins (1844–1889): A Study of Poetic Idiosyncrasy in Relation to Poetic Tradition.* 2 vols. London: Oxford University Press, 1949.

Gilkey, Langdon. *Naming the Whirlwind: The Renewal of God Language.* New York: Bobbs-Merrill, 1969.

Goldberg, S. L. *The Classical Temper.* London: Chatto & Windus, 1961.

Guggenheimer, Richard. *Creative Vision in Artist and Audience.* New York: Harper, 1950.

Harding, Rosamond E. M. *An Anatomy of Inspiration.* Cambridge: Cambridge University Press, 1940.

Hartman, Geoffrey. "Toward Literary History." In *Beyond Formalism: Literary Essays, 1958–1970.* New Haven: Yale University Press, 1970.

_____. *Wordsworth's Poetry, 1787–1814.* New Haven: Yale University Press, 1964.

Heaney, Seamus. *Field Work.* New York: Farrar, Straus & Giroux, 1979.

―――. *The Fire i' the Flint: Reflections on the Poetry of Gerard Manley Hopkins*. Proceedings of the British Academy. London: Oxford University Press, 1974.

―――. *Poems, 1965–1975*. New York: Farrar, Straus & Giroux, 1980.

―――. *Preoccupations: Selected Prose, 1968–1978*. New York: Farrar, Straus & Giroux, 1980.

Hendry, Irene. "Joyce's Epiphanies." *Sewanee Review* 54 (1946): 449–67.

Honan, Park. *Browning's Characters*. New Haven: Yale University Press, 1961.

Hopkins, Gerard Manley. *Letters of Gerard Manley Hopkins to Robert Bridges*. 2d ed. Edited by C. C. Abbott. London: Oxford University Press, 1955.

―――. *The Poems of Gerard Manley Hopkins*. 4th ed., rev. and enl. Edited by W. H. Gardner and N. H. MacKenzie. Oxford: Oxford University Press, 1970.

Houghton, Walter E. *The Victorian Frame of Mind: 1830– 1870*. New Haven: Yale University Press, 1957.

Hume, David. *A Treatise of Human Nature*. Edited by L. A. Selby-Bigge. Oxford: Clarendon Press, 1888.

James, William. *The Varieties of Religious Experience*. New York: Longmans Green, 1902.

Jauss, Hans Robert. *Aesthetic Experience and Literary Hermeneutics*. Translated by Michael Shaw. Minneapolis: University of Minnesota Press, 1982.

Johnson, E. D. H. "*In Memoriam:* The Way of the Poet." *Victorian Studies* 2 (1958): 139–48.

Johnston, Kenneth. "The Idiom of Vision." In *New Perspectives on Coleridge and Wordsworth*, edited by Geoffrey H. Hartman. New York: Columbia University Press, 1972.

Joyce, James. "Epiphanies." In *The Workshop of Daedalus: James Joyce and the Raw Materials for "A Portrait of the Artist as a Young Man,"* edited by Robert Scholes and Richard M. Kain. Evanston, Ill.: Northwestern University Press, 1965.

―――. *A Portrait of the Artist as a Young Man*. New York: Viking Penguin, 1967.

―――. *Stephen Hero*. New York: New Directions, 1963.

Jump, John. "Tennyson's Religious Faith and Doubt." In *Tennyson*, edited by D. J. Palmer. London: G. Bell, 1973.

Jung, C. G. *The Structure and Dynamics of the Psyche*. Vol. 8 of *Collected Works*. Princeton: Princeton University Press, 1960.

Keats, John. *Letters of John Keats*. Edited by Robert Gittings. Oxford: Oxford University Press, 1970.
Kenner, Hugh. "Eliot's Moral Dialectic." *Hudson Review* 2, no. 3 (1949): 421–48.
Kermode, Frank. *The Sense of an Ending: Studies in the Theory of Fiction*. New York: Oxford University Press, 1967.
Kierkegaard, Søren. *Concluding Unscientific Postscript*. Translated by David F. Swenson and Walter Lowrie. Princeton: Princeton University Press, 1944.
Kincaid, James R. *Tennyson's Major Poems*. New Haven: Yale University Press, 1975.
King, Roma A., Jr. *The Focusing Artifice: The Poetry of Robert Browning*. Athens: Ohio University Press, 1968.
Knowles, James. "Aspects of Tennyson: A Personal Reminiscence." *Nineteenth Century* 33 (1893): 164–88.
Kroeber, Karl. *Romantic Narrative Art*. Madison: University of Wisconsin Press, 1960.
Langbaum, Robert. "Hardy, Frost, and the Question of Modern Poetry." *Virginia Quarterly Review* 58, no. 1 (1982): 69–80.
―――. *The Poetry of Experience*. 1957. Rev. ed. New York: Norton, 1971.
―――. "Wordsworth and the Epiphanic Mode in Modern Poetry." *New Literary History* 14, no. 2 (1983): 335–58.
Lee, Umphrey. *John Wesley and Modern Religion*. Nashville: Cokesbury Press, 1936.
Lewin, Bertram D. *The Image and the Past*. New York: International Universities Press, 1968.
Lindenberger, Herbert. *On Wordsworth's "Prelude."* Princeton: Princeton University Press, 1963.
Loder, James. *The Transforming Moment: Understanding Convictional Experiences*. San Francisco: Harper & Row, 1981.
Lowes, John Livingston. *The Road to Xanadu: A Study in the Ways of the Imagination*. Boston: Houghton Mifflin, 1927.
Macquarrie, John. *God-Talk: An Examination of the Language and Logic of Theology*. New York: Harper & Row, 1967.
Martin, Loy D. *Browning's Dramatic Monologues and the Post-Romantic Subject*. Baltimore: Johns Hopkins University Press, 1985.
―――. "The Inside of Time: An Essay on the Dramatic Monologue." In *Robert Browning: A Collection of Critical Essays*, edited by Harold Bloom and Adrienne Munich. Englewood Cliffs, N.J.: Prentice-Hall, 1979.

Martin, Robert Bernard. *Tennyson: The Unquiet Heart*. Oxford: Clarendon Press, 1980.

Mellor, Anne K. *English Romantic Irony*. Cambridge: Harvard University Press, 1980.

Moore, Carlisle. "Faith, Doubt, and Mystical Experience in 'In Memoriam.'" *Victorian Studies* 7 (1963): 155–69.

Miller, J. Hillis. *The Disappearance of God: Five Nineteenth-Century Writers*. Cambridge: Harvard University Press, Belknap Press, 1963.

———. *The Linguistic Moment: From Wordsworth to Stevens*. Princeton: Princeton University Press, 1985.

Myerhoff, Hans. *Time in Literature*. Berkeley: University of California Press, 1960.

Newsome, David. *Two Classes of Men: Platonism and English Romantic Thought*. London: Murray, 1974.

Nock, A. D. *Conversion: The Old and the New in Religion from Alexander the Great to Augustine of Hippo*. Oxford: Oxford University Press, 1933.

Noon, William T. *Joyce and Aquinas*. New Haven: Yale University Press, 1957.

Nuttall, A. D. *A Common Sky: Philosophy and the Literary Imagination*. London: Chatto & Windus, 1974.

Olney, James. *Metaphors of Self: The Meaning of Autobiography*. Princeton: Princeton University Press, 1972.

———, ed. *Autobiography: Essays Theoretical and Critical*. Princeton: Princeton University Press, 1980.

Otto, Rudolf. *The Idea of the Holy*. 1923. Translated by John W. Harvey. London: Oxford University Press, 1957.

Paffard, Michael. *Inglorious Wordsworths*. London: Hodder & Stoughton, 1973.

Palmer, D. J. "Tennyson's Romantic Heritage." In *Tennyson*, edited by D. J. Palmer. London: Bell & Sons, 1973.

Pater, Walter. *The Renaissance: Studies in Art and Poetry*. 1893. Edited by Donald L. Hill. Berkeley: University of California Press, 1980.

Patrides, C. A. *Aspects of Time*. Manchester: Manchester University Press, 1976.

Peake, C. H. *James Joyce: The Citizen as Artist*. London: Arnold, 1977.

Phillips, John L., Jr. *Piaget's Theory: A Primer*. San Francisco: Freeman, 1981.

Piaget, J. *The Child's Conception of Space.* 1948. Translated by F. J. Langdon and J. L. Lunzer. New York: Norton, 1956.
———. *Memory and Intelligence.* 1968. Translated by A. J. Pomerans. New York: Basic Books, 1972.
Pick, John. *A Hopkins Reader.* London: Oxford University Press, 1953.
Poulet, Georges. *Studies in Human Time.* Translated by Elliott Coleman. Baltimore: Johns Hopkins University Press, 1956.
Pound, Ezra. *Pavannes and Divisions.* New York: Knopf, 1918.
Preyer, Robert. "Tennyson as an Oracular Poet." *Modern Philology* 55 (1958): 239–51.
Prickett, Stephen. *Coleridge and Wordsworth: The Poetry of Growth.* Cambridge: Cambridge University Press, 1970.
Pynchon, Thomas. *Gravity's Rainbow.* New York: Bantam Books, 1974.
Raymond, William O. *The Infinite Moment and Other Essays in Robert Browning.* Toronto: University of Toronto Press, 1950.
Reardon, B. M. G. *Religious Thought in the Nineteenth Century.* Cambridge: Cambridge University Press, 1966.
Rehder, Robert. *Wordsworth and the Beginnings of Modern Poetry.* Totowa, N.J.: Barnes & Noble, 1981.
Reiman, Donald H. "Structure, Symbol, and Theme in 'Lines Written among the Euganean Hills.'" *PMLA* 77 (1962): 404–13.
———. "Wordsworth, Shelley, and Romantic Inheritance." *Romanticism Past and Present* 5, no. 2 (1981): 1–22.
Ricoeur, Paul. *The Symbolism of Evil.* Translated by Emerson Buchanan. Boston: Beacon Press, 1967.
Riddel, Joseph N. *The Clairvoyant Eye: The Poetry and Poetics of Wallace Stevens.* Baton Rouge: Louisiana State University Press, 1965.
Roppen, George. *Evolution and Poetic Belief.* 1956. Oxford: Blackwell, 1978.
Rosenthal, M. L., and Gall, Sally M. *The Modern Poetic Sequence: The Genius of Modern Poetry.* New York: Oxford University Press, 1983.
Rousseau, J. J. *The Confessions of J. J. Rousseau.* 1767. Translated by W. Conyngham Mallory. New York: Tudor Publishing, 1935.
———. *La Nouvelle Héloïse: Julie, or the New Heloise.* 1761. Translated by Judith McDowell. University Park: Pennsylvania State University Press, 1968.

----. *The Reveries of a Solitary Walker.* Translated by Charles E. Butterworth. New York: New York University Press, 1979.

Rutherford, Mark. *The Autobiography of Mark Rutherford, Dissenting Minister.* Edited by Reuben Shapcott and published pseudonymously. London: Trubner, 1881. Reprint. New York: Garland Publishing, 1976.

Ryskamp, Charles. "Wordsworth's Lyrical Ballads in Their Time." In *From Sensibility to Romanticism,* edited by Frederick W. Hilles and Harold Bloom. New York: Oxford University Press, 1965.

Salaman, Ester. *A Collection of Moments: A Study of Involuntary Memories.* London: Longmans, 1970.

Salvesen, Christopher. *The Landscape of Memory: A Study of Wordsworth's Poetry.* Lincoln: University of Nebraska Press, 1965.

Schenk, H. G. *The Mind of the European Romantics.* 1966. Rev. ed. Oxford: Oxford University Press, 1979.

Schug, Charles. *The Romantic Genesis of the Modern Novel.* Pittsburgh: University of Pittsburgh Press, 1979.

Scully, James, ed. *Modern Poetics.* New York: McGraw-Hill, 1965.

Shelley, P. B. *Shelley's Poetry and Prose.* Edited by Donald H. Reiman and Sharon B. Powers. New York: Norton, 1977.

Sherry, Charles. *Wordsworth's Poetry of the Imagination.* Oxford: Clarendon Press, 1980.

Sinfield, Alan. *The Language of Tennyson's "In Memoriam."* Oxford: Blackwell, 1971.

Smith, Brian. *Memory.* London: Allen & Unwin, 1966.

Spencer, Theodore. "*Stephen Hero:* The Unpublished Manuscript of James Joyce's *Portrait of the Artist as a Young Man.*" *Southern Review* 7, no. 1 (1941): 174–86.

Steinberg, Erwin R. *The Stream of Consciousness and Beyond in Ulysses.* Pittsburgh: University of Pittsburgh Press, 1973.

Stevens, Wallace. *The Collected Poems of Wallace Stevens.* New York: Knopf, 1954.

----. *The Necessary Angel: Essays on Reality and the Imagination.* New York: Knopf, 1951.

----. *Opus Posthumous.* Edited by Samuel French Morse. New York: Knopf, 1957.

Symons, Arthur. *The Symbolist Movement in Literature.* 1899. New York: Dutton, 1958.

Tennyson, Alfred. *In Memoriam.* Edited by Robert H. Ross. New York: Norton, 1973.

―――. *The Poems of Tennyson.* Edited by Christopher Ricks. London: Longmans, 1969.
Tennyson, Hallam. *Alfred, Lord Tennyson: A Memoir.* 2 vols. New York: Macmillan, 1897.
Thorpe, Clarence DeWitt. "Coleridge on the Sublime." In *Wordsworth and Coleridge,* edited by Earl Leslie Griggs. New York: Russell & Russell, 1962.
Tillich, Paul. *Dynamics of Faith.* New York: Harper & Row, 1958.
Toulmin, Stephen, and Goodfield, June. *The Discovery of Time.* New York: Harper & Row, 1965.
Trosse, George. *The Life of the Reverend Mr. George Trosse: Written by Himself and Published Posthumously according to His Order in 1714.* Edited by A. W. Brink. Montreal: McGill-Queen's University Press, 1974.
Tucker, Herbert F., Jr. *Browning's Beginnings: The Art of Disclosure.* Minneapolis: University of Minnesota Press, 1980.
van der Leeuw, G. *Religion in Essence and Manifestation.* 2 vols. Translated by J. E. Turner. Gloucester, Mass.: Peter Smith, 1967.
von Franz, M.-L. "Time and Synchronicity in Analytic Psychology." In *The Voices of Time,* edited by J. T. Fraser. Amherst: University of Massachusetts Press, 1981.
Wasserman, Earl R. *Shelley: A Critical Reading.* Baltimore: Johns Hopkins University Press, 1971.
Weiskel, Thomas. *The Romantic Sublime: Studies in the Structure and Psychology of Transcendence.* Baltimore: Johns Hopkins University Press, 1976.
Wells, Henry W. *Introduction to Wallace Stevens.* Westport, Conn.: Greenwood Press, 1976.
Wesley, John. *Journal.* 8 vols. Edited by Nehemiah Curnock. London: Epworth Press, 1909–16.
―――. *The Letters of John Wesley.* 8 vols. Edited by John Telford. London: Epworth Press, 1931.
Willey, Basil. *The Eighteenth-Century Background.* London: Chatto & Windus, 1940.
―――. "In Memoriam." In *More Nineteenth-Century Studies: A Group of Honest Doubters.* London: Chatto & Windus, 1956.
―――. *The Seventeenth-Century Background: Studies of the Thought of the Age in Relation to Poetry and Religion.* New York: Doubleday, 1934.

Bibliography

Wittgenstein, Ludwig. *Philosophical Investigations.* Translated by G. E. M. Anscombe. Oxford: Blackwell, 1972.

Wordsworth, Dorothy. *Journals of Dorothy Wordsworth.* Edited by Mary Moorman. Oxford: Oxford University Press, 1971.

Wordsworth, Jonathan. "As with the Silence of the Thought." In *High Romantic Argument: Essays in Honor of M. H. Abrams,* edited by Lawrence Lipking. Ithaca: Cornell University Press, 1981.

———. *William Wordsworth: The Borders of Vision.* Oxford: Clarendon Press, 1982.

Wordsworth, William. *Letters of William and Dorothy Wordsworth.* 3 vols. Edited by E. de Selincourt, revised by Chester L. Shaver. Oxford: Clarendon Press, 1967.

———. *The Poetical Works of William Wordsworth.* 5 vols. Edited by E. de Selincourt and Helen Darbishire. Oxford: Clarendon Press, 1940–49.

———. *The Prelude: 1799, 1805, 1850.* Edited by Jonathan Wordsworth, M. H. Abrams, and Stephen Gill. New York: Norton, 1979.

———. *The Prose Works of William Wordsworth.* 3 vols. Edited by W. J. B. Owen and Jane Worthington Smyser. Oxford: Clarendon Press, 1974.

Yeats, W. B. *The Collected Poems of W. B. Yeats.* New York: Macmillan, 1956.

———. *Essays and Introductions.* New York: Collier Books, 1968.

———. *Explorations.* Selected by Mrs. W. B. Yeats. London: Macmillan, 1962.

———. *Mythologies.* New York: Macmillan, 1959.

Zaehner, R. C. *Mysticism, Sacred and Profane: An Inquiry into Some Varieties of Praeternatural Experience.* Oxford: Clarendon Press, 1957.

Index

Abrams, M. H., 3, 8, 213 (n. 7)
Accident (coincidence), 32–33, 35, 37–38, 54, 69, 81–82, 127, 149, 159, 161, 165, 172, 182, 185, 188, 205–06, 219 (n. 49), 229 (n. 23). *See also* Randomness
Altick, Richard, 136
Ambiguity, 45, 59, 139, 148. *See also* Indeterminacy of meaning
Aphrodite (Venus), 209
Apocalypse, 2, 75, 109, 119, 142, 150
Apollinaire, Guillaume, 235 (n. 5)
Aquinas, Thomas, 10–12, 168
Arnold, Matthew, 4–5, 30, 33, 117–18; "The Buried Life," 117; "A Dream," 118; "To a Gipsy Child by the Sea-Shore," 118; "Mortality," 118; "Rugby Chapel," 172–73; "The Strayed Reveller," 118
Association (of ideas), 11, 26, 43, 53, 57, 72, 84, 86, 88, 92, 101, 114, 116, 122, 126, 138, 177, 183, 185, 206
Augustine, Saint, 3, 14–19, 30, 40, 64, 191
Autobiography, 16–17, 19, 38–39, 46, 49–50, 59, 86, 97, 109, 114, 139, 143, 147, 154
Avatar, 6, 193

Bachelard, Gaston, 41, 213 (n.1), 221 (n. 10)
Baker, Carlos, 61, 224 (n. 36)
Baum, Paull F., 163
Beer, John, 24, 217 (n. 39)
Beja, Morris, 3
Beresford, Anne, 1
Bergson, Henri, 131, 229 (n. 20), 236 (n. 22)
Berkeley, George, 22, 226 (n. 22)

Bidney, Martin, 1, 213 (n. 1)
Blake, William, 3, 184, 186, 218 (n. 45), 230 (n. 26)
Bloom, Harold, 91, 95, 102, 226 (n. 18)
Bradley, F. H., 196
British Quarterly Review, 39
Browning, Elizabeth Barrett, 109, 114, 139
Browning, Robert, 4, 29–30, 107–43, 152–53, 155, 166, 170, 172, 174, 186, 190, 193, 197, 201, 211–12; "Abt Vogler," 110, 120, 139; "Andrea del Sarto," 110, 120; "Bishop Blougram's Apology," 111; "By the Fireside," 114–16, 139, 152, 164, 203; "Childe Roland to the Dark Tower Came," 109, 142, 176; "Cristina," 110–11; "Fra Lippo Lippi," 108, 110, 120; "infinite moment," 5, 22, 31, 82, 98, 129, 148–49, 170, 190; "Love among the Ruins," 112, 201; "My Last Duchess," 112; "Meeting at Night—Parting at Morning," 112; "Now," 120; "One Word More," 114; "Pictor Ignotus," 110; "Porphyria's Lover," 111; "Rabbi Ben Ezra," 115; *The Ring and the Book*, 122–41, 168; "Sordello," 116; "A Toccata of Galuppi's," 110; "Two in the Campagna," 113
Buckler, William, 131
Buckley, Jerome H., 111, 121, 147
Bunyan, John, 17–19
Burke, Edmund, 73
Byron, George Gordon, 30

Campbell, Oscar, 85
Cardinal, Roger, 1, 235 (n. 5)
Carlyle, Thomas, 26, 119
Characterization, 107–08, 120, 123

250

Index

Chekov, Anton, 2, 121
Chiari, Joseph, 224 (n. 35)
Childhood, 51, 55, 57–60, 62, 70–71, 73, 89, 219 (n. 49)
Christ, Carol T., 30, 108, 119, 219 (n. 47)
Claritas, 10, 12, 169
Clark, Kenneth, 214 (n. 7)
Clausen, Christopher, 122
Coincidence. *See* Accident
Coleridge, Ernest Hartley, 83
Coleridge, Hartley, 91
Coleridge, Samuel Taylor, 4–5, 25–28, 30, 36, 38, 49, 53, 59, 66, 71, 80, 95, 97–98, 124, 128, 132, 153, 155, 166, 174, 186, 211–12, 213 (n. 2), 226 (n. 17); "Apologia Pro Vita Sua," 81; "Christabel," 30, 84; "Frost at Midnight," 84–93, 101–02, 164; "Kubla Khan," 84; "Limbo," 92; "To Nature," 84; "The Pains of Sleep," 92; "Phantom," 82; "Phantom or Fact," 83; "Religious Musings," 187; "Rime of the Ancient Mariner," 81–82, 84; "Sonnet: Composed on a Journey Homeward," 83; "Time, Real and Imaginary," 25
Collins, Philip, 157
Comte, Auguste, 133
Conrad, Joseph, 107, 121, 214 (n. 7)
Consciousness, 3, 8, 13, 22, 24–25, 47, 58, 69, 75, 90, 155, 184, 199, 226 (n. 17); elevations of, 78, 88, 101, 132, 135, 154, 162, 180–82; subconscious, 37–38, 186, 193, 207
Conversion, 4, 14, 16, 27, 156
Crashaw, Richard, 175
Culler, A. Dwight, 146
Culler, Jonathan, 1, 213 (n. 2)

Daimon, 184–85
Darwin, Charles, 132–33
Davie, Donald, 192
Decadents, 141, 182–83
De Quincey, Thomas, 32, 37, 53, 165
Descartes, René, 44
DeVane, William Clyde, 114
Dickens, Charles, 123
Dionysius, 6

Divinity, 6–8, 23, 184, 190; defined in human terms, 43, 67, 130–31, 156–57, 204, 209
Donne, John, 175
Dostoevsky, Feodor, 225 (n. 5)
Dramatic monologue, 30–31, 107–08, 117, 120, 123–24, 130–41
Dreams, 32, 59, 72, 77, 83–84, 88, 96, 115, 118, 133, 195, 235 (n. 13)

Eclectic Review, 38
Edinger, Edward, 58
Edwards, Jonathan, 17
Eliot, George, 123, 235 (n. 18)
Eliot, T. S., 107, 121–22, 138, 141, 147, 157, 167, 181–82, 190–98, 202, 205; "Burnt Norton," 191; "The Dry Salvages," 192–94; *Four Quartets*, 163, 190; "Little Gidding," 194, 197; objective correlative, 30, 63; "The Waste Land," 232 (n. 21)
Elisha, 123, 126
Emerson, Ralph Waldo, 8–9, 169, 208, 215 (n. 15)
Emotion: distinguished from interpretation, 121, 148, 171, 191; heightened by memory, 67; intensifies experience, 26, 40–43, 46–47, 73, 84–85, 96, 111, 201, 203; linked to perception, 5, 14, 52, 93, 95, 152, 183–84; and objective correlative, 63; and poetry, 38, 76, 90–91, 122, 180, 201
Empiricism, 20, 23, 60, 97, 105, 121
Engell, James, 44, 221 (n. 13)
Epicurus, 74–75
Epiphany: accidental, 4; adelonic, 75, 77, 92, 121; benedictional, 75, 80, 135; demonic, 2; epiphanic imagination, 34, 87, 90, 107, 122, 135, 143, 163, 203; fearful, 56, 58, 62, 68, 75, 80, 83, 135, 209, 211; ironic, 11–12, 215 (n. 18); of loss, 118; negative, 99, 118; memory, 62; phainein, 5, 84, 165; proleptic, 74, 92, 121. *See also* chapter titles in table of contents
Euripides, 6
Evolution, 132, 234 (n. 37)

251

Index

Examiner, 47
Ezekiel, 13, 218 (n. 45)

Fantasy, 5, 71, 83–84, 96, 101, 170
Faulkner, William, 3, 123, 141, 214 (n. 7)
Fernandez, Ramon, 200
Flaubert, Gustave, 11
Flowers, Betty, 132, 229 (n. 21)
Frazer, James G., 7, 192
Freud, Sigmund, 225 (n. 5)
Frost, Robert, 237 (n. 33)
Frye, Northrop, 2, 144, 155, 213 (n. 4)

Galvani, Luigi, 124
Galvanism, 124, 229 (n. 18)
Gilkey, Langdon, 218 (n. 46)
Godwin, William, 84
Goethe, Johann Wolfgang von, 26
Goodfield, June, 132
Graham's Magazine, 39
Graves, Robert, 206
Guggenheimer, Richard, 227 (n. 30)

Haecceitas, 168
Hallam, Arthur Henry, 110, 152–53, 156–58, 161–62, 164
Hardy, Thomas: "The Darkling Thrush," 176; "Moments of Vision," 181; "In Time of 'The Breaking of Nations'", 201
Hartley, David, 89
Hartman, Geoffrey, 3–4, 64, 214 (n. 9)
Hazlitt, William, 36, 45
Heaney, Seamus, 29, 121, 166, 181, 204–12; "Bogland," 207; "Digging," 207; "Exposure," 211; "Death of a Naturalist," 211; "Feeling into Words," 204; "Fosterage," 208; "Girls Bathing, Galway 1965," 209; "Glanmore Sonnets," 207; "Personal Helicon," 211; "Vision," 210
Hegel, George Wilhelm Friedrich, 133, 222 (n. 21)
Hendry, Irene, 11
Heraclitus, 203
Herbert, George, 175
Herodotus, 6
Hierophany, 218 (n. 46)

History, 21, 116, 123, 126–27, 132–33, 192–93, 229 (n. 22)
Hölderlin, Friedrich, 26
Hopkins, Gerard Manley, 4, 138, 157, 166–81, 190, 192, 196–98, 202, 205, 215 (n. 18); "Ashboughs," 179; "The Candle Indoors," 171–72; "Carrion Comfort," 177; "Il Mystico," 170; "I wake and feel the fell of dark," 178; "The Lantern out of Doors," 172; "Nondum," 180; "No worst, there is none," 177; "The Starlight Night," 170; "To seem the stranger lies my lot," 177–78; "The Windhover," 175; "Winter with the Gulf Stream," 175
Houghton, Walter, 131
Hume, David, 22–23, 40, 43, 89, 91, 185, 217 (n. 36)
Huxley, Thomas Henry, 133

Iliad, 6
Illumination, 8, 10, 24, 32, 67, 90, 97, 101, 109, 135, 163, 188, 192, 200
Imagination, 2, 9, 11, 21, 34, 36, 43, 59, 64, 67, 74, 79, 97, 104–05, 125, 131, 146, 158, 163, 182
Imagism, 128, 182–83, 199
Imouthes, 6
Indeterminacy of meaning, 4, 17, 20, 28, 30, 33, 52, 56, 74, 80, 93, 121–22, 125–26, 152, 165, 177, 180, 200, 212. *See also* Ambiguity
Inspiration, 2–4, 13, 15, 30, 95, 134, 167, 191; reversal of traditional, 190
Interpretation: distinguished from emotion, 191–92; distinguished from perception, 82, 91, 110, 115, 143, 168, 171, 175; indeterminacy of, 73, 77, 87, 113, 147, 163; in modern literary epiphany, 16–17; multiplicity of, 27, 29, 33–34, 138; in Puritan autobiography, 18; and role of reader, 130; in traditional inspiration, 13–15
Isaiah, 180, 218 (n. 45)
Istrus, 6

James, Henry, 107, 214 (n. 7), 226 (n. 26)
James, William, 132, 231 (n. 7)

252

Index

Jauss, Hans Robert, 110, 228 (n. 7)
Jeremiah, 13–14
Jesus, 14–17, 19, 30, 139, 171, 174–75, 196
Johnson, E. D. H., 156
Johnston, Kenneth, 223 (n. 30)
Joyce, James, 1–11, 27, 32, 34, 43, 61, 68, 75, 78, 82, 92–93, 103–07, 114, 116, 120, 123, 125, 141, 158, 165, 181–82, 185, 206; *Dubliners*, 216 (n. 18); "Epiphanies," 10, 35, 70, 190; *Finnegans Wake*, 10; *A Portrait of the Artist as a Young Man*, 9–10; *Stephen Hero*, 1–2, 8, 10, 12, 108; *Ulysses*, 164, 233 (n. 24)
Joyce, Stanislaus, 215 (n. 18)
Jump, John, 156
Jung, Carl Gustav, 31–32, 192, 219 (n. 49)

Keats, John, 3–5, 20, 26–27, 30, 38, 47–48, 71, 128, 145, 153, 161, 174
Kenner, Hugh, 192
Kermode, Frank, 24, 30
Kierkegaard, Søren, 147, 150
Kincaid, James, 152
King, Roma, 113
Kroeber, Karl, 223 (n. 30)

Laforgue, Jules, 233 (n. 28)
Langbaum, Robert, 1, 3, 213 (n. 3)
Language, 5, 10, 31–34, 40, 46, 90, 96–97, 165, 167, 184, 212
Lawrence, D. H., 31, 80, 121, 123
Leibniz, Gottfried Wilhelm von, 44
Locke, John, 22–23, 43, 91, 185
Loucks, James, 136
Lowes, John Livingston, 85
Lyric, 1, 5, 30–31, 49, 117, 122, 216 (n. 19)

McDowell, Judith, 41
Magic, 99, 102
Magician, 7, 102, 123, 163–64
Magus (magi), 34, 123, 186
Mallarmé, Stéphane, 182
Mann, Thomas, 3
Martin, Loy D., 227 (n. 1), 230 (n. 25)
Martin, Robert B., 146
Marx, Karl, 133, 230 (n. 25)

Maurice, Frederick Denison, 47
Mellor, Anne, 227 (n. 26)
Memory, 21, 24–25, 31, 40–41, 46, 57, 58, 61, 65, 70, 74, 85, 88, 91, 161
Mill, John Stuart, 33, 45
Miller, J. Hillis, 30, 74, 178
Milton, John, 19, 23, 126, 135
Moore, Carlisle, 144, 156, 159
Music, 9, 120, 127, 158, 164
Myerhoff, Hans, 132
Mysticism, 4, 144–48, 154, 158, 161, 166, 230 (n. 1), 231 (n. 7)
Myth, 2, 32, 186, 193, 209

Narrative, 5, 12, 30–31, 50, 117, 123, 130, 141–42
Negative capability, 20
Newsome, David, 133
Nicolson, Harold, 144
Nietzsche, Friedrich Wilhelm, 133, 192
Noon, William T., 10–11
Novalis, 26
Novel, 30–31, 106, 117, 123
Nuttall, A. D., 48

Olney, James, 46, 221 (n. 18)
Otto, Rudolph, 58
Oxford English Dictionary, 145

Paffard, Michael, 223 (n. 35)
Pater, Walter, 116, 119, 173–74, 183, 187, 191, 199, 228 (n. 11)
Perception: and aesthetic experience, 110; leads to emotion, 4–5, 14, 41, 47, 52, 55, 60; fleeting, 112–14; distinguished from intellect, 15–16, 29, 178; distinct from interpretation, 15–16, 18, 23, 29, 57, 66, 168; and memory, 25; power of, 8, 21, 31, 43, 83, 169, 183; primacy of, 17, 33, 89, 199; transformed in epiphany, 28, 69, 71–72, 81–82, 101–02, 153, 198; triggers epiphany, 4, 34, 37, 46, 67, 77, 87, 92
Petrarch, 64
Phanes, 25
Phantom, 5, 82, 83, 97, 128, 186
Phenomenology, 1, 131, 221 (n. 10)
Phylarchus, 6
Piaget, Jean, 58

253

Index

Pick, John, 169
Poetic composition, 9, 38–40, 140, 148, 179, 199, 206
Pope, Alexander, 38, 42
Poulet, Georges, 22, 45, 217 (n. 35)
Pound, Ezra, 5, 30, 107, 128, 141, 182–83
Preyer, Robert, 146
Prickett, Stephen, 74
Proust, Marcel, 24, 72, 214 (n. 7), 229 (n. 21)
Puritan, 16–20, 27, 30
Pynchon, Thomas, 141–42

Quidditas, 12, 82, 168–69

Randomness, 2, 46, 223 (n. 30). *See also* Accident (coincidence)
Raymond, William O., 108
Reader (role of), 12, 31, 66, 130, 142–43, 208, 231 (n. 7)
Rehder, Robert, 219 (n. 2)
Reiman, Donald H., 44
Rembrandt van Rijn, 45
Reverie, 40–41, 104
Ricoeur, Paul, 32
Riddel, Joseph, 202
Rilke, Rainer Maria, 1
Rimbaud, Arthur, 182
Roppen, George, 229 (n. 23)
Rossetti, Dante Gabriel, 144
Rousseau, Jean Jacques, 17, 40–42, 220 (n. 7), 221 (n. 9)

Sartre, Jean-Paul, 48, 218 (n. 42), 222 (n. 25)
Schelling, Friedrich Wilhelm Joseph von, 26
Schenk, H. G., 217 (n. 35)
Schiller, Friedrich von, 87
Schug, Charles, 226 (n. 26)
Scotus, Duns, 168
Scully, James, 168
Shakespeare, William, 106
Shelley, Mary Wollstonecraft, 124, 229 (n. 18)
Shelley, Percy Bysshe, 4–5, 31, 34, 36, 41, 93–106, 123, 180, 184, 186; "Adonais," 130, 220 (n. 8); "A Defence of Poetry," 93, 97, 102; "Epipsychidion," 97; "Hymn to Intellectual Beauty," 94–95; "To Jane. The Invitation," 98; "To Jane. The Recollection," 114; *Laon and Cythna, (The Revolt of Islam)*, 93–95; "Lines Written among the Euganean Hills," 99; "On Life," 96; "On Love," 96; "Mont Blanc," 100–02, 212; "Peter Bell the Third," 35; *Queen Mab*, 26; *The Revolt of Islam*, 96; "The Sensitive Plant," 176; "To a Sky-Lark," 97–98; "Stanzas Written in Dejection," 99; "The Triumph of Life," 30
Sherry, Charles, 221 (n. 12)
Sinfield, Alan, 144
Solipsism, 99, 170
Spencer, Herbert, 133
Spencer, Theodore, 216 (n. 19)
Stauffer, Donald A., 92
Stevens, Wallace, 2, 5, 29–30, 84, 167, 181, 198–204, 212; "Adagia," 199; "The Idea of Order at Key West," 151, 153, 200; "Martial Cadenza," 201; "The Noble Rider and the Sound of Words," 198; "Notes toward a Supreme Fiction," 200; "An Ordinary Evening in New Haven," 199
Strauss, D. F., 14
Sublime, 73
Surrealism, 199
Symbol, 33, 79, 93, 128, 130, 132–33, 141, 182, 184–85
Symbolists, 128, 145, 182–83, 206
Symons, Arthur, 181–83
Synchronicity, 31–32
Synesthesia, 59, 62

Tait's Edinburgh Magazine, 39
Tasso, Torquato, 123
Tennyson, Alfred, 4–5, 29–30, 110, 128, 144–66, 172, 174, 212; "The Ancient Sage," 149; "Armageddon," 150; "Audley Court," 151–53; "De Profundis," 154; "Far-Far-Away," 154; "The Higher Pantheism," 165; "The Lotus-Eaters," 159; "Maud," 164; *In Memoriam*, 145, 147–48, 152, 156–63, 165, 193; "Merlin and the Gleam," 164;

Index

"Morte D'Arthur," 145; "The Palace of Art," 128; "Timbuctoo," 150; trances, 145–47, 156, 160–61; "In the Valley of Cauteretz," 161
Tennyson, Charles, 144
Thackeray, William Makepeace, 123
Theology, 7, 13, 135, 166–69, 174, 181, 190, 195
Theophany (distinguished from epiphany), 30, 34, 138–39, 157, 169–70, 177, 180, 192, 195–96, 202
Thomas, Dylan, 213 (n. 5)
Thoreau, H. D., 215 (n. 16)
Thorpe, Clarence DeWitt, 225 (n. 14)
Tillich, Paul, 150
Time, 3–4, 21, 24–26, 31, 43, 50, 52, 116, 119, 129, 131–32, 136, 149, 196, 217 (n. 41); aion, 25–26, 28, 158–59, 174, 190, 202, 217 (n. 40); chronos (chronology), 24–25, 111–12; kairos, 24–25, 72, 113, 140, 159, 174, 190, 217 (n. 39, n. 40); moment, 2, 22–23, 25, 27, 41, 44, 46–47, 90, 95, 108–09, 112, 131, 173, 181–82, 187, 191; timelessness, 24, 115, 118–19, 133, 136, 182, 184, 191
Toulmin, Stephen, 132, 229 (n. 22). *See also* Goodfield, June
Traherne, Thomas, 17
Trosse, George, 18–19
Tucker, Herbert F., 228 (n. 6)

Vagueness, 43–44, 76, 139, 183. *See also* Indeterminacy of meaning
Valéry, Paul, 213 (n. 5)
van der Leeuw, G., 58
Vaughan, Henry, 29
Verlaine, Paul, 182
Vico, Giambattista, 133

Wasserman, Earl, 96, 99
Weiskel, Thomas, 225 (n. 4)
Wells, Henry, 202
Wesley, John, 19–20, 27
Westminster Review, 174
Weston, Jessie, 192
White, William Hale (Mark Rutherford), 45
Willey, Basil, 72, 144–45, 156

Wittgenstein, Ludwig, 170
Wolfe, Thomas, 214 (n. 7)
Woolf, Virginia, 3, 21, 26, 31, 49, 93, 107, 121–22, 141, 198, 214 (n. 7)
Wordsworth, Dorothy, 39, 49, 66, 75, 207
Wordsworth, Jonathan, 51, 222 (n. 28)
Wordsworth, William, 35–80, 110–11, 118, 121, 128, 148, 150, 158, 163, 166; "The Cock is crowing," 39; "Composed after a Journey," 40; "Composed upon an Evening," 40; elevation of ordinary, 85, 87, 153, 155; and Eliot, 191–94; "Essay, Supplementary to the Preface," 38; "An Evening Walk," 42, 179; *The Excursion*, 50, 71, 80; and Heaney, 206–07, 210–12; *Home at Grasmere*, 50; indeterminacy in, 16–17; and Joyce, 2–5, 9–12, 27–29, 92–93, 105–06, 108, 114, 125; kairos in, 23–25; "Ode to Duty," 196; "Ode: Intimations of Immortality," 70, 96; "I wandered lonely as a cloud," 74; "Lines Written in Early Spring," 40; *Lyrical Ballads*, 2–3, 30, 33, 37, 45, 104; "Michael," 39; "A Night-Piece," 40, 53, 203, 212; "Preface" to *Lyrical Ballads*, 42, 104–05; *The Prelude*, 30, 37–38, 43, 47, 49–69, 70, 75–76, 88, 116, 122, 162, 204; *The Recluse*, 50; "Resolution and Independence," 64, 70–80, 99, 102, 164, 194; "Rural Architecture," 46, 57; and Shelley, 97–98, 101, 105–06; "A slumber did my spirit seal," 53; spots of time, 9, 20–21, 31, 44, 49–51, 99–100, 147–48, 151, 170, 174, 186, 209; "Stepping Westward," 154; and Stevens, 200–01; "The Thorn," 39, 45, 208; "Tintern Abbey," 72–73; "We are Seven," 40; "A whirl-blast from behind the hill," 39; "Written in March . . . ," 39; and Yeats, 186

Yeats, William Butler, 1, 5, 30, 46, 123, 128, 141, 181–90, 194–95, 197–99, 212, 213 (n. 5), 226 (n. 17); "Among School Children," 189; "Byzantium," 189; "The Cap and Bells," 186; "The

(*Yeats, continued*)
  Circus Animals' Desertion," 125, 189; "The Cutting of an Agate," 187; "A Dialogue of Self and Soul," 185; "The Magi," 189; "A Memory of Youth," 187; "Modern Poetry," 187; "Per Amica Silentia Lunae," 184–85; *Responsibilities*, 187; "The Symbolism of Poetry," 183; "Two Songs from a Play," 189; "Under Ben Bulben," 190; "Vacillation," 121, 185; *A Vision*, 186

Zaehner, R. C., 146